# Lecture Notes
# in Business Information Processing     231

More information about this series at http://www.springer.com/series/7911

Joseph Barjis · Robert Pergl
Eduard Babkin (Eds.)

# Enterprise and Organizational Modeling and Simulation

11th International Workshop, EOMAS 2015, Held at CAiSE 2015
Stockholm, Sweden, June 8–9, 2015
Selected Papers

 Springer

*Editors*
Joseph Barjis
Delft University of Technology
Delft, Zuid-Holland
The Netherlands

Robert Pergl
Czech Technical University in Prague
Prague
Czech Republic

Eduard Babkin
Higher School of Economics
National Research University
Nizhny Novgorod
Russia

ISSN 1865-1348 ISSN 1865-1356 (electronic)
Lecture Notes in Business Information Processing
ISBN 978-3-319-24625-3 ISBN 978-3-319-24626-0 (eBook)
DOI 10.1007/978-3-319-24626-0

Library of Congress Control Number: 2015949467

Springer Cham Heidelberg New York Dordrecht London

Printed on acid-free paper

Springer International Publishing AG Switzerland is part of Springer Science+Business Media
(www.springer.com)

# Preface

A number of factors contribute to challenges in enterprises study spanning from organizational complexity to intricacy of business processes and sophistication in workflows. While these are only internal factors, there are a myriad external factors and uncertainties such as competition, politics, emergence of innovative technologies, and so on. All this raises constant challenges for enterprises to change and redesign. In doing so, efficiency is the primary indicator enterprises use as a measuring stick while producing tangible and intangible goods. For studying efficiency or, in general, studying dynamic behavior of any aspect of an enterprise and impact of external factors, quantitative methods have emerged as a viable tool. Among these quantitative tools, simulation is becoming more and more popular tool. With simulation, the importance of modeling or conceptual modeling also becomes of paramount importance.

The Enterprise and Organization Modeling and Simulation (EOMAS) Workshop was founded to become a forum among researchers and practitioners to share their research and practical findings. In this forum we encourage dissemination of research results under a more generic umbrella called enterprise engineering.

Like any system, an enterprise is an object of continuous improvements, redesign, and reimplementation. The departure point for any design or redesign activity pertinent to an enterprise is first to understand the enterprise business processes. Therefore, in the overall enterprise engineering activities, business process modeling plays a central role. However, an extended enterprise and organizational study involves both analysis and design activities, in which not only modeling but also simulation plays a prominent role. Therefore this growing importance of modeling and simulation in the context of enterprises is attracting the attention of researchers. Today, modeling and simulation are the tools and methods that are effective, efficient, economic, and widely used in enterprise engineering, organizational study, and business process management, especially when inspired and/or combined with other approaches and paradigms.

Complementary insights of modeling and simulation in enterprise engineering constitute a whole cycle of study of enterprises. For monitoring and studying business processes and the interaction of actors in a realistic and interactive environment, simulation has proven to be a powerful tool and method, especially if simulation is supported with rich animation and gaming elements. In order to explore these topics, address the underlying challenges, find and improve solutions, and demonstrate applications of modeling and simulation in the domain of enterprise, its organization, and underlying business processes, peer-reviewed papers were accepted for presentation at EOMAS 2015, which was held during June 8–9, 2015, Stockholm, Sweden.

June 2015                                                                 Joseph Barjis
                                                                          Robert Pergl

# Organization

The EOMAS workshop is annually organized as an international forum for researchers and practitioners in the field of enterprise and organization modeling and simulation. Organization of this workshop, planning, and review of the contributions were accomplished by an international team of researchers.

## Workshop Organizers

### General Chair

Joseph Barjis                    Delft University of Technology, The Netherlands

### Program Chair

Martin Molhanec                 Czech Technical University in Prague, Czech Republic
Robert Pergl                     Czech Technical University in Prague, Czech Republic
Eduard Babkin                    National Research Univeristy Higher School of
                                 Economics in Nizhny Novgorod, Russia

### Program Committee

Jean-Paul Arnaout               Gulf University for Science and Technology, Kuwait
Anteneh Ayanso                  Brock University, Canada
Eduard Babkin                   State University - Higher School of Economics, Russia
Ygal Bendavid                   University of Quebec in Montreal (UQAM), Canada
Kawtar Benghazi                 University of Granada, Spain
Anna Bobkowska                  Gdansk University of Technology, Poland
Peter Bollen                    University of Maastricht, The Netherlands
Mahmoud Boufaida                Mentouri University of Constantine, Algeria
Manuel I. Capel-Tuñón           University of Granada, Spain
José Luis Garrido               University of Granada, Spain
Rafael Gonzalez                 Javeriana University, Colombia
Frantisek Hunka                 University of Ostrava, Czech Republic
P. Radha Krishna                Infosys Technologies Ltd., India
Petr Kroha                      Czech Technical University in Prague, Czech Republic
Russell Lock                    Loughborough University, UK
Vojtech Merunka                 Czech University of Life Sciences, Czech Republic
Navonil Mustafee                University of Exeter, UK
Murali-Mohan Narasipuram        University of Porto, Portugal
Manuel Noguera                  University of Granada, Spain
Maria Ntaliani                  Agriculture University of Athens, Greece
Ghaith Rabadi                   Old Dominion University, USA

## Sponsoring Institutions

- SIGMAS (Special Interest Group on Modeling And Simulation of the Association for Information Systems)
- CAiSE 2015 (International Conference on Advanced Information Systems Engineering)
- Czech Technical University in Prague (Faculty of Information Technology Department of Software Engineering)

# Contents

**Enterprise Conceptual Modelling and Simulation**

**Enterprise Modelling Formal Foundation**

## Enterprise Optimisation

# Enterprise Conceptual Modelling
# and Simulation

# Natural Language Generation for Declarative Process Models

Lars Ackermann(✉), Stefan Schönig, Michael Zeising, and Stefan Jablonski

University of Bayreuth, Bayreuth, Germany
{lars.ackermann,stefan.schoenig,michael.zeising,
stefan.jablonski}@uni-bayreuth.de
http://www.uni-bayreuth.de

**Abstract.** Two different types of processes can be distinguished: well-structured routine processes and agile processes where the control-flow cannot be predefined a priori. In a similar way, two modeling paradigms exist whereby procedural models are more adequate for routine processes and declarative models are more suitable for agile processes. Often business analysts are not confident in understanding process models; this holds even more for declarative process models. Natural language support for this kind of processes in order to improve their readability is desirable. In the work at hand we define a technique that transforms declarative models to intuitive natural language texts. Hereof, the approach focuses on content determination and structuring the output texts.

**Keywords:** Declarative process models · Natural language generation · Model transformation · Process model validation

## 1 Introduction

*Business Process Management (BPM)* is a well accepted method for structuring activities carried out in an organization. BPM usually covers modeling, executing and analyzing processes [1]. Two different types of processes can be distinguished [2]: well-structured routine processes with exactly prescribed control flow and agile processes with control flow that evolves at run time without being fully predefined a priori. The former are common, e.g., in manufacturing industry where it is well and strictly defined what steps have to be executed in what sequence. Agile processes can be encountered frequently in, for instance, customer relationship management. There processes are greatly driven by customer data. Depending on these data each customer case has to be treated differently. So a huge number of similar but finally different process executions results.

In a similar way, two different representations for process models can be distinguished: procedural models focus on describing in what sequence steps have to be executed while declarative models focus on defining execution constraints: every execution that do not violate these constraints is acceptable. Consequently, due to the flexible nature of agile processes, they can often be captured more easily using a declarative rather than a procedural modeling approach [3,4].

© Springer International Publishing Switzerland 2015
J. Barjis et al. (Eds.): EOMAS 2015, LNBIP 231, pp. 3–19, 2015.
DOI: 10.1007/978-3-319-24626-0_1

Business analysts often do not feel confident in understanding and interpreting process models (PMs) [1]. In this context, the problem is not only that domain experts are often not trained to create process models themselves, but also that they are not capable reading process models created by other people. Hence, the interpretation of these models frequently has to rely on a discourse in natural language [1,5]. Due to this lack of expertise, a transformation of process models into a natural language description of these processes is desired.

Though it is usually possible to use canned text snippets or plain templates to create appropriate descriptions in natural language, this is unanimously not recommended in many contexts due to the enormous effort creating the texts, inflexible representations and many other reasons [5–9]. This is where techniques of *Natural Language Generation (NLG)* can be applied effectively. However, there are only few sophisticated verbalization techniques for procedural [5] and even none for declarative process models. Since the latter are even less comprehensible [4], verbalization methods for declarative PMs are strongly required. Thus, the aim of this paper is to provide an approach to generate natural language models for declarative process models. The latter must be easily comprehensible and intuitive for the users.

The remainder of this paper is structured as follows: in Sect. 2 we explain the background upon which our approach is built. In Sect. 3 we describe the related work and challenges our approach has to deal with. Section 4 describes our approach to transform declarative process models to natural language texts. Section 5 finally concludes this paper.

## 2   Background and Preliminaries

Procedural and declarative process models are likewise represented using formal languages whose artifacts are the transformation input. This section describes the syntax and usage of *Declarative Process Intermediate Language (DPIL)* which we prefer for describing declarative process models due to several reasons [10]. First, it is multi-perspective, i.e., it allows representing several business process perspectives, namely, control flow, data and resources. The expressiveness of DPIL and its suitability for business process modelling have been evaluated in [10]. Second, it is multi-modal, meaning that it allows for defining two different types of rules: rules representing mandatory relations (called **ensure** in DPIL) and rules representing recommended relations (called **advice** in DPIL). The latter are useful, e.g., to reflect good practices. In order to express organizational relations, DPIL builds upon a generic organizational meta model that comprises, for instance, concepts for modeling concrete identities (called **identity** in DPIL) and roles that may be assigned to identities (called **group**). DPIL provides a textual notation based on the use of *macros* to define reusable rule templates. For instance, the **sequence** macro (**sequence(a,b)**) states that the existence of a *start event* of task b implies the previous occurrence of a *complete event* of task a; and the **role** macro (**role(a,r)**) states that an activity a is assigned to a role r. In contrast, the **direct** macro (**direct(a,id)**) assigns a task a directly to an identity id. The following example shows a process for trip management modeled with DPIL:

```
1     use identity SJ
2     use group Professor
3
4     process BusinessTrip {
5         task Book Flight
6         task Approve Application
7
8         advice direct(Approve Application, SJ)
9         ensure role(Approve Application, Professor)
10         advice sequence(Approve Application, Book Flight)
11    }
```

The model states that it is recommended to approve a business trip before booking a flight (line 10). Moreover, it is mandatory that the approval is carried out by a resource with the role *Professor* (line 9). Within the group of professors the task should be performed by the concrete identity *SJ* (line 8).

When transforming process models like the one above, one has to consider that NLG is usually purpose-driven and context-sensitive [6]. Hence, for our approach we distinguish between two contexts, namely *report* and *execution assistance*. In the former case, a process mining tool, in our case the DpilMiner [11], generates a declarative process model by extracting knowledge from event logs [1]. Since event logs represent a history of an already executed process, the generated texts should be written in past tense. In contrast, a process execution tool gives instructions to guide a process attendee. These instructions should be written in present tense and, in contrast to a report, do not require a sophisticated sentence ordering, since they usually are very short.

An exemplary report for the process above is shown in Fig. 1. There may be individual preferences concerning verbosity, word order, active and passive voice and other stylistic variations. However, this paper illustrates the *general* approach of transforming declarative models to natural language.

## 3   Related Work and Challenges

Natural language generation systems are a suitable means to provide intuitive interfaces for communication of information from different data sources. Though applications and goals vary considerably, a common reference methodology and architecture emerged. Probably the best known is Reiter and Dale's pipeline model for natural language generation [6].

The DPIL model above is used as a running example in the following sections for both illustrating the challenges to deal with and their solution approaches.

**Overview**
Two tasks have been performed where one role and one concrete person were involved. The involved role is professor. SJ is the only fixed identity, which means that he was involved very frequently.
One mandatory rule seems to restrict the process and in two cases there is a recommendation.
**Performed Tasks**
We only consider tasks that were performed with a certain frequency. These tasks are Approve Application and Book Flight. All restrictions are explained in the following section.
**Constraints and Advice**
1: The application was always approved by a professor and usually by SJ.
2: Furthermore, the flight was booked after approval of the application.

**Fig. 1.** Natural language report for the exemplary DPIL process model

### 3.1 Pipeline Model

Many NLG approaches for diverse domains and applications have been developed and as early as in 1994 the question came up if any consensus NLG architecture can be found [12]. Even if Reiter argues that there is no real consensus he clearly identified a tendency that manifested over the past years. Many current NLG approaches are based on the three-step pipeline model shown in Fig. 2.

**Fig. 2.** Pipeline model

During the *Document Planning* phase the system has to select the formal contents to be included in the output texts and to embed them in an appropriate text structure plan. *Microplanning* is in charge of organizing the sentence's structure and lexical contents, in introducing referring expressions and in aggregating sentences. The latter usually means merging sentences and referring expressions are words or phrases that can be used instead of an entity. A common example is a personal pronoun. *Surface Realization* is the final step and is responsible for generating grammatically and orthographically correct sentences based on the decisions made in the two preceding phases.

Though there are also drawbacks for this unidirectional, generalized model, we chose this structure for the following reasons: First, modularization is easy and recommended due to a large variety of approaches for partial solutions. Second, separating *Surface Realization* is reasonable because it can be treated as largely domain-independent and can be solved generically [13] and third, debugging intermediate results is easier than in interwcaved systems.

Reiter and Dale's pipeline approach describes four input parameters and the three mentioned processing stages they influence. Their equivalents and utilization details in the domain of generating texts for declarative process models are described in Sect. 4. For more details regarding the general processing pipeline we refer to [6]. According to Reiter and Dale, our approach has to deal with a multitude of issues. However, we focus on Document Planning as well as on the sentence structuring and lexical choice part of the Microplanning phase, since these are the most domain-dependent tasks [6].

In the following subsection challenges that refer to the different processing stages are discussed in context of transforming declarative process models to natural language texts.

## 3.2   Challenges

The pipeline model introduced in the previous subsection is a general approach for transforming formal input to natural language text. While there are existing approaches for transforming procedural process models [5,14] and other formal input [7,8,15,16], there is currently none for declarative process models. However, some of the challenges arising in the procedural world and none-process domains are also relevant to the transformation process for declarative process models. Table 1 gives an overview over these challenges as well as over related work that provide solutions to some issues in their particular domain and how far they are applicable in the context of transforming declarative process models. Some solutions are completely ($\checkmark$) or partially ($\circlearrowright$) applicable and can therefore be reused or extended. Others ($\times$) are not handled in an applicable manner and have to be solved independently.

Considering the introduced pipeline model, the first challenge involves the selection and population of messages that serve as a transmission medium of information about the process model to explain. None of the existing approaches deal with declarative process models, which is why we discuss a holistic principle for selecting and populating messages in "Content Determination" is referred under Subsect. 4.2.

The second challenge, *Text Structuring*, has been discussed in multiple previous approaches. Existing approaches create domain-dependent schemata based on empirically retrieved document structures and discourse relations providing a good flow of reading. Natural language texts are sequential in that terms that they have fixed starting and end points and therefore a fixed reading direction. The DPIL process model shown in Sect. 2 has also a particular structure which, in contrast, is declarative. This means that the complete semantic is preserved even if the order of all tasks and rules may be shuffled. However this is not applicable to procedural processes models because of their restrictive execution paths. This connotes an amplification of the general structuring problem compared to [5] which cannot be solved using the same approach. Other approaches

**Table 1.** Challenges for generating text from declarative process models

| Phase | Challenge | Related Work | Applicable |
|---|---|---|---|
| Document Planning | **Information Extraction** | | |
| | Message Selection and Population | [5, 7, 8, 14] | × |
| | **Text Structuring** | | |
| | Inferring Document Plans | [5, 7–9, 14–16] | ○ |
| | Model Linearization | [5, 9, 14, 15] | × |
| Micro-planning | **Lexicalization** | | |
| | Linguistic Label Analysis | [5, 8] | ✓ |
| | Choosing Words | [5, 7–9, 15, 16] | ○ |
| | **Aggregation** | | |
| | Detecting Aggregation Potential | [5, 8] | ○ |
| | Applying Aggregation | [5, 8] | ○ |
| | **Improving Reading Flow** | | |
| | Referring Expressions | [5, 7] | ○ |
| | Discourse Marker | [5] | ○ |
| Surf. Real. | **Flexible Realization** | [5, 16] | ✓ |
| Flexibility, Crosscut | **Varying Input Complexity** | - | × |
| | **Tailoring Output** | [7, 16] | × |

also provide solutions but structure their texts tailored to the needs of the respective domain and target audience [14, 15] and are therefore not applicable for the approach at hand. We address this challenge in "Text Structuring" is referred under Subsect. 4.2.

The challenge in *Lexicalization* is to dynamically choose words for expressing the message contents [6]. In contrast our approach can reuse already verbalized process data like task labels. Regarding this, *Linguistic Label Analysis* means that, for instance, the task label "Approve application" must be decomposed into "Approve" and "application" or in general *Action* and *Business Object*. There are two reasons for this decomposition. First of all the system needs to know which of the two words depicts the verb in, order to structure the sentence reasonably [5]. Furthermore a verb may be transformed to a different word class, as it is shown in Fig. 1: "[...]after **approval** of the application.". This issue is solved, e.g., in [5, 8] using WordNet [17] and tagging techniques. WordNet is a lexical database of linked English words. One can retrieve, for instance, hypernyms of a given word. While object labels can be reused an appropriate word choice for, e.g., the task's relation to *Professor* in the DPIL rule `ensure role(Approve Application, Professor)` must be inferred. Most of the existing approaches use linguistic templates. We reuse some of the concepts in "Lexicalization" is referred under Subsect. 4.3.

In an NLG system, rules for detecting *Aggregation* potential and for the transformation are required [6]. *Referring Expressions* and *Discourse Markers* are used to reduce word redundancies and to provide a more fluent reading experience. However, existing linguistic approaches largely operate on natural language level and hence do not consider any related resources like the input process model [5]. Leopold et al. aggregate explanations of sequential activities in case of shared roles, business objects or actions utilizing the procedural process model. Since declarative process models do not provide any ordering, neighboring constraints only can be identified in the document plan itself. Detecting shared properties and objects in rules of declarative process models is further impeded due to the arbitrary rule complexity. Though our approach focuses on the document planning part, we provide principles to deal with these issues in "Aggregation, Referring Expressions and Discourse Markers" is referred under the Subsect. 4.3, reusing principles in a modified manner from related approaches.

While the previous stages encode linguistic information on a more abstract level a surface realization component uses this knowledge to make plain and explicit linguistic decisions. Beyond that grammatical function words (e.g. articles), capitalization and punctuation are covered, too. Several solutions have been developed but most of the existing approaches use the realizer described in [13]. While they differ in terms of the underlying theory and required inputs they all can be used independently from the particular domain. This probably is the reason why this stage is the best-investigated research field in NLG [6].

As already stated in [5] *Flexibility* is an important criterion and requires stage-crossing support. For now we assume that declarative input models follow certain conventions (cf. 4.1). *Varying Input Complexity* considers that DPIL is a formal language allowing for rule composition through Boolean operators. Hence, message selection and filling have to deal with arbitrary complex input rules. None of the comparable previous approaches encountered this issue, mostly because of the absence of Boolean operations.

*Tailoring Output* deals with varying generation purposes. The NLG system has to be able to generate textual descriptions of declarative process models either as report or as execution assistance. The main differences are geared to the possible input constructs and the desired textual output form. Existing approaches vary their outputs according to individual user needs but do not distinguish between a report and individual rule explanation messages due to different domains and input models. We address the challenges regarding flexibility in general in all generation steps in Sect. 4.

## 4 Natural Language Generation for DPIL Models

Considering the challenges discussed in Subsect. 3.2 this section describes our approach for transforming declarative process models to natural language texts.

### 4.1 Generation Inputs

In this section the described input concepts are mapped to the domain of declarative process modeling using DPIL.

In theory our *Knowledge Base (KB)* is an infinite set of DPIL rules, since DPIL supports Boolean operations. Each DPIL rule has a hierarchical object structure, i.e. an object tree. Since our approach is based on a grammar formalism that works on sequential data, we first rewrite the *direct* object tree using in-order traversal to a sequential representation[1]. In order to focus on the contained information rather than on their technical implementation we chose a reduced view on each DPIL rule which means that we only consider nodes and properties that are relevant to the NLG problem. Hence, the two introduced exemplary rule macros `direct` and `role` are represented as follows:

- `direct(a,id):= T:a Start implies T:a And ID:id Start`
- `role(a,r):= T:a And ID:id Start implies ID:id Subject And`
  `RT:hasRole Predicate And Var:r Object Relation`

Though we elaborated solution suggestions for all mentioned challenges, we now introduce some assumptions that are either driven by limitations of the current research in NLG or by characteristics of DPIL models. First it is necessary that each task is labeled with a noun-verb combination without being limited to a particular order. This is necessary since we need to extract the action as well as the business object. This assumption is valid since it follows a quality criteria for processes [18]. As a starting point, we support a set of commonly used rule types according to the well-known Workflow Patterns [19]. This means that each DPIL rule contains an *implication*, having a *condition* to the right and a *consequence* on the opposite site [10]. Considering DPIL's huge variability, this restriction allows for a more concise discussion but does not cause any changes to the main concepts if this assumption is discarded. In the previous section the challenge of arbitrary rule complexities has been illustrated. To the current state of research we prescribe a fixed maximum number of Boolean operations but later the system should be able to deal with arbitrary complex rules.

The *Communicative Goal (CG)* parameter has two possible manifestations, namely *report* and *execution assistance*. In the case of a report the input is always a complete process model. However, for assisting a user during execution time the KB input would be a set of rules only.

A *User Model (UM)*, applied to DPIL, corresponds to an instance of the mentioned generic organizational meta model, covering information about the user's position and relations. DPIL allows for consideration of identity management systems supporting the concepts *Identity*, *Group* and *Relation*. Without this user model it would be impossible to generate the first sentence in the example report, due to the missing relation between SJ and Professor.

Creating a *Discourse History (DH)*, remembering already mentioned entities and concepts, it is possible to avoid stilted texts and to reduce verbosity of the output texts using referring expressions [6]. In the case of a report, the necessary information are given implicitly after the document planning stage. In contrast, for the purpose of execution assistance this does not pertain since the user navigates through a process model step by step.

---

[1] Our binary trees are object trees without optional associations. Hence, the meta model prevents information loss during serialization.

Within the next sections we describe our approach for transforming DPIL rules to adequate texts influenced by all input parameters mentioned above.

## 4.2  Document Planning

As discussed in Subsect. 3.1 this stage consists of two steps, namely Content Determination and Text Structuring. The input for this stage are the parameters discussed in the previous subsection. The result, a Document Plan, is forwarded to the Microplanner.

**Content Determination.** Retrieving a set of DPIL rules this step is responsible for constructing messages that express the contained information appropriately and making them easy to access. Our approach utilizes the formalism of *Categorial Unification Grammars (CUG)* [20] as a basis for building pattern matching rules. Matched DPIL rules are transformed into an intermediate representation, namely *CUG messages*.

Categorial Unification Grammars denote a grammar family that combines the advantages of two other grammar types: *Categorial Grammars* and *Unification Grammars* [20]. A Categorial Grammar, as defined in [21] consists of basic and derived categories or functions that constitute how other categories can be derived. These functions consist of a functor and an argument to its right, separated by a direction indicator. Lexical categories complement this kind of grammar system by assigning terminal symbols to basic or derived categories. A simple CU Grammar[2] for parsing the sequentialized DPIL rule `direct` is:

- Basic categories: `Ta, Id, TPEvent, TPBy, TPEventBy, IdCE`
- Lexical categories:
  - `T: Ta`
  - `ID: Id`
  - `And: (TPBy\Ta)/Id`
  - `Start: TPEvent\Ta`
  - `TPEventBy\TPBy`
  - `implies: (IdCE\TPEvent)/TPEventBy`
- Feature Structures:
  - `TPEvent[ctask=<task>]`
  - `TPEventBy[ctask=<task>]`

Ta is the grammar symbol for a task and Id for an identity. The other categories denote more complex structures. `TPEvent\Ta` means that this constituent can be combined to `TPEvent` if it is preceded by a constituent of category `Ta`. If the `\` is turned into `/` this means that the current terminal symbol or category must have a `Ta` as successor. Both, lexical and derived categories denote semantic rather than syntactic groups. Hence, `TPEventBy` means that somebody is involved in a particular task or process through causing an event. This abstraction allows for

---

[2] Notations vary; we have chosen the notation used in [20].

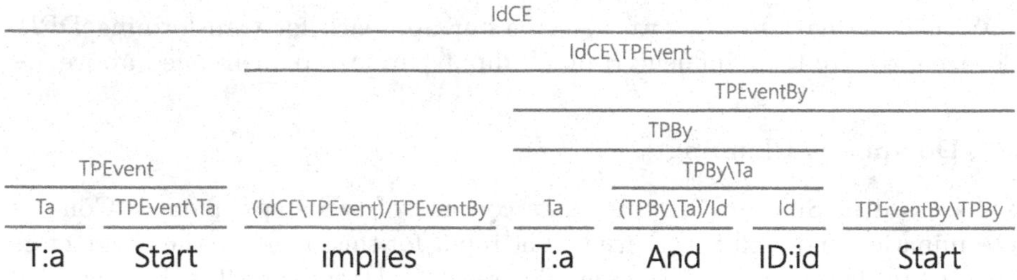

| | | | | | IdCE | | | |
| --- | --- | --- | --- | --- | --- | --- | --- | --- |
| | | | | | IdCE\TPEvent | | | |
| | | | | | | TPEventBy | | |
| | | | | | | TPBy | | |
| | TPEvent | | | | | TPBy\Ta | | |
| Ta | TPEvent\Ta | (IdCE\TPEvent)/TPEventBy | | Ta | (TPBy\Ta)/Id | Id | TPEventBy\TPBy |
| T:a | Start | implies | | T:a | And | ID:id | Start |

**Fig. 3.** CUG parse tree for DPIL rule `direct`

unifying different events like `Start`, `Complete` or `Write` below a single grammar symbol. Finally `IdCE`, an *Identity Constrained Event*, states that the parsed rule restricts an event through constraints on the identity causing it, which is the same general description that can be used for `role`. Using the grammar rules above, the system is able to parse the full `direct` rule's sequential object hierarchy, as Fig. 3 shows.

Unification grammars are based on *Feature Structures* that allow for specifying partial information about constituents [20,22]. In a Categorial Unification grammar this allows for specifying also non-structural feature constraints for combining constituents. Additionally, when combining two constituents, the process of unification means merging the two associated feature structures as well, given that they agree on common features. The Unification aspect is used to specify constraints that, considering the exemplary DPIL rule in Fig. 3, the subsequences left and right of `implies` contain identical task objects. This is necessary because the `TPEventBy` restricts the task only if the corresponding `Ta` is part of its subject-matter. Hence, both the `TPEvent` and the `TPEventBy` in the `direct` example are annotated with the feature structure [ctask = < task >]. Now the two nodes can be combined to an `IdCE` node only if they agree on their common feature `ctask`. By adding a few grammar rules the system is enabled to parse the `role` rule as an `IdCE`, too. Both the rules `direct` and `role` restrict the execution of a particular task in terms of the performer. This commonality is stated through the common top node in both parse trees. Building this tree structure allows for mapping each top level node to a linguistic template which is discussed in "Lexication" is referred under the Subsect. 4.3.

**Text Structuring.** As described later in "Lexication" is referred under Subsect. 4.3 each CUG message is mapped to a linguistic specification of exactly one sentence. *Text Structuring* therefore means planning the ordering of the sentences as well as the embedding of this ordered set in a superordinate structure. The result is a document plan. In the presented approach no text structuring is required, if the generation result is used for execution assistance. The reason is that these texts only comprise the description of a very small set of rules and are presented in message dialogue style [10]. In contrast, generating appropriate reports like the running example requires a structuring. McKeown introduced a

schema-based approach that combines fixed structures for the document frame
and rhetorical relations for message ordering [23]. The latter are discussed more
centrally in the context of another formalism called *Rhetorical Structure Theory
(RST)* that describes relations between utterances [24]. `Sequence`, for instance,
organizes sentences in a sequential flow. `Contrast` is useful for relating opposed
utterances, that are usually indicated by phrases like *"however, ..."*. Based on
McKeown's principles, our approach defines the following schema:

```
SEQ(
    Title: title-template(process-model-name)
    Overview: SEQ(intro-template(nT,...), roles-template(roles),...)
    PerformedTasks: SEQ(consider-canned, tasks-template(tasks),...)
    ConstraintsAndAdvice: SEQ(<CUG messages>)
)
```

`SEQ` corresponds to the rhetorical relation `sequence` and can be nested. The
top-level sequence organizes the document title and three sections. Each section
covers either another sequential relation or a single template. A template is a
canned text with placeholders for information from the particular process model.
For instance, the first sentence in the running example only varies regarding
the number of tasks, roles and concrete persons but not in terms of the structure and the subject-matter. For this reason a template is used, replacing the
placeholders with the particular statistical information. The `PerformedTasks`
make use of canned sentences that cover non-varying information to provide a
brief introduction to the section and to segue to the next section. Finally the
`ConstraintsAndAdvice` section organizes all CUG messages in a sequence. This
sequence construction solves the model linearization issue and is produced using
an extendable set of ordering rules: (i) shared rule, shared arguments (highest
count first); (ii) shared arguments (highest count first); (iii) shared rule. The
enumeration corresponds to a ranking with (i) as the highest priority. If multiple structure pairs share arguments they are ordered according to the number of
sharings, starting with the highest. So far, the document plan still contains CUG
messages which still do not contain verbalized information. Hence, the following
subsection describes the verbalization of the document plan's messages.

## 4.3   Microplanning

The current stage is responsible for determining an appropriate linguistic representation for each CUG message.

**Lexicalization.** After building the CUG messages, we map them directly to
message templates that are based on the *Meaning-Text Theory (MTT)* [25].
Therein natural language sentences are specified on multiple abstraction levels,
whereby one is called *Deep-Syntactic Representation*. There sentence semantic
is represented by *Deep Syntactic Trees (DSynT)* whose nodes are so called *Full
Lexemes*. This means that words like auxiliary verbs, conjunctions and other

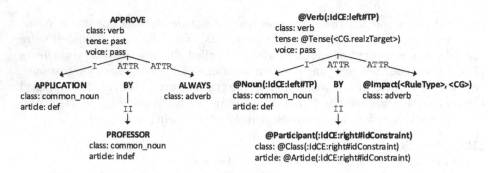

**Fig. 4.** DSynT message and corresponding template for rules `role` and `direct`

words with minor semantic meanings are excluded. Each node is annotated with grammatical information regarding, for instance, number and definiteness for nouns or voice, tense and person for verbs. Each arc between two of these nodes is directed and labeled with one of a small set of *Deep-Syntactic Relations*. I, II and so on are actant labels and carry parts of the most conspicuous information like subject and object of a sentence. A higher number means lesser conspicuousness. For the purpose of generating texts, two complementing relations are utilized, which is consistent with [5]. The first is the ATTR relation and the second is called COORD, whereby the former describes all kinds of modifiers, like conditions, circumstantials and attributes. The latter is used for conjoined constructions like comma-separated enumerations of entities. An appropriate DSynT for expressing the meaning of the DPIL rule pattern `role` is shown in Fig. 4. In the figure, the full lexemes are boldfaced and the corresponding grammemes are listed below, respectively. Combining the lexeme APPLICATION with the word class information common_noun and restricting the article to be definite enables the realizer to generate the clause "*The application*". The predicate, "*was approved*" is derived using its base form, APPROVE, and the grammemes of class, tense and voice. All other parts of the sentence are generated in an analogous manner. The word order depends on both the grammemes and the edge labels. In the example I and II express that the clause with the corresponding edge is a predecessor or a successor of APPROVE, respectively. Using the class adverb and the edge label ATTR the system is able to generate the phrase "*was always approved*". More information about the Meaning-Text Theory can be found in [25]. Similar to [5], we utilize the MTT paradigm and its DSynT structures as our linguistic message representation. This means that each CUG message in the Document Plan is transformed into a DSyn tree. This transformation can be accomplished by assigning an appropriate DSynT message template to each possible top node of the CUG trees. An example template is given in Fig. 4, too. As shown earlier, the rule patterns `direct` and `role` produce the same CUG top node, namely IdCE. According to our one-to-one mapping the same DSynT message template is assigned to the `role` rule's CUG tree. An appropriate verbalization of these DSynT messages and, by association, the two source rules is: (i) `role(Approve Application, Professor)`: The application has been approved by a professor; (ii) `direct(Approve Application, SJ)`: The application has been approved by SJ. Both verbalizations obviously have a very similar structure and wording and it is therefore desired to map at least these two rules to the same DSynT.

The expressions marked with a preceded @ symbol are directives for our actual Lexicalization engine. Each expression follows the pattern `@<ResultType> (<query>)` and is mapped to a function that determines the respective lexeme or grammatical feature. The Impact function simply performs a binary decision based on the type of the rule and the Communicative Goal to compute the importance of following the corresponding rule. Both functions, Class and Article depend on the result of the lexeme function. Similar to [5], we use WordNet to determine whether the Participant function returns a role or a real person name. If it is a person or a proper name, we return "proper_noun" and otherwise "common_noun" for our Class function. Article evaluates to "indef", which later is realized to "a", if the related noun is a role otherwise it returns "no_art" indicating the article has to be omitted. Leopold discusses the decomposition of activity labels in BPMN models [18]. Using the elaborated techniques, our system is able to extract noun and verb from task labels. These are the results of the two functions Noun and Verb. Tense evaluates to "past" if the sentence is realized in the context of a report otherwise "pres" is inserted. Finally the DSynT message is identical to the DSynT structure shown in Fig. 4(left).

The required function arguments can be retrieved using a suitable query language, as it is shown in the example above. But because of the recently introduced mapping mechanism there is no warranty that the queried information are present. The `direct` rule, for instance, does not provide any Relation in the right subtree below the implies node. Hence, we do not use full but partial queries which hand over the responsibility for providing requested information to the respective subtrees in the CUG message. So the system can access information for the Lexicalization more generally. The task that is constrained can be retrieved from the left subtree in both rules. Hence, the opposite subtree contains the constraint information. In case of a Relation subtree, the corresponding CUG substructure provides the content of the Var(iable) and in case of an `TPEventBy` it returns the identity. After this processing step the document plan only contains fully lexicalized DSynT messages, one for each CUG tree previously forming the leaf level.

**Aggregation, Referring Expressions and Discourse Markers.** In case that there are multiple rules that share arguments or structural features, generating a separate sentence for each of them would result in an enumeration instead of fluent text. Hence, for procedural process models Leopold et al. [18] perform *Aggregation* on the input level by triggering merging techniques based on the detection of activities that are performed by the same role, that share the same business objects or that contain the same actions. However, we choose an intermediate way by working on the CUG trees produced during the content determination step. Considering that each top level node is annotated with a feature structure that covers all available information about involved entities like tasks, roles and business objects, the aggregation component is able to find commonalities between rules. Though declarative process models do not provide a sequential structure, the system is able to identify neighboring rules using the document plan. Aggregation potential is detected using the rules 1 and 2 that are used for message ordering during the text structuring phase. Shared arguments are marked so that they will be materialized only once. Aggregation is performed using a set of conjunction rules that merge DSynT messages using MTT COORD relations. In order to prevent the generation of too complex sentences, Leopold et al. introduced a configurable threshold that restricts the number of aggregations. In contrast, we introduce a configurable threshold for the maximum number of lexemes in the aggregated DSynT message. This change is necessary because of the potential arbitrary rule complexity in declarative process models if we discard the assumption of a limited number of Boolean operations at a later juncture.

The generation of *Referring Expressions* works on messages that are adjacent and share arguments or have the same structure but were not aggregated. Shared arguments are materialized only once and are referenced by pronouns in succeeding sentences [5]. Additionally to shared arguments, we detect structure similarities with additive differences. If the structure with the addition has the type ensure and the other is an advice, a referring DSynT message is generated, that expresses the content of the additional structure part as a conditional phrase, extended by the phrase *"this was always the case"* in the case of a report or *"this is obligatory"* if the communicative goal is execution assistance.

Finally, the system inserts discourse markers as ATTR relations to existing DSynT messages, where applicable. We have defined a simple mapping of RST relations, that define the Document Plan's internal structure, to discourse markers like *"furthermore"*. In order to vary between the markers, we perform a random choice. Since the NLG system currently supports only sequence relations, there is a single set of discourse markers: {furthermore, in addition, additionally, ...}.

Discourse markers, referring expressions and aggregation are likewise style improvements but are not necessary to produce readable texts. That is why we currently keep these steps simple.

## 4.4   Surface Realization

Many previous NLG approaches showed that the process of serializing all DSynT messages, namely Surface Realization, is practically domain independent [5,6,16]. Hence, general solutions have been worked out. CoGenTex' *RealPro*[3] is able to transform fully lexicalized DSynT messages into natural language sentences and is, therefore, utilized in our approach's final stage. The Meaning-Text Theory defines a set of *Lexical Functions* that reduce the required linguistic knowledge [25], e.g. through functions like $Adv_0(x)$   which accepts

---

[3] http://www.cogentex.com/technology/realpro/index.shtml, l.a.: March 13th, 2015.

words of different types and determines the corresponding adverb. Other functions return weak verbs for given strong verbs as in *"go swimming"*. However, RealPro currently does not support Lexical Functions. For that reason, the DSynT messages in our approach do not contain any.

Using such a standard realizer technology this final task is simplified so that the document plan's leaf nodes are realized from left to right. The result is a natural language text that describes few DPIL rules or a complete model considering all introduced input parameters.

# 5 Conclusion and Outlook

Though DPIL does not force the user to use the structure pattern <consequence> implies <condition>, we assume it. This simplification is valid since we currently consider only the introduced frequent patterns which are consistent with this structure. As a future conceptual extension it is necessary to discard this assumption and to provide a more general way to access information in a CUG message. A possible solution is the assignment of appropriate unification features to the corresponding top level node of each CUG tree, providing access information.

Another limitation of the approach is the fixed maximum number of Boolean operations per DPIL rule. However, the person who creates the DPIL model is not restricted to this constant. It is therefore necessary to develop techniques that are able to deal with arbitrary rule complexity. As a starting point, the DSynT messages currently used should be reduced to partial DSyn trees that express an atomic part of a DPIL rule and can therefore be reused. Furthermore this requires techniques for combining partial DSyn trees to a message that can be realized to a valid natural language text snippet.

Finally, the approach in general and the usage of techniques and frameworks have to be evaluated properly. [5] suggest metrics for text quality, model coverage and performance, which we will use as a starting point. Applying the approach to real-world scenarios is planned and will probably raise further requirements for improvement and extension. According to discussions with non-academic stakeholders we identified possible applications in health care and administration environments, where declarative process modeling becomes more and more attractive.

# References

1. Dumas, M., Rosa, M.L., Mendling, J., Reijers, H.A.: Fundamentals of Business Process Management. Springer, Heidelberg (2013)
2. Jablonski, S.: MOBILE: A modular workflow model and architecture. In: Working Conference on Dynamic Modelling and Information Systems (1994)
3. van der Aalst, W., Pesic, M., Schonenberg, H.: Declarative workflows: balancing between flexibility and support. Comput. Sci. Res. Dev. **23**(2), 99–113 (2009)

4. Pichler, P., Weber, B., Zugal, S., Pinggera, J., Mendling, J., Reijers, H.: Imperative versus declarative process modeling languages: an empirical investigation. In: Daniel, F., Barkaoui, K., Dustdar, S. (eds.) Business Process Management Workshops. LNBIP, vol. 99, pp. 383–394. Springer, Heidelberg (2012)
5. Leopold, H., Mendling, J., Polyvyanyy, A.: Supporting process model validation through natural language generation. IEEE TSE **40**(8), 818–840 (2014)
6. Reiter, E., Dale, R.: Building Natural Language Generation Systems. Cambridge University Press, New York (2000)
7. Dalianis, H.: A method for validating a conceptual model by natural language discourse generation. In: Loucopoulos, P. (ed.) Advanced Information Systems Engineering. LNCS, vol. 593, pp. 425–444. Springer, Heidelberg (1992)
8. Meziane, F., Athanasakis, N., Ananiadou, S.: Generating natural language specifications from uml class diagrams. Req. Eng. **13**(1), 1–18 (2008)
9. Malik, S., Bajwa, I.S.: Back to origin: transformation of business process models to business rules. In: La Rosa, M., Soffer, P. (eds.) Business Process Management Workshops. LNBIP, vol. 132, pp. 611–622. Springer, Heidelberg (2013)
10. Zeising, M., Schönig, S., Jablonski, S.: Towards a common platform for the support of routine and agile business processes. In: Collaborative Computing: Networking, Applications and Worksharing (2014)
11. Schönig, S., Cabanillas, C., Jablonski, S., Mendling, J.: Mining the organisational perspective in agile business processes. In: Gaaloul, K., Schmidt, R., Nurcan, S., Guerreiro, S., Ma, Q. (eds.) Enterprise, Business-Process and Information Systems Modeling. LNBIP, vol. 214, pp. 37–52. Springer, Heidelberg (2015)
12. Reiter, E.: Has a consensus nl generation architecture appeared, and is it psycholinguistically plausible?. In: Proceedings of the 7th INLG, pp. 163–170 (1994)
13. Lavoie, B., Rambow, O.: A fast and portable realizer for text generation systems. In: 5th ANLP Conference, ANLC 1997, pp. 265–268. ACL (1997)
14. Coşkunçay, A.: An Approach for Generating Natural Language Specifications by Utilizing Business Process Models, Master's thesis, Middle East TU (2010)
15. Burden, H., Heldal, R.: Natural language generation from class diagrams. In: Proceedings of the 8th International Workshop on MoDeVVa. ACM (2011)
16. Lavoie, B., Rambow, O., Reiter, E.: Customizable descriptions of object-oriented models. In: Proceedings of the 5th Conference on ANLP, pp. 253–256 (1997)
17. Fellbaum, C.: WordNet: An Electronic Lexical Database. Bradford Books, Cambridge (1998)
18. Leopold, H., Smirnov, S., Mendling, J.: Refactoring of process model activity labels. In: Hopfe, C.J., Rezgui, Y., Mètais, E., Preece, A., Li, H. (eds.) Natural Language Processing and Information Systems. LNCS, vol. 6177, pp. 268–276. Springer, Heidelberg (2010)
19. Russell, N., van der Aalst, W.M., Ter Hofstede, A.H., Edmond, D.: Workflow resource patterns: identification, representation and tool support. In: Pastor, O., e Cunha, J.F. (eds.) Advanced Information Systems Engineering. LNCS, vol. 3520, pp. 216–232. Springer, Heidelberg (2005)
20. Uszkoreit, H.: Categorial Unification Grammars. In: Proceedings of COLING (1986)
21. Bar-Hillel, Y.: A quasi-arithmetical notation for syntactic description. Language **29**, 47–58 (1953)
22. Shieber, S.M.: An Introduction to Unification-Based Approaches to Grammar. CSLI Lecture Notes Series, vol. 4. Center for SLI, Stanford (1986)

23. McKeown, K.R.: Text Generation: Using Discourse Strategies and Focus Constraints to Generate Natural Language Text. Cambridge University Press, New York (1985)
24. Mann, W.C., Thompson, S.A.: Rhetorical structure theory: toward a functional theory of text organization. Text 8(3), 243–281 (1988)
25. Melčuk, I.A.: Dependency Syntax: Theory and Practice. Daw Book Collectors, State University Press of New York, New York (1988)

# Generating Event Logs Through the Simulation of Declare Models

Claudio Di Ciccio[1], Mario Luca Bernardi[2], Marta Cimitile[3],
and Fabrizio Maria Maggi[4(✉)]

[1] Vienna University of Economics and Business, Vienna, Austria
claudio.di.ciccio@wu.ac.at
[2] University of Sannio, Benevento, Italy
mlbernar@unisannio.it
[3] Unitelma Sapienza University, Rome, Italy
marta.cimitile@unitelma.it
[4] University of Tartu, Tartu, Estonia
f.m.maggi@ut.ee

**Abstract.** In the process mining field, several techniques have been developed during the last years, for the discovery of declarative process models from event logs. This type of models describes processes on the basis of temporal constraints. Every behavior that does not violate such constraints is allowed, and such characteristic has proven to be suitable for representing highly flexible processes. One way to test a process discovery technique is to generate an event log by simulating a process model, and then verify that the process discovered from such a log matches the original one. For this reason, a tool for generating event logs starting from declarative process models becomes vital for the evaluation of declarative process discovery techniques. In this paper, we present an approach for the automated generation of event logs, starting from process models that are based on Declare, one of the most used declarative modeling languages in the process mining literature. Our framework bases upon the translation of Declare constraints into regular expressions and on the utilization of Finite State Automata for the simulation. An evaluation of the implemented tool is presented, showing its effectiveness in both the generation of new logs and the replication of the behavior of existing ones. The presented evaluation also shows the capability of the tool of generating very large logs in a reasonably small amount of time, and its integration with state-of-the-art Declare modeling and discovery tools.

**Keywords:** Declare · Regular expressions · Declarative process models · Process simulation · Log generation

## 1 Introduction

Process mining is a rising research discipline allowing for the analysis of business processes starting from event logs. XES (eXtensible Event Stream) [1] has been

© Springer International Publishing Switzerland 2015
J. Barjis et al. (Eds.): EOMAS 2015, LNBIP 231, pp. 20–36, 2015.
DOI: 10.1007/978-3-319-24626-0_2

recently developed as the standard for storing, exchanging and analyzing event logs. In this standard, each event refers to an activity (i.e., a well-defined step in some process) [2,3] and is related to a particular case (i.e., a process instance). The events belonging to a case are ordered and can be seen as one execution of the process (often referred to as a trace of events). Event logs may store additional information about events such as the resource (i.e., person or device) executing or initiating the activity, the timestamp of the event, or data elements recorded with the event.

One of the main branches of process mining is the automated discovery of process models from event logs. The main idea of process discovery is to extract knowledge from logs concerning control flow, data, organizational and social structures. Therefore, testing and evaluation of process discovery techniques and tools require the availability of event logs. There are several real life logs publicly available that can be used for this purpose [4,5]. However, these logs usually contain imperfections and have some missing information that can alter the evaluation of the discovery algorithms (e.g., they can be incomplete and/or contain noise). For this reason, a common approach adopted for testing process discovery algorithms is based on the use of synthetic logs created via simulation. Simulations can produce event logs with different predefined characteristics and allow the researchers to have more control on the experimental settings to fine tune the developed algorithms.

Starting from these needs, several model simulators and log generators have been developed and are available in the literature [6–9]. However, all these tools generate synthetic logs through the simulation of a procedural process model. This makes them not suitable for the evaluation of process discovery techniques based on declarative process models. Such techniques have recently attracted the attention of the process mining community and are useful to mine processes working in dynamic environments [10–16]. Indeed, differently from procedural process models that work in a closed world assumption and explicitly specify all the allowed behaviors, declarative models are open. Therefore, they enjoy flexibility and are more suitable to describe highly variable behaviors in a compact way.

To test process discovery techniques based on declarative models, tools for the generation of event logs based on the simulation of declarative models are needed and, to the best of our knowledge, they are not available in the literature. To close this gap, in this paper, we present a tool for log generation based on Declare models [17]. This model simulator is based on the translation of Declare constraints into regular expressions and the utilization of Finite State Automata for the simulation of declarative processes. The tool allows the user to generate logs with predefined characteristics (e.g., number and length of the process instances), which is compliant with a given Declare model.

The paper is structured as follows. In Sect. 2, some background concepts are discussed. Section 3 describes the proposed approach. Section 4 reports the experimental setup and the results of the experiments. Section 5 discusses the related work. Section 6 contains conclusive remarks and briefly presents future work.

## 2    Background

In this section, we describe some background elements of our proposed research, i.e., the concepts of event log, Declare-based modeling of processes, and essential theoretical notions about regular expressions and Finite State Automata.

### 2.1    Event Logs

A basic functionality of the core component of Business Process Management Systems (BPMSs) is the recording, in the so-called *event logs* [18], of reporting information during the execution of a workflow [19]. An event log is a structured text file documenting the executions of a single process. Each event log indeed contains a collection of *traces*, each representing the enactment of a unique case (a process instance). Traces are in turn sequences of *events*, i.e., single data entries related to the carry-out of an activity, within the process instance evolution. In 2010, the IEEE Task Force on Process Mining has adopted XES (eXtensible Event Stream) [1] as the standard for storing, exchanging and analyzing event logs. Event logs are typically stored during the Business Process Management System (BPMS)-aided execution of a process. Therefore, logs tend to respect the process model that the BPMS's execution engine loads to coordinate the workflow. In the next section, we introduce Declare, a process modeling notation that is alternative to the older well-established procedural languages, such as Petri nets [20], Workflow Nets [21], YAWL [22] and BPMN [19].

### 2.2    Declare

In this work, the process models are meant to be defined using Declare, a declarative process modeling language introduced by Pesic and van der Aalst in [24]. Declare is qualified as "declarative" because it does not explicitly specify every possible sequence of activities leading from the start to the end of a process execution. Instead, it bases models upon a set of constraints, which must hold true during the enactment. All behaviors that respect the constraints are thus allowed. Constraints are meant to be exerted on sets of activities and mainly pertain to their temporal ordering. In particular, Declare specifies an extensible set of standard templates (see Table 1) that a process analyst can use to model a process. Constraints are concrete instantiations of templates. The adoption of templates makes the model comprehension independent of the logic-based formalization. Indeed, analysts can work with the graphical representation of templates while the underlying formulas remain hidden. Graphically, a Declare process model is a diagram, where activities are presented as nodes (labeled rectangles), and constraints as arcs between activities.

Compared with procedural approaches, Declare models are more suitable to describe processes working in unstable environments and characterized by many exceptional behaviors. Since all what is not explicitly specified is allowed, few constraints can specify many possible behaviors at once.

**Table 1.** Semantics of Declare templates as POSIX regular expressions [23].

| | Template | Regular Expression | Notation |
|---|---|---|---|
| Existence | Participation(a) | `[^a]*(a[^a]*)[^a]*` | |
| | AtMostOne(a) | `[^a]*(a)?[^a]*` | |
| | Init(a) | `a.*` | |
| | End(a) | `.*a` | |
| Relation | RespondedExistence(a, b) | `[^a]*((a.*b.*)|(b.*a.*))*[^a]*` | |
| | Response(a, b) | `[^a]*(a.*b)*[^a]*` | |
| | AlternateResponse(a, b) | `[^a]*(a[^a]*b[^a]*)*[^a]*` | |
| | ChainResponse(a, b) | `[^a]*(ab[^a]*)*[^a]*` | |
| | Precedence(a, b) | `[^b]*(a.*b)*[^b]*` | |
| | AlternatePrecedence(a, b) | `[^b]*(a[^b]*b[^b]*)*[^b]*` | |
| | ChainPrecedence(a, b) | `[^b]*(ab[^b]*)*[^b]*` | |
| Coupling Relation | CoExistence(a, b) | `[^ab]*((a.*b.*)|(b.*a.*))*[^ab]*` | |
| | Succession(a, b) | `[^ab]*(a.*b)*[^ab]*` | |
| | AlternateSuccession(a, b) | `[^ab]*(a[^ab]*b[^ab]*)*[^ab]*` | |
| | ChainSuccession(a, b) | `[^ab]*(ab[^ab]*)*[^ab]*` | |
| Negative Relation | NotChainSuccession(a, b) | `[^a]*(aa*[^ab][^a]*)*([^a]*|a)` | |
| | NotSuccession(a, b) | `[^a]*(a[^b]*)*[^ab]*` | |
| | NotCoExistence(a, b) | `[^ab]*((a[^b]*)|(b[^a]*))?` | |

Declare templates can be divided into two main groups: *existence templates* and *relation templates*. The former is a set of unary templates. They can be expressed as predicates over one variable. The latter comprises rules that are imposed on target activities, when activation tasks occur. Relation templates thus correspond to binary predicates over two variables. Starting from the first row of Table 1, *Participation*(a) is an existence template, which requires the execution of a at least once in every process instance. *AtMostOne*(a) is its dual, as it details that a is not executed more than once in a process instance. *Init*(a) and *End*(a) specify that a occurs in every case as the first and the last activity, respectively. *RespondedExistence*(a, b) is a relation template imposing that if a is performed at least once during the process execution, b must occur at least once as well, either in the future or in the past, with respect to a. *Response*(a, b) adds to *RespondedExistence*(a, b) the condition that b must occur eventually *after* a. *AlternateResponse*(a, b) adds to *Response*(a, b) the condition that no other a's occur between an execution of a and a subsequent b. *ChainResponse*(a, b) is even stronger and specifies that whenever a occurs, b must occur immediately after. *Precedence*(a, b) specifies that a must occur *before* b. *AlternatePrecedence*(a, b)

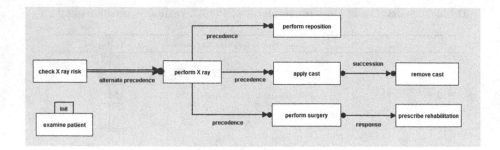

**Fig. 1.** The Declare model for a fracture treatment process.

adds to $Precedence(a, b)$ the condition that no other b's occur between an execution of b and a precedent a. $ChainPrecedence(a, b)$ specifies that whenever b occurs, a must occur immediately before.

Two specializations of the relation templates are *coupling relation templates* and *negative relation templates*. In the first group there are templates where both the constrained activities are together activation and target. For instance, $CoExistence(a, b)$ is a coupling relation template requiring that if a is executed, then b must be performed as well, and vice-versa. In the second group, the occurrence of one activity excludes the occurrence of the other. For instance, $NotCoExistence(a, b)$ is a negative relation template requiring that if a is executed, then b cannot be performed in the same trace, and vice-versa.

An example of Declare process model (fracture treatment) is depicted in Fig. 1. The process comprises activities *examine patient, check X ray risk, perform X ray, perform reposition, apply cast, remove cast, perform surgey,* and *prescribe rehabilitation.* Its behavior is specified by the following constraints $C_1$–$C_7$:

$C_1$ $Init(examine\ patient)$
$C_2$ $AlternatePrecedence(check\ X\ ray\ risk, perform\ X\ ray)$
$C_3$ $Precedence(perform\ X\ ray, perform\ reposition)$
$C_4$ $Precedence(perform\ X\ ray, apply\ cast)$
$C_5$ $Succession(apply\ cast, remove\ cast)$
$C_6$ $Precedence(perform\ X\ ray, perform\ surgery)$
$C_7$ $Response(perform\ surgery, prescribe\ rehabilitation)$

According to these constraints, every process instance starts with activity *examine patient.* Moreover, if activity *perform X ray* occurs, then *check X ray risk* must be carried out before it, without other occurrences of *perform X ray* in between. Activities *perform reposition, apply cast* and *perform surgery* require that *perform X ray* occurs before they are executed. If *perform surgery* occurs, then *prescribe rehabilitation* occurs eventually after it. Finally, after every execution of *apply cast,* eventually *remove cast* occurs and, vice-versa, before every occurrence of *remove cast, apply cast* must be carried out.

Declare templates semantics have been expressed in the literature as formulations of several formal languages: as Linear Temporal Logic over Finite Traces

(LTL$_f$) formulas [25], as shown in [26]; in the form of $\mathcal{SCIFF}$ integrity constraints [27], as exploited in [28]; as First Order Logic (FOL) formulas interpreted over finite traces, as described in [13,25]. In this work, we use regular expressions (REs), as described in [23]. Table 1 reports the translation of Declare constraints into regular expressions (REs).

## 2.3  Regular Expressions

Regular expressions are a formal notation to compactly express finite sequences of characters, a.k.a. matching patterns. The syntax of REs consists of any juxtaposition of characters of a given alphabet, optionally grouped by enclosing parentheses ( and ), to which the following well-known operators can be applied: the binary alternation | and concatenation, and the unary Kleene star *. Thus, the regular expression a(bc)*d|e identifies any string starting with a, followed by any number of repetitions of the pattern (sub-string) bc (optionally, none), and closed by either d or e, such as ad, abcd, abcbce and ae. Table 1 adopts the POSIX standard for the following additional shortcut notations: (i) . and [^x] respectively denote any character, or any character but $x$, (ii) the + and ? operators respectively match from one to any, and none to one occurrences of the preceding pattern. In the reminder of this paper, we will also make use of (iii) the parametric quantifier $\{,m\}$, with $m$ integer higher than 0, which specifies the maximum number of repetitions of the preceding pattern, and (iv) the parametric quantifier $\{n,\}$, with $n$ integer higher than or equal to 0, which specifies the minimum number of repetitions of the preceding pattern. We recall here that (i) REs are closed under the conjuction operation & [29], and (ii) the expressive power of REs completely covers regular languages, thus (iii) for every RE, a corresponding deterministc Finite State Automaton (FSA) exists, accepting all and only the matching strings.

## 2.4  Finite State Automata

A deterministc FSA is a labeled transition system $\mathcal{A} = \langle A, S, \delta, s_0, S_f \rangle$ defined over states $S$ and an alphabet $A$, having $\delta : S \times A \to S$ as transition function, i.e., a function that, given a starting state and a character, returns the target state (if defined). $s_0 \in S$ is the initial state of $\mathcal{A}$, and $S_f \subseteq S$ is the non-empty set of its accepting states ($S_f \neq \emptyset$). For the sake of simplicity, we will omit the qualification "deterministic" in the remainder of this paper. A finite path $\pi$ of length $n$ over $\mathcal{A}$ is a sequence $\pi = \langle \pi^1, \ldots, \pi^n \rangle$ of tuples $\pi^i = \langle s^{i-1}, \sigma^i, s^i \rangle \in \delta$, for which the following conditions hold true: (i) $\pi^1$, the first tuple, is such that $s^0 = s_0$ (it starts from the initial state of $\mathcal{A}$), and (ii) the starting state of $\pi^i$ is the target state of $\pi^{i-1}$: $\pi = \langle \langle s^0, \sigma^1, s^1 \rangle, \langle s^1, \sigma^2, s^2 \rangle, \ldots \langle s^{n-1}, \sigma^n, s^n \rangle \rangle$. A finite string of length $n \geqslant 1$, i.e., a concatenation $t = t_1 \ldots t_n$ of characters $t_i \in A$ is accepted by $\mathcal{A}$ if a path $\pi$ of length $n$ is defined over $\mathcal{A}$ and is such that (i) for every $i \in [1, n]$, $\pi^i = \langle s^{i-1}, t_i, s^i \rangle$, and (ii) $\pi^n = \langle s^{i-1}, t_n, s^n \rangle$ is s.t. $s^n \in S_f$.

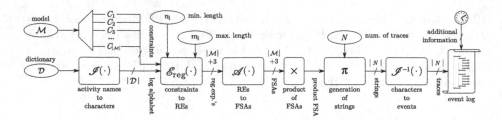

**Fig. 2.** The log-generation framework.

FSAs are closed under the product operation ×. A product of two FSAs accepts the intersection of languages (sets of accepted strings) accepted by each operand. The product of FSAs is an isomorphism for the conjunction of RE, i.e., the product of two FSAs respectively corresponding to two REs is equivalent to the FSA that derives from the conjunction of the two REs.

## 3  Approach

Figure 2 sketches the modular framework upon which our approach is based. The output is an event log $L$, synthesized on the basis of a Declare process model that must regulate the composition of the traces. The input indeed consists of *(i)* the set of activity names of the process, henceforth activity dictionary $\mathcal{D}$, *(ii)* a Declare model $\mathcal{M}$, i.e., a set of constraints $C_1, \ldots, C_{|\mathcal{M}|}$ expressed on the activities of the process, *(iii)* the minimum and maximum number of events per trace, respectively $n_l$ and $m_l$, and *(iv)* the number $N$ of traces that the output event log must contain.

The overall approach goes through six consecutive steps, as listed below. The idea is to create a Finite State Automaton that accepts all and only those traces complying with the conditions imposed by the user. The event log will result in a collection of traces, generated by running paths along the automaton, from its initial state, to an accepting one.

*From Activity Names to Characters.* The first step is the mapping of process activity names to single terminal characters, henceforth *process alphabet* $\Sigma$, by means of the function $\mathscr{I} : \mathcal{D} \to \Sigma$. $\mathscr{I}$ is bijective, i.e., every activity maps to a distinct character, and all characters can be referenced to the related activity. Therefore, it admits an inverse function $\mathscr{I}^{-1} : \Sigma \to \mathcal{D}$. In the example of Fig. 1, activities of the process are *apply cast, check X ray risk, examine patient, perform X ray, perform reposition, perform surgery, prescribe rehabilitation*, and *remove cast* in $\mathcal{D}$, respectively mapped by $\mathscr{I}$ to a, b, c, d, e, f, g, and h in $\Sigma$. Thus, e.g., $\mathscr{I}(perform\ surgery) = $ f, and $\mathscr{I}^{-1}($g$) = prescribe\ rehabilitation$.

*From Constraints to Regular Expressions.* Every constraint is thereafter translated into the corresponding RE during the second step, as per Table 1 [23]. The translation function is henceforth indicated with $\mathscr{E}_{\text{reg}}$. In the example,

$\mathscr{E}_{\text{reg}}\left(Response(\text{f},\text{g})\right) = $ [^f]*(f.*g)*[^f]*, being $\text{f} = \mathscr{I}(perform\ surgery)$ and $\text{g} = \mathscr{I}(prescribe\ rehabilitation)$.

For the generation of logs, an additional regular expression is considered, specifying that accepted strings can only comprise those characters that belong to the process alphabet [30]: $[\sigma_1\sigma_2\ldots\sigma_{|\Sigma|}]$ *, for all $\sigma_i \in \Sigma, i \in [1,|\Sigma|]$. In the example, such RE is [abcdefgh]*. By means of regular expressions, we also specify (a) the minimum, and (b) the maximum length of traces. Given the user-defined parameters $n_l$ and $m_l$, such REs are (a) .*{$n_l$,}, and (b) .*{,$m_l$}.

Therefore, the specification of the traces for the fracture treatment process $\mathcal{M}$ consisting of constraints $C_1$–$C_7$ (Fig. 1, Sect. 2.2) defined over activities in $\mathcal{D}$, where the length of traces ranges between $n_l = 3$ and $m_l = 20$, would result in the following list of REs, $R_1$–$R_{10}$:

$R_1$ .*c $= \mathscr{E}_{\text{reg}}(C_1)$     $R_6$ [^f]*(d.*f)*[^f]* $= \mathscr{E}_{\text{reg}}(C_6)$

$R_2$ [^d]*(b[^d]*d[^d]*)*[^d]*     $R_7$ [^f]*(f.*[g])*[^f]* $= \mathscr{E}_{\text{reg}}(C_7)$
$\quad = \mathscr{E}_{\text{reg}}(C_2)$     $R_8$ [abcdefgh]*

$R_3$ [^e]*(d.*e)*[^e]* $= \mathscr{E}_{\text{reg}}(C_3)$     $R_9$ .*{3,}

$R_4$ [^a]*(d.*a)*[^a]* $= \mathscr{E}_{\text{reg}}(C_4)$     $R_{10}$ .*{,20}

$R_5$ [^ah]*(a.*h)*[^ah]* $= \mathscr{E}_{\text{reg}}(C_5)$

Out of these regular expressions, $R_1$–$R_7$ are the respective translation of constraints $C_1$–$C_7$ given in Sect. 2.2. $R_8$ defines the characters that are admissible for the strings, whilst $R_9$ and $R_{10}$ limit their length. The output of this phase is thus a set of $|\mathcal{M}| + 3$ REs.

*From Regular Expressions to Finite State Automata.* For each RE, a FSA accepting all and only the matching strings is derived, by means of function $\mathscr{A}$. Figure 3 shows the FSAs deriving from those regular expressions that express the relation constraint templates in our example model (*AlternatePrecedence, Response, Precedence* and *Succession*). In particular, $\mathcal{A}_2 = \mathscr{A}(R_2)$ is depicted in Fig. 3a, $\mathcal{A}_7 = \mathscr{A}(R_7)$ in Fig. 3b, $\mathcal{A}_4 = \mathscr{A}(R_4)$ in Fig. 3c, and $\mathcal{A}_5 = \mathscr{A}(R_5)$ in Fig. 3d, respectively referring to constraints $C_2$, $C_7$, $C_4$, and $C_5$. Hence, the outcome of this phase is a set of $|\mathcal{M}| + 3$ FSAs, i.e., $\mathcal{A}_1, \ldots \mathcal{A}_{|\mathcal{M}|+3}$.

*Product of Finite State Automata.* The constraints representing the process behavior, and the conditions on the length of traces must hold true at the same time. This entails that the conjunction of all regular expressions $R_1$–$R_{10}$ must be verified. In turn, this means that the product of the derived FSAs is the generator of the traces. We will denote this automaton with $\mathcal{A}^\times = \mathcal{A}_1 \times \cdot \times \mathcal{A}_{|\mathcal{M}|+3}$.

*Generation of Strings.* The traces of the event log are created on the basis of the strings accepted by $\mathcal{A}^\times$. To this extent, a random path is chosen along $\mathcal{A}^\times$ that terminates in an accepting state, and characters of traversed transitions are concatenated. The resulting string corresponds to the backbone of a trace for the event log. The strings are indeed made of characters that uniquely identify activities, in a sequence that complies with the constraints of the input model $\mathcal{M}$.

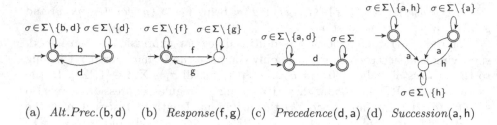

(a)  *Alt.Prec.*(b, d)   (b)  *Response*(f, g)   (c)  *Precedence*(d, a)   (d)  *Succession*(a, h)

**Fig. 3.** FSAs accepting the traces that verify Declare constraints.

*From Strings to Event Log.* We create traces in the event log by deriving the corresponding activities from each character in the strings, keeping the sequences unaltered. Each activity is retrieved through the application of the inverse translation mapping function $\mathscr{I}^{-1}$ to the single-character identifiers. Further information such as timestamps can also be specified for the events: custom attributes can indeed be seamlessly added to enhance the information conveyed by the event log. However, such enrichment goes beyond the scope of this paper.

This procedure is repeated $N$ times, being $N$ the user-specified parameter indicating the number of desired traces in the log. At the end of the $N$ iterations, the log is returned. This last step concludes the overall approach.

## 4   Evaluation

Our framework has been implemented as a working prototype integrated within the modeling tool Declare designer [17].[1] Figure 4 shows a screenshot of its main dialog window, where the user can specify the input parameters affecting the length and the number of the traces in the generated log, once the model has been drawn or loaded from an external Declare XML specification file. The output log can be either encoded using XES [1] or MXML (another XML-based standard format for logs), or as plain text.

In order to evaluate the efficiency of the proposed approach, we have run an extensive set of experiments to assess the time to generate event logs of different sizes, following the trailing example provided in Sect. 2.2. The results are described in Sect. 4.1. To validate it from the perspective of the effectiveness, we have used as reference models the fracture treatment example process of Fig. 1, and a real case study. We have generated an event log on the basis of each model, and run two different Declare discovery algorithms, in order to check whether the simulated and the discovered models match. The tests confirm the compliance of the log w.r.t. the input model, as detailed in Sect. 4.2.

All tests have been conducted on a machine equipped with an Intel i7 CPU quad processor at 2.8 Ghz and 12 GB of dedicated RAM. We have used Java SE 1.7 as the coding language for the implementation of the framework.

---

[1] https://github.com/processmining/synthetic-log-generator.

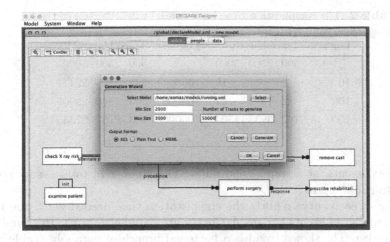

**Fig. 4.** A screenshot of the implemented prototype.

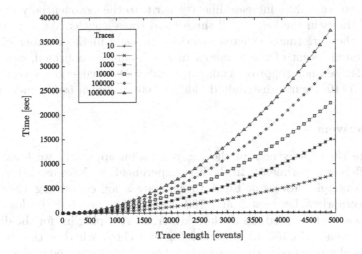

**Fig. 5.** Generation times with respect to number of traces and trace size.

## 4.1 Efficiency

In order to assess the performance of the log generation approach, we considered as reference model the sample process described in Sect. 2.2 and depicted in Fig. 1. A set of logs with different characteristics has been generated. In particular, we have sampled the generation times that resulted by varying the following user parameters: *(i)* the number of events per trace, keeping minimum and maximum values equal ($n_l = m_l$), and *(ii)* the number of traces in the log $N$. In order to show that the generator can be used in real contexts also to generate very large logs within acceptable times, we increased the number of traces from 10 to $10^6$ at a base-10 logarithmic step, and raised the length of each trace from

**Table 2.** The computation time (in seconds) w.r.t. the size of the log.

| Log size | Trace length | | | Log size | Trace length | | |
|---|---|---|---|---|---|---|---|
| | 500 | 2500 | 5000 | | 500 | 2500 | 5000 |
| 10 | 2 | 51 | 191 | 10000 | 242 | 5875 | 22477 |
| 100 | 82 | 1992 | 7620 | 100000 | 323 | 7816 | 29906 |
| 1000 | 162 | 3933 | 15049 | 1000000 | 403 | 9757 | 37335 |

10 to 5,000 events, at a step of 500 units. The number of total events per log ranged from 100 up to $5 \cdot 10^9$.

In Fig. 5, each curve reports the computation time needed w.r.t. the incremented number of events per trace. Curves are parametric w.r.t. the number of traces per log. The shown trend is a flattened branch of parabola. Table 2 lists the sampled times w.r.t. the logarithmic progression of the number of traces instead, fixing three values for the trace length (500, 2500, and 5,000). As the reader can notice, values increase linearly w.r.t. to the exponentially increasing number of traces in the log, for all three fixed trace lengths. We can thus conclude that the performance increases logarithmically in the number of traces. The moderated ascent of the parabola in Fig. 5 is here confirmed, e.g., by the fact that 242 seconds (approx. 4 min) are sufficient to generate a very big log containing $5 \cdot 10^6$ events, distributed along 10,000 traces of 500 events each.

### 4.2   Effectiveness

To evaluate the effectiveness of the log generation approach, we have carried out two different experiments. In the first experiment, we have used the fracture treatment example process of Fig. 1 to generate a log containing 1,000 traces of length comprised between 2 and 100 events. We exported the log in XES format. Then, we have used the Declare Miner, a ProM plug-in[2] for the discovery of Declare models [14,15], to mine the log and check whether the discovered Declare model was in line with the simulated one. The discovered model is shown in Fig. 6. The figure shows the list of constraints that are satisfied in 100 % of the cases. The model contains the same constraints as the simulated one, thus experimentally confirming the correctness of the generated log.

In our second experiment, we have tried to reproduce with our tool the behavior of a real-life log. To this aim, we have used the log provided for the BPI challenge 2014 by Rabobank Netherlands Group ICT [31]. The log pertains to the management of calls or mails from customers to the Service Desk concerning disruptions of ICT-services. The log contains 46,616 traces and amounts to 466,737 events referring to 39 different activities. We have used the Declare Miner to discover a model from this log. The discovered model is shown in Fig. 7. Starting from this model, we generated a log with 46,616 cases of length between

---

[2] www.processmining.org/prom/start.

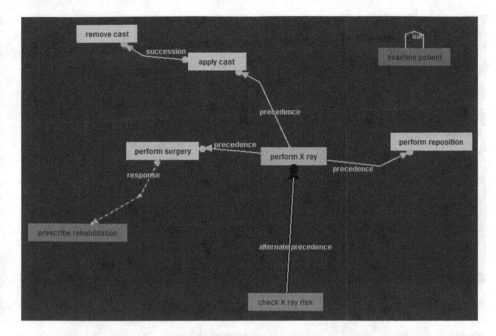

**Fig. 6.** Discovered model from the log generated starting from the fracture treatment process model.

1 and 173. These parameters were chosen according to the characteristics of the original real life log. We exported the log in XES format. Figure 8 shows the ProM log visualizer dashboard window, listing the main statistics about the loaded log. In this second experiment, we have used MINERful [32] to rediscover the model. Using again the option that in this tool allows the user to discover only the constraints always satisfied, we obtain the same model shown in Fig. 7.

We can conclude that the logs generated by our approach reproduce exactly the behavior of the input models, regardless of the discovery algorithm adopted to verify it, and irrespectively of whether the aim is to simulate a hand made reference model, or rather to replicate the behavior of an existing real life event log. Furthermore, our tool is highly integrated with the state-of-the-art software for modeling and mining Declare processes.

## 5   Related Work

The automated generation of event logs to test process mining algorithms has been studied extensively in the context of procedural modeling languages. The work of Hee and Liu [8] introduces a framework for the automated generation of classes of Petri nets (PNs), according to user-defined topological rules. Generated Petri nets (PNs) are meant to be used as benchmarks for algorithms. This work is of inspiration for us, in that we also create a graph-based structure as a means to create benchmarking data (event logs). In [33], an approach based

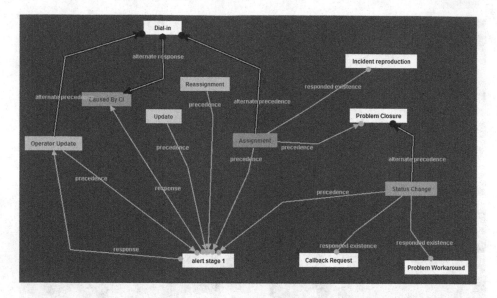

**Fig. 7.** Discovered model from the log provided for the BPI challenge 2014.

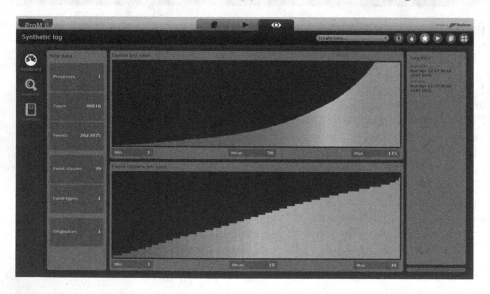

**Fig. 8.** Information about the log generated starting from the Declare model in Fig. 7.

on CPN Tools [7] is described, to generate XML event logs by the simulation of a Colored Petri net (CPN). In [6], Burattin and Sperduti propose an approach for the generation of logs. Process descriptions are meant to be provided via a (stochastic) context-free grammar, whose definition is based on well-known process patterns. The work of [6] relates to the one presented in this paper in that we adopt regular expressions to generate logs, and the REs express regular languages, hence, languages accepted by left-linear context-free grammars. However, we use REs as translations of business rules, and not as production rules for the topology of the process.

All the approaches described so far support indeed only procedural business process models. Procedural business process models show some limitations when the represented process is characterized by several possible execution paths, high variability and continuous changes [11], as in the case of knowledge-intensive processes [34]. In this context, declarative process models such as Declare [35] are proven to perform better in terms of compactness [36] and customizability [37]. The newest version of CPN Tools [38] allows the user to graphically add Declare constraints to the transitions of a CPN, thus obtaining hybrid models. The simulation tool allows both user-driven and random executions of such models. Our framework differs from CPN Tools in that it is not an extension of a procedural-based modeler, but inherently a tool for the management of Declare process models, specialized in the generation of event logs. For instance, the number of traces to be generated is here a parameter. In CPN Tools, instead, a workaround would be needed, resorting on the initial marking of user-specified fictitious places linked to process activities/transitions. In addition, notions outside the Declare specification are needed for simulation (marking, places, tokens), and a Declare model could not thus be simply loaded to generate the logs.

Preliminary versions of log generators based on Declare models were presented in [13,32,39,40] for testing the time performance of the proposed process mining tools. A discussion on the adoption of a product of FSAs to represent a conjunction of declarative constraints can also be found in [30]. Here, we present the complete approach, which is detached from any discovery algorithm and can be used for the creation of platform-independent benchmarks.

# 6    Conclusions and Future Work

In this paper, we have presented an approach for generating event logs based on the simulation of declarative models. The proposed approach is based on the translation of Declare constraints into regular expressions. The framework has been presented in its execution flow, which undergoes a sequence of steps leading from a set of Declare constraints to a simulation automaton, to the final event log. The evaluation has shown that the implemented solution, integrated within the Declare designer tool, correctly reproduces user-defined models and replicates the behavior of existing logs. Two experiments have been conducted as an experimental evidence of such claims, respectively using as input an example reference model, and a model stemming from the BPI Challenge 2014 benchmark event log. The generated logs have been subject to the processing of two different declarative process discovery techniques, and in both cases the retrieved model matched the input one. Performance tests also showed that the algorithm is capable of generating very large logs in a fairly small amount of time. It is in the future plans to extend the framework towards the creation of logs containing user specified data attributes and complex activity life-cycles.

**Acknowledgments.** The work of Claudio Di Ciccio has received funding from the EU Seventh Framework Programme (FP7/2007-2013) under grant agreement 318275 (GET Service).

# References

1. Verbeek, H.M.W., Buijs, J.C.A.M., van Dongen, B.F., van der Aalst, W.M.P.: XES, XESame, and ProM 6. In: Soffer, P., Proper, E. (eds.) CAiSE Forum 2010. LNBIP, vol. 72, pp. 60–75. Springer, Heidelberg (2011)
2. Scheer, A.-W., Nüttgens, M.: ARIS Architecture and reference models for business process management. In: van der Aalst, W.M.P., Desel, J., Oberweis, A. (eds.) Business Process Management. LNCS, vol. 1806, p. 376. Springer, Heidelberg (2000)
3. Scheer, A.: ARIS toolset: a software product is born. Inf. Syst. **19**(8), 607–624 (1994)
4. van Dongen, B.: BPI challenge 2011 (2011)
5. van Dongen, B.: BPI challenge 2012 (2012)
6. Burattin, A., Sperduti, A.: PLG: a framework for the generation of business process models and their execution logs. In: Muehlen, M., Su, J. (eds.) BPM 2010 Workshops. LNBIP, vol. 66, pp. 214–219. Springer, Heidelberg (2011)
7. Jensen, K., Kristensen, L.M., Wells, L.: Coloured petri nets and cpn tools for modelling and validation of concurrent systems. Int. J. Softw. Tools Technol. Transf. **9**(3), 213–254 (2007)
8. Hee, K.V., Liu, Z.: Generating benchmarks by random stepwise refinement of petri nets. In: Donatelli, S., Kleijn, J., Machado, R., Fernandes, J. (eds.) PETRI NETS 2010, pp. 403–417. CEUR-ws.org (2012)
9. Bergmann, G., Horváth, A., Ráth, I., Varró, D.: A benchmark evaluation of incremental pattern matching in graph transformation. In: Ehrig, H., Heckel, R., Rozenberg, G., Taentzer, G. (eds.) ICGT 2008. LNCS, vol. 5214, pp. 396–410. Springer, Heidelberg (2008)
10. Pesic, M., van der Aalst, W.M.P.: A declarative approach for flexible business processes management. In: Eder, J., Dustdar, S. (eds.) BPM Workshops 2006. LNCS, vol. 4103, pp. 169–180. Springer, Heidelberg (2006)
11. Fahland, D., Lübke, D., Mendling, J., Reijers, H., Weber, B., Weidlich, M., Zugal, S.: Declarative versus imperative process modeling languages: the issue of understandability. In: Halpin, T., Krogstie, J., Nurcan, S., Proper, E., Schmidt, R., Soffer, P., Ukor, R. (eds.) Enterprise, Business-Process and Information Systems Modeling. LNBIP, vol. 29, pp. 353–366. Springer, Heidelberg (2009)
12. Pichler, P., Weber, B., Zugal, S., Pinggera, J., Mendling, J., Reijers, H.A.: Imperative versus declarative process modeling languages: an empirical investigation. In: Daniel, F., Barkaoui, K., Dustdar, S. (eds.) BPM Workshops 2011, Part I. LNBIP, vol. 99, pp. 383–394. Springer, Heidelberg (2012)
13. Di Ciccio, C., Mecella, M.: On the discovery of declarative control flows for artful processes. ACM Trans. Manage. Inf. Syst. **5**(4), 24:1–24:37 (2015)
14. Maggi, F.M.: Declarative process mining with the Declare component of ProM. In: BPM (Demos) (2013)
15. Maggi, F.M., Bose, R.P.J.C., van der Aalst, W.M.P.: Efficient discovery of understandable declarative process models from event logs. In: Ralyté, J., Franch, X., Brinkkemper, S., Wrycza, S. (eds.) CAiSE 2012. LNCS, vol. 7328, pp. 270–285. Springer, Heidelberg (2012)

16. Bernardi, M.L., Cimitile, M., Di Francescomarino, C., Maggi, F.M.: Using discriminative rule mining to discover declarative process models with non-atomic activities. In: Bikakis, A., Fodor, P., Roman, D. (eds.) RuleML 2014. LNCS, vol. 8620, pp. 281–295. Springer, Heidelberg (2014)

17. Pesic, M., Schonenberg, H., van der Aalst, W.M.P.: DECLARE: full support for loosely-structured processes. In: EDOC, pp. 287–300 (2007)

18. van der Aalst, W.M.P.: Process Mining: Discovery, Conformance and Enhancement of Business Processes. Springer, New York (2011)

19. Dumas, M., La Rosa, M., Mendling, J., Reijers, H.A.: Fundamentals of Business Process Management. Springer, Heidelberg (2013)

20. van der Aalst, W.M.P.: The application of petri nets to workflow management. J. Circ. Syst. Comput. 8(1), 21–66 (1998)

21. van der Aalst, W.M.P.: Verification of workflow nets. In: Azéma, P., Balbo, G. (eds.) ICATPN 1997. LNCS, vol. 1248, pp. 407–426. Springer, Heidelberg (1997)

22. van der Aalst, W.M.P., ter Hofstede, A.H.M.: YAWL: yet another workflow language. Inf. Syst. 30(4), 245–275 (2005)

23. Di Ciccio, C., Mecella, M., Scannapieco, M., Zardetto, D., Catarci, T.: MailOfMine – analyzing mail messages for mining artful collaborative processes. In: Aberer, K., Damiani, E., Dillon, T. (eds.) SIMPDA 2011. LNBIP, vol. 116, pp. 55–81. Springer, Heidelberg (2012)

24. van der Aalst, W., Pesic, M., Schonenberg, H.: Declarative workflows: balancing between flexibility and support. Computer Science - R&D 23, 99–113 (2009)

25. De Giacomo, G., Vardi, M.Y.: Linear temporal logic and linear dynamic logic on finite traces. In: IJCAI (2013)

26. De Giacomo, G., De Masellis, R., Montali, M.: Reasoning on ltl on finite traces: Insensitivity to infiniteness. In: AAAI (2014)

27. Alberti, M., Chesani, F., Gavanelli, M., Lamma, E., Mello, P., Torroni, P.: Verifiable agent interaction in abductive logic programming: the sciff framework. ACM Trans. Comput. Log. 9(4), 29:1–29:43 (2008)

28. Chesani, F., Lamma, E., Mello, P., Montali, M., Riguzzi, F., Storari, S.: Exploiting inductive logic programming techniques for declarative process mining. In: Jensen, K., van der Aalst, W.M.P. (eds.) Transactions on Petri Nets and Other Models of Concurrency II. LNCS, vol. 5460, pp. 278–295. Springer, Heidelberg (2009)

29. Gisburg, S., Rose, G.F.: Preservation of languages by transducers. Inf. Control 9(2), 153–176 (1966)

30. Prescher, J., Di Ciccio, C., Mendling, J.: From declarative processes to imperative models. In: SIMPDA, pp. 162–173, CEUR-WS.org (2014)

31. van Dongen, B.: BPI challenge 2014 (2014)

32. Di Ciccio, C., Mecella, M.: A two-step fast algorithm for the automated discovery of declarative workflows. In: CIDM, IEEE, pp. 135–142 (2013)

33. de Medeiros, A.A., Günther, C.W.: Process mining: Using CPN tools to create test logs for mining algorithms. In: Proceedings of the sixth workshop on the practical use of coloured Petri nets and CPN tools (CPN 2005), vol. 576 (2005)

34. Di Ciccio, C., Marrella, A., Russo, A.: Knowledge-intensive Processes: Characteristics, requirements and analysis of contemporary approaches. J. Data Semant. 4(1), 29–57 (2015)

35. van der Aalst, W.M.P., Pesic, M.: DecSerFlow: towards a truly declarative service flow language. In: Bravetti, M., Núñez, M., Zavattaro, G. (eds.) WS-FM 2006. LNCS, vol. 4184, pp. 1–23. Springer, Heidelberg (2006)

36. van der Aalst, W.M.P., Pesic, M., Schonenberg, H.: Declarative workflows: Balancing between flexibility and support. Comput. Sci. R&D 23(2), 99–113 (2009)

37. Schunselaar, D.M.M., Maggi, F.M., Sidorova, N., van der Aalst, W.M.P.: Configurable declare: designing customisable flexible process models. In: Meersman, R., et al. (eds.) OTM 2012, Part I. LNCS, vol. 7565, pp. 20–37. Springer, Heidelberg (2012)
38. Westergaard, M., Slaats, T.: Cpn tools 4: A process modeling tool combining declarative and imperative paradigms. In: BPM (Demos) (2013)
39. Di Ciccio, C., Maggi, F.M., Mendling, J.: Discovering target-branched declare constraints. In: Sadiq, S., Soffer, P., Völzer, H. (eds.) BPM 2014. LNCS, vol. 8659, pp. 34–50. Springer, Heidelberg (2014)
40. Di Ciccio, C., Mecella, M., Mendling, J.: The effect of noise on mined declarative constraints. In: Ceravolo, P., Accorsi, R., Cudre-Mauroux, P. (eds.) SIMPDA 2013. LNBIP, vol. 203, pp. 1–24. Springer, Heidelberg (2015)

# Towards a Business Process Model Transformations Framework

Khoutir Bouchbout[✉], Sarah Khaldoun, and Saber Marouf

Computer Science Research Unit, EMP University, Algiers, Algeria
{kbouchbout, skhaldoun, smarouf}@gmail.com

**Abstract.** The essential purpose of Business Process Management (BPM) is to construct processes which yield a profit for enterprise. In today's business world, there is a strong need for adopting a BPM approach based on Service Oriented Architecture (SOA) paradigm that can be applied to execute and manage IT-enabled business processes. Hence, the proposed BP model transformations framework combines BPM concepts and Web services which is an application of SOA technology. Two basic categories of BP modelling languages can be recognized: block-oriented languages and graph-oriented languages. Our work details the implementation of the transformation of Business Process Modelling Notation (BPMN) process model to Business Process Execution Language (BPEL) process model by means of transformation rules implemented as an Eclipse plug-ins. Finally, we develop also a software tool by applying Petri Nets analysis techniques to statically check if it satisfies a number of semantic conditions.

**Keywords:** Business process modelling · BPMN · ATL · Web services · BPEL · Business process formal verification

## 1 Introduction

A modern enterprise is a heavily wired and networked system where multiple components play in symphony to yield a competitive position in the ear of digital economy. Therefore, collaboration and interaction in modern enterprises are the only way that the complex activities and processes are carried out [3]. The importance of BPM has been widely recognized, leading to a variety of approaches and proposed solutions to their design and implementation [29].

Moreover, due to the close relationship between BPM and SOA, the objective of business process modelling should be to design processes that could be eventually executed in the service-oriented environment. Accordingly, to align the business requirements with the executable processes, the modelling should start from high level processes, which would be refined to more detailed and exact models and finally to executable code.

In addition, there is a technical separation between the business process models developed by business analysts and the process representations required by the systems designed to implement and execute those processes. Many business process modelling languages have been proposed [17]. They are classified into two categories:

© Springer International Publishing Switzerland 2015
J. Barjis et al. (Eds.): EOMAS 2015, LNBIP 231, pp. 37–48, 2015.
DOI: 10.1007/978-3-319-24626-0_3

block-oriented and graph-oriented languages. BPEL is for the most part block-oriented. BPMN is the most representative of graph-oriented languages. Transformations between these fundamentally different languages are problematic, because graph-oriented languages can express process patterns that block-oriented cannot. Additionally, the business process model transformation tools check that the BPMN model [21] is valid in the sense that a BPEL file [20] can be generated, but there is no way to automatically ensure that the process terminates correctly, meaning that the process is free of deadlocks, for example. Henceforth, it is necessary to provide support for checking the correctness of both models using Petri Net analysis techniques [1].

As case study, the diagram of Fig. 1 involves two participants with their own processes including the points of interaction according to certain pre-agreed rules. The buyer first sends an order to the seller. Having accepted the order, the seller sends the goods which are received by the buyer. After that, the seller sends an invoice to the seller. This is followed by payment whose sending ends the process from the buyer's point of view and acceptance from the seller's point of view (white boxes represent public activities and grey boxes represent the private ones).

The rest of the paper proceeds as follows. In Sect. 2, we overview the different business process modelling languages. Section 3 analyses the current literature on process model transformations. Subsequently, Sect. 4 presents the details of our framework. Next, Sect. 5 assesses the capabilities of proposed solution. Finally, Sect. 6 closes the paper with a conclusion and future work.

## 2  Business Process Modelling: An Overview

Below, we discuss some issues related to business process modelling and transformation of process models.

### 2.1  Process Modelling Languages

Many surveys comparing different types of BP modelling languages are provided in [7, 15, 16, 18, 28]. They have compared these languages based on their expressive power, status and support. Two basic categories can be recognized: block-oriented languages and graph-oriented languages. Business process languages such as EPC – Event-driven Process Chain [27], BPMN, BPEL – Business Process Execution Language and WS-CDL - Web Service Choreography Description Language [7, 16] have emerged as a key instrument for achieving integration of business applications in a SOA setting [25].

Obviously, most authors agree that for business process definition well known graphical language - BPMN has been proposed. Meanwhile, the most popular and supported by industry for defining executable processes is BPEL. Thus, BPEL is an XML-based language for the composition of executable business processes based on Web services technology. Additionally, the relevance of BPEL's evaluation is hindered by the fact that it has no real competitors as an execution language standard in the industry.

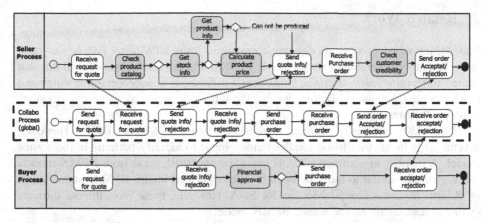

**Fig. 1.** An example of business process (procurement process)

## 2.2 BPMN to BPEL Processes Transformation

Initially, it was necessary to manually translate the original business process models to execution models. These translations were subject to misinterpretations and they made difficult the analysis of process evolution and performance by process owners. Henceforth, the goal is to describe a formal transformation from BPMN to BPEL which would support business process definition objectives (we should verify whether intended semantics are preserved and the process model certainly yields a profit generated by the model).

BPMN has had a close relationship with BPEL from the beginning and preliminary mappings to BPEL are provided already in the BPMN specification [21]. Accordingly, a standards-based method for developing process-oriented systems is to start with BPMN models and to translate these models into BPEL definitions for subsequent refinement by software developers. The problem of defining these transformations turns out to be rather complex because of inherent differences between these two languages: BPMN process models are graph-oriented, while BPEL process definitions are block-structured. So, the definition of BPMN-to-BPEL model transformations is straightforward for some classes of BPMN models, but less obvious for others [2, 26].

Regarding to the transformation languages, there are several options such as ATL – AtlanMod Transformation Language [12] or MOLA [19], both capable of providing an adequate solution for the definition of 1:1 and 1: n mappings. In our work, we have used ATL to create transformation rules. ATL is MDA (Model-Driven Architecture) [22] compliant and uses a repository to store and to manipulate the source and target meta-models [11]. ATL is a declarative language allowing the specification of transformation rules matched over the source model which create elements in the target model. It contains also an imperative part allowing handling cases that can be too difficult to manage declaratively [4].

# 3  Related Work

The definition of process model transformations from BPMN to BPEL has been investigated by several authors [2, 8, 13, 14, 26]. These contributions found out that some shortcomings stem from the fundamental differences between graph-oriented and block-oriented languages. Below, we briefly introduce some of these contributions found in the literature.

White [30] informally outlines a translation from BPMN to BPEL. However, several steps in his translation require human input to identify patterns in the source model. A number of commercial tools can generate BPEL code from BPMN models using methods similar to those outlined by White such as Intalio BPM Systems/Suites or eClarus Business Process Modeler for SOA. However, these tools impose intricate syntactic restrictions on the source BPMN model.

Additionally, another valuable work made by Mendling et al. [17] review a number of techniques for translating graph-oriented process models to BPEL and classify them into four strategies depending on the structure of the source model. Another relevant contribution made by Ouyang et al. [23] present a mapping from a graph-oriented language BPMN into block-structured language BPEL. They propose an overall translation algorithm which makes greater use of BPEL's block-structured constructs and control links.

In our case, focusing on BPM and web services technology, we use existing technology and standards to realize our vision of MDA [22] software development in the context of business collaborations. Therefore, the intended semantics of business process should also to be preserved. For this aim, we apply Petri Net analysis techniques to statically check if it satisfies a number of semantic conditions such as absence of deadlock/livelock and soundness on the source BPMN model and on the target BPEL model [1, 6, 24].

# 4  Process Transformation Framework

The MDA is a framework for software development driven by the Object Management Group (OMG) [22]. It uses different kind of models to define a valid separation between business, software and technological platforms in the information systems: (1) Computation Independent Model (CIM); (2) Platform Independent Model (PIM); (3) Platform Specific Model (PSM). So, using an MDA approach, the interaction between business analysts and software engineers can be improved. In addition, MDA approach is characterized by a set of vertical transformations across different phases (PIM to PSM and PSM to Code) using model transformation languages. A PIM is transformed into a PSM for each specific technology platform. Processes at PIM level shall be described in such a way, that they can be transformed to process execution languages on PSM level. The vertical transformation corresponds to process automation approaches where conceptual models are transformed to executable processes. A transformation definition is a set of rules that, all together, describe how a model, expressed in a source language, can be mapped into a model in a target language.

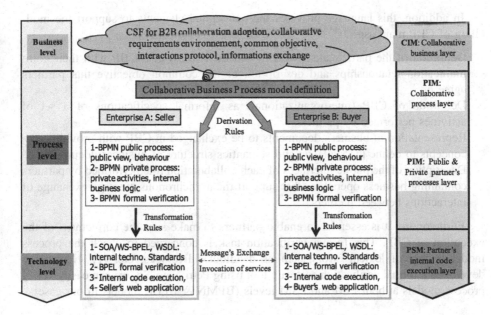

**Fig. 2.** MDA-based framework for process model transformations

Having these considerations in mind, in Fig. 2 we depict the proposed framework which supports: the design of Collaborative BP (CBP) independent of particular process model standard; and the automatic generation of each partner's side specifications based on a process model standards (in our case BPMN and BPEL). It is mainly based on the technique of meta-model transformations [11]. The framework is organized into three levels [10] from the abstract conceptual level (collaborative interactions) to the technical execution level (Web services).

## 4.1 Collaborative Business Agreement Definition Phase

The collaborative business requirements phase at CIM level consists in analyzing the problem and identifying the collaborative business requirements. Hence, it depicts the different roles involved in the collaboration and their specific responsibilities with regard to the collaboration scenario. So, it needs close coordination among partners which requires an agreement (common objective that partners agree on) on how to interact and exchange information without revealing internal operations.

## 4.2 Collaborative Process Modelling Phase

In this work, modelling CBP follows an MDA-based approach, proposing a set of models at different levels of abstraction and model transformations to connect them. At the PIM level, we model CBP using an UML profile [5] which adds semantics and constraints to the UML AD meta-model (with stereotypes, constraints and tagged values) and provide a vocabulary more suitable to model CBP.

In addition, this language provides the conceptual elements to support the modelling of CBP main aspects:

– Definition of the participants (partners and their roles) of a CBP with their communication relationships and description of the common objective that partners agree on.
– Definition of CBP (interorganizational) as informal specifications of a set of activities performed by partners.
– Representation of business documents to be exchanged in CBP with providing the concepts to define the syntactic and semantics structure of business documents.
– Description of the public interfaces of each collaboration role performed by partners containing business operations that support the asynchronous message exchange of interactions between partners.

Furthermore, it is essential to enable partners to make sure the correctness of the execution of CBP. This formal verification task is concerned to check the process model is free of logical errors such as deadlocks, livelocks, etc. [1]. Hence, we developed a formal verification software tool using Petri Nets. So, we can easily verify process models at both PIM and PSM levels (BPMN & BPEL models in our case).

### 4.3   Generation of Partner's Public Processes Phase

As we are shown before, CBPs are not executable. Hence, CBP requires the definition of public and private processes each organization has to implement for executing collaborative process. A public process defines, at PIM layer, the externally visible behaviour of a business partner in terms of the activities that support the receiving and sending of messages and business documents with each other.

For this purpose, we define automated process model transformation method. Henceforth, UML Activity Diagram and BPMN models have some elements share the same semantic meaning. These elements are transformed directly without considering about the element context or neighbourhood elements (one-to-one transformation rule). In addition, some UML Activity Diagram element types cannot be transferred directly to BPMN elements. To be able to remain the same semantic meaning, two or more elements in UML Activity Diagram will be translated to one BPMN element (many-to-one transformation rule).

### 4.4   Definition of Partner's Private Processes Phase

The private executable process is derived from a public process at each partner's side. It adds the private logic of the enterprise required to achieve the role within a global CBP. The internal business logic includes the activities for producing and processing the exchanged information/documents as well as data transformations and invocations to internal systems. Internal or private activities which are required for generating the information to be sent and processing the information to be received from partners, have to be added to the public process to define the corresponding private process.

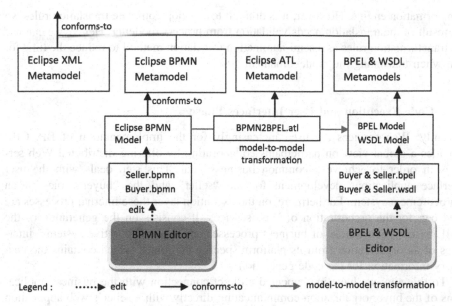

**Fig. 3.** Main steps of the MDA-based process model transformations engine

Beside the process model transformation engine, we consider the business process as the key focal point of Web services design. Henceforth, each of the activities in the process model must be implemented with one or more services. Below we describe this task in two steps:

*Step1: Determine objectives and describe the business process structure*: The business process structure refers to the logical flow or progression of the business process. The functions of a business process are expressed in terms of the activities or the services that need to be performed by a specific business process.

*Step2: Describe business activity responsibilities (roles)*: Each activity within a business process is associated with a particular Web service provider who fulfils a defined role (responsibility) within the process. Each service provider is expected to properly fulfil the business responsibility of implementing the Web service, or set of Web services, which perform that activity within the process under the role that the provider is expected to undertake.

In this paper we are concerned mainly with BPMN-to-BPEL model transformation. Our approach clearly shows that mapping between both languages is not always straightforward and requires a trade-off between different design special cases, for example the benefit of readable structured activities versus the burden of analyzing the BPMN graph. So, we implement an algorithm inspired from Ouyang et al. [23]. It takes as input a BPD (BPMN Business Process Diagram) represented in XML format and produces the correspondent BPEL code as an XML file. Figure 3 illustrates this model transformation engine. However, it is difficult to develop complete translation rules, so the result of the translation needs validation from process modeller. Hence, we can use the transformation rules as a semi-automation translation method to reduce the time for him when translating the models manually.

### 4.5   Code Execution and User Interfaces Phase

Recently, Web services are used increasingly for the implementation of BP. CBP provides a global view on participants collaborating by offering distributed Web services in order to achieve a common business goal. This step deals with the user interface applications development for the "seller" and the "buyer" roles in an e-procurement system. Furthermore, on the execution layer these internal processes are used e.g. for the orchestration of Web services. It consists on the generation of the XML-based specifications of business processes and the collaborative systems' interfaces of an organization from its platform-specific IT model, which contains the necessary information for the code generation.

To this aim, we have implemented a direct connection with the business applications of the buyer organization communicating directly with a seller's web application to send and receive information. After collaborating, both of the two partners' applications progress independently.

## 5   Implementation

To master the complexity of the design and implementation of process model transformation engine reported in the previous section, we developed a software tool which achieves two main functions. The first one is related to process model transformations (shown in Fig. 3) and the second one is related to formal verification of these process models. As case study, we implemented the basic business process scenario « Procurement process » (see Fig. 1).

Accordingly, we use an Eclipse-based integrated platform [9] to guarantee the interoperability of the different plug-ins, tools and ATL transformation languages and Fig. 3 illustrates the main program of the transformation. Thus, we develop an Eclipse-based ATL code for process model transformations (from BPMN to BPEL). Our meta-models of the source language BPMN and the target language BPEL are conform to the meta-modelling quasi-standard of the Eclipse Modelling Framework EMF [9]. Finally, we implemented an e-procurement application for each partner's side, implementing the executable private business processes as Web services.

For example, we develop transformation rule related to the mapping of BPMN "task" to BPEL "invoke" (shown in Listing 1) and transformation rule related to mapping of BPMN "input message" to BPEL "receive message" (shown in Listing 2). Due to page number limitations we cannot present all defined ATL transformation rules.

```
1    <vertices xmi:type="bpmn:Activity"
2              xmi:id="_CAcWEW1XEeGTTs94ELTy5Q"
3              iD="_CAcWEG1XEeGTTs94ELTy5Q"
4              outgoingEdges="_LauCsW1YEeGTTs94ELTy5Q"
5              incomingEdges="_eIW3kXMsEeGFF-oZDAXduw"
6              name="consulterCatalogue"/>
```

a.   The corresponding ATL code is:

```
1  helper context bpmn!Activity def : isTask : Boolean =
2      self.activityType = #Task;
3
4  rule Pool2Process {
5      from
6          s: bpmn!Pool
7      to
8
9  rule Task2Invoke {
10     from
11         s: bpmn!Activity(s.isTask)
12     to
13         t: bpel!Invoke(name <- s.name, partnerLink <- s.name+'PL'),
14         u: bpel!partnerLink(name <- s.name+'PL'),
15         v: bpel!Variable(name <- s.name+'Request'),
16         w: bpel!Variable(name <- s.name+'Response')
17 }
18
```

b.   The target (BPEL code) model is:

```
1    <activities xsi:type="Invoke" name="ConsulterCatalogue"/>
2
3    <partnerLink name="ConsulterCataloguePL"/>
4
5    <variable name="ConsulterCatalogueRequest"/>
6    <variable name="ConsulterCatalogueResponse"/>
```

Listing 1: An example of Transformation rule

```
1  helper context bpmn!Activity def : isMSGReceive : Boolean =
2      self.activityType = #EventStartMessage or
3      self.activityType = #EventIntermediateMessage or
4      self.activityType = #EventEndMessage or
5  and if not self.name.oclIsUndefined()
6      then self.name->toSequence()->includes('Receive')
7      else false
8      endif;
9
10 rule inMSG2Receive {
11     from
12         s: bpmn!Activity(s.isMSGReceive)
13     to
14         t: bpel!Receive(name <- s.name)
15 }
```

Listing 2: ATL code for transforming BPMN "input message" to BPEL "message receive"

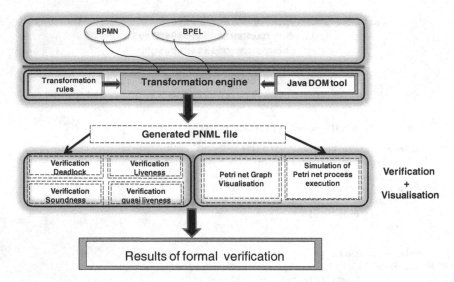

**Fig. 4.** Architecture of process model verification software module

In addition, we have developed in parallel a software tool implementing formal verification techniques which have to be applied to corresponding Petri Nets representation of business process (BPMN and BPEL models). We note that four verification properties (deadlock, bounded, liveness and quasi-liveness) are implemented. The source (BPMN) model is:

Figure 4 outlines the different phases of the process of formal verification. After that, Fig. 5 highlights the interface Petri-Nets based verification software tool for "Procurement process model" outlined before.

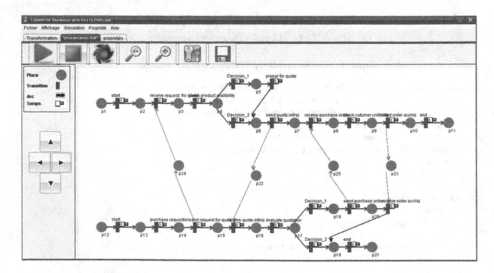

**Fig. 5.** Verification of "Procurement process" using Petri-Net based software tool

## 6 Conclusion and Future Research

In the frame of this work, we have proposed a process model transformations engine based on BPM and Web services. So, we have used the BPMN standard language in the process modelling phase and BPEL at the execution phase. Then, we have defined the transformation rules in ATL language. Moreover, a software tool for verifying process models was developed in order to provide a complete methodology that supports the specification, modelling and verification of the business processes.

Moreover, we are currently working along two lines of actions. Firstly; we push the stepwise implementation by the development of custom modelling tools and plug-ins. Secondly; we aim at testing reverse process model transformations. So, the modified BPEL models can be viewed in BPMN and any deviations can be easily identified.

**Acknowledgment.** The work published in this paper was achieved within the ISID research team of CEDRIC/CNAM-Paris, France that the authors want to thank Prof. Jacky Akoka and all members for their valuable help.

## References

1. van der Aalst, W.M.P., Van Hee, K., ter Hofstede, A., Sidorova, N., Verbeek, H.: Soundness of workflow nets: classification, decidability, and analysis. Formal Aspects Comput. **3**, 1–31 (2010)
2. van der Aalst, W.M.P., Lassen, K.: Translating unstructured workflow processes to readable BPEL: theory and implementation. Inf. Softw. Tech. **50**(3), 131–159 (2008)
3. Joseph, B., Ashish, G., Sharda, R.: Knowledge work and communication challenges in networked enterprises. Inf. Sys. Front. **13**(5), 615–619 (2011)
4. Bézivin, J., Hammoudi, S., Lopes D., Jouault, F.: Applying MDA approach to B2B Applications: a road map. In: Workshop on Model Driven Development (WMDD 2004), ) at ECOOP 2004, 14–18 June, Oslo, Norway. LNCS, vol. 3344, pp. 148–157, Springer-Verlag (2004)
5. Bouchbout, K., Akoka, J., Alimazighi, Z.: An MDA-Based framework for collaborative business process modelling. BPMJ **18**(6), 919–948 (2012)
6. Decker, G., Weske, M.: Behavioral consistency for B2B process integration. In: Krogstie, J., Opdahl, A.L., Sindre, G. (eds.) CAiSE 2007 and WES 2007. LNCS, vol. 4495, pp. 81–95. Springer, Heidelberg (2007)
7. Dorn, J., Grün, C., Werthner, H., Zapletal, M.: A survey of B2B methodologies and technologies: from business models towards deployment artifacts. In: Proceedings of HICSS 2007, USA (2007)
8. Dumas, M.: BPMN to BPEL Model Transformation. University of Tartu, Estonia. A *GraBaTs 2009* Case Study (2009)
9. Eclipse Oranisation: Eclipse Platform. http://www.eclipse.org. Accessed on June 2013
10. Paul, G., Heiko, L., Samuil, A.: A three-level framework for process and data management of complex e-services. Int. J. Coop. Inf. Sys. **12**(4), 487–531 (2003)
11. Hammoudi, S., Alouini, W., Lopes, D., Huchard, M.: Towards a semi-automatic transformation process in MDA: architecture. Method. First Exp. IJISMD **1**(4), 48–76 (2010)

12. Jouault, F., Allilaire, F., Bézivin, J., Kurtev, I.: ATL: a model transformation tool. Sci. Comput. Program. **72**(3), 31–39 (2008)
13. Ivanna, L.M., Omar, C., Pablo, V.D.: Transforming collaborative process models into interface process models by applying an MDA approach. AIS Trans. Enterp. Sys. **2**, 13–23 (2009)
14. Christine, L., Tobias, V., Jan, L., Christian, M.: Transforming inter-organizational business processes into service-oriented architectures. method and application. In: Proceedings of KiVS 2007, Bern (2008)
15. List, B., Korherr, B.: An evaluation of conceptual business process modelling languages. In: Proceedings of the 2006 ACM Symposium on Applied Computing, pp. 1532–1539 (2006)
16. Medjahed, B., Benatallah, B., Bouguettaya, A., Elmagarmid, A.: Business-to-business interactions issues. VLDB J. **12**, 59–85 (2003)
17. Mendling, J., Lassen, K., Zdun, U.: Transformation Strategies between Block- Oriented and Graph-Oriented Process Modelling Languages. In: Lehner, F., Nösekabel, H., Kleinschmidt, P (eds.) Multikonferenz Wirtschaftsinformatik, GITO-Verlag, Berlin, pp. 297–312 (2006)
18. Mendling, J., Neumann, G., Nuttgens, M.: A Comparison of XML Interchange Formats for Business Process Modelling. In: Feltz, F., Oberweis, A., Otjacques, B (eds.) EMISA2004 of Lecture Notes in Informatics (LNI), **56** .pp. 129–140, Luxembourg (2004)
19. MOLA Project. http://www.mola.mii.lu.lv. Accessed on May 2013
20. OASIS, Web Services Business Process Execution Language. http://www.oasis-open.org/committees/download.php/23964/wsbpel-v2.0-primer.htm. Accessed on May 2013
21. OMG: BPMN 2.0 (2011). http://www.omg.org/BPMN/
22. OMG: Model Driven Architecture (2003). http://www.omg.org/mda/
23. Ouyang, C., Dumas, M., Aalst, W.M.P., Ter Hofstede, A.H.M.: From business process models to process-oriented software systems. ACM Trans. Softw. Eng. Method. **19**(1), 1–37 (2009)
24. Ouyang, C., Verbeek, H.M.W., Aalst, W.M.P., Van der Breutel, S., Dumas, M., Ter Hofstede, A.H.M.: Formal semantics and analysis of control flow in WS-BPEL. Sci. Comput. Program. **67**(2–3), 162–198 (2007)
25. Papazoglou, M., Traverso, P., Dustdar, S., Leymann, F.: Service-Oriented Computing. Research Roadmap. Morgan Kaufmann, San Francisco (2006)
26. Recker, J., Mendling, J: On the translation between BPMN and BPEL: conceptual mismatch between process modeling languages. In: Proceedings of CAISE (2006)
27. Scheer, A.-W.: ARIS Business Process Modeling. Springer Verlag, Heidelberg (1999)
28. Söderström, E., Andersson, B., Johannesson, P., Perjons, E., Wangler, B.: Towards a framework for comparing process languages. In: Proceedings of the 14th International Conference on Advanced Information Systems Engineering; pp. 600–611 (2002)
29. Weske, M.: Business Process Management, Concepts, Languages, Architectures. Springer, Heidelberg (2007)
30. White, S.: Using BPMN to Model a BPEL Process. BPTrends **3**(3), 1–18 (2005)

# Object-Oriented Conceptual Modeling
# and Simulation of Health Care Processes

Radek Hřebík(⊠), Vojtěch Merunka, Zuzana Kosejková,
and Pavel Kupka

Faculty of Nuclear Sciences and Physical Engineering,
Department of Software Engineering, Czech Technical University in Prague,
115 19 Břehová 7, Prague, Czech Republic
{radek.hrebik,vmerunka,knoflice,kupka.pavel}@gmail.com

**Abstract.** This paper presents our own approach to modeling, visualization and simulation of biology-related processes. It presents the own BORM (Business and Object Relation Modeling) approach, which is an application of the object-oriented paradigm and finite-state machines. The first part of this paper discusses the motivation for the new approach and explains its theoretical foundation. The second part presents our practical experience with BORM as the method enabling necessary capture of requirement and verification activities for the analysis and design of information systems. The real example of the largest Prague Hospital is used. The BORM method has been used in the last 17 years on various projects in the Czech Republic and Central-European region.

**Keywords:** BORM · Requirement engineering · Process modeling and simulation · Biology-related processes · Sociotechnical processes · Object-oriented approach · Finite-state machines

## 1 Introduction

Business process models show and animate (when they are simulated) the collaboration of more participants within the solved system. Such approach is needed for simulation, validation and verification of the real problems [1]. The issue is stressed in specific areas of technical systems analysis and design, e.g. in area of agriculture, landscape management and also, as it is used in this paper, in the visualization of law-based processes of country planning. A very important purpose of such business model is to create and simulate an interconnected complex system where local actors, citizens, regional government, various interested organizations and partners and other participants mutually communicate [3, 7]. In addition to that, business process models are also the foundation of subsequent system modeling activities of software engineering, organizational design and management consulting. Typical way of performing these activities is to start directly with drawing process diagrams just during the initial interviews. But in this paper, we present the idea, that for better modeling, we need to use a specific textual technique, which helps us to recognize, define and refine our initial set of business process participants and their properties before the graphical business process model is assembled.

© Springer International Publishing Switzerland 2015
J. Barjis et al. (Eds.): EOMAS 2015, LNBIP 231, pp. 49–60, 2015.
DOI: 10.1007/978-3-319-24626-0_4

## 2 Motivation

Expected output of the business process modeling and simulation activities is information or data in a form that can be directly used as an input for implementation of the system in the spirit of software engineering and organizational modeling and management consulting. However, this is not the easy case; there are following issues described by Ilgen and Hulin [7] and Aalst [1]:

*Oversimplification* - while trying to at least finish business and organizational model we are forced to simplify the problem being modeled, and

*Inability* - some important details cannot be recorded because of the poorly used method.

A perennial problem with the development of business systems is the existing communication gap between analysts and domain experts; each live in their own well defined and complex cultures. This gap is represented in the constant failure of simulation model designers to fully capture the requirements of any proposed business system. In our experience, gathered during the last ten years working on major projects, not all system requirements are known at the start of the project, and the customer expects that their discovery and refinement will form part of the project [7]. This problem is complicated further, since the function of any major system developed has a significant impact on the organizational and management structure of the company or organization where the system is being implemented.

## 3 Borm Approach

### 3.1 Method Basics

Business Object Relation Modeling (BORM) is an approach to both process modeling and the subsequent development of information systems [8, 9]. It provides an approach that facilitates the description of how real business systems evolve, change and behave. BORM - Business Object Relation Modeling was originally developed in 1993 and was intended to provide seamless support for the building of object oriented software systems based on pure object-oriented languages, databases and distributed environments. Subsequently, it has been realized that this method has significant potential in business process modeling and other related business issues. BORM has been used in last 17 years (1998−2015) for a number of business consulting and software engineering projects including the health care processes IS, as a tool for business process reengineering in the electricity supply, gas supply industry and telecommunication network management, several business process simulation projects in various areas of modeling and simulation with subsequent IS development as well as in organizational modeling and simulation of regional management project concerning the analysis of the legislation and local officials' knowledge such as living situations, law, country planning etc.

Process approach and object orientation are the pillars of the BORM method. It is the application of principles that are successful in the field of modeling and software. The basis of the object approach is the notion that each action must have an object that executes it; or, vice versa; that each object must have some activity in a conceptual model. It is impermissible to have an action without an object, or an object without an action. This is BORM interpretation of the Model-driven architecture (MDA) approach [10].

Any modeling and simulation tool and any diagramming technique used at this kind of business projects should be comprehensible to the stakeholders, many of whom are not software engineering literate [5]. Moreover, these diagrams must not deform or inadequately simplify requirement information. It is our experience that the correct mapping of the problem into the model and subsequent visualization and possible simulation is very hard task with standard diagramming techniques. We believe that the business community needs a simple yet expressive tool for process modeling; able to play an equivalent role to that played by Entity-Relation Diagrams, Data-Flows Diagrams or Flow-Charts over the past decades. One of the strengths of these diagrams was that they contained only a limited set of concepts (about 5) and were comprehensible by problem domain experts after few minutes of study. Unfortunately UML approach (as well as BPMN) lost this power of simplicity and clarity [17].

## 3.2 Combination of the OOP and FSM

Currently there is not a 'standard solution' to the problem of gathering and representing knowledge. That is reason why we developed and successfully used our own UML-based BORM process diagramming technique [17] and our own way to start object-oriented business system analysis recommended by Taylor [16] and together with Scheldbauer [13] prefer this approach before the semantically different BPMN [6, 15].

BORM innovation is based on the reuse of old thoughts from the beginning of 1990s regarding the description of object properties and behaviour using finite state machines (FSM). The first work expressing the possible merge of Object-Oriented Paradigm (OOP) and FSM was the book by Shaller and Melor [12]. One of the best books speaking about the applicability of OOP to the business modeling was written by Taylor [16]. These works together with our practical experience is the reason to believe that the business requirement modeling and simulation and software modeling could be unified on the platform of OOP and FSM.

The object-oriented approach has its origins in the researching of operating systems, graphic user interfaces, and particularly in programming languages, that took place in the 1970s. It differs from other software engineering approaches by incorporating non-traditional ways of thinking into the field of informatics. We look at systems by abstracting the real world in the same way as in ontological, philosophical streams. The basic element is an object that describes data structures and their behavior. In other modeling approaches, data and behavior are described separately, and, to a certain extent, independently. OOP has been and still is explained in many books (in [14], for example), but we think that this one by Rubin and Goldberg [11] is written by OOP pioneers and belong to the best.

In the field of theoretical informatics, the theory of automata is a study of abstract automatons and the problems they can save. An automaton is a mathematical model for a device that reacts to its surroundings, gets input, and provides output. Automatons can be configured in a way that the output from one of them becomes input for another. An automaton's behavior is defined by a combination of its inner structure and its newly - accepted input. The automata theory is a basis for language and translation theory, and for system behavior descriptions. Its usage for modeling and simulation in software engineering activities has been described by Shlaer and Mellor in [12] and many newer publications. The idea of automata also inspired behavioral aspects of the UML.

### 3.3   Modeling Cards

The BORM development methodology starts from an informal problem specification and provides both methods and techniques, to enable this informal specification to be transformed into an initial set of interacting objects. The main technique used here are modified modeling cards from the Object Behavior Analysis (OBA) being firstly published in [11]. Original OBA is an only text-based method and used a large set of form sheets, textual lists and tables for storing and manipulating the information being processed. Modeling cards are structured texts, various lists and tables and so-called modeling cards (textual forms).

In BORM, we do not start directly by drawing the process diagrams. Process diagrams are the subsequent refined visual representation of the information collected by the modeling cards.

1. *Modeling card of a scenario* clarifies the entire process contours, process participants, necessary legislation, documents etc. (see example in Fig. 1)
2. *Modeling card of a participant* is a textual description of some role in a process. It
   has similar structure as scenario card, but seen from the different perspective of
   particular participant (e.g. process actor). Participant modeling cards are subsequently refined into several FSM. (see examples in Figs. 2 and 3)

Business process diagrams in BORM, or Object-Relationship Diagrams (ORD), are visual representation of processes and objects inside of processes obtained by modeling

| Patient in the hospital - scenario | |
|---|---|
| *initiation*<br>Patient needs to stay in the hospital. | *participants*<br>Patient<br>Doctor |
| *actions*<br>Receiving the patient, his inclusion<br>on the bed, procedures and transfers. | Medical records<br>Insurance account<br>Release report |
| *result*<br>Patient is released from the hospital<br>or the patient's death. | |

**Fig. 1.** Patient in hospital - scenario example

| Patient | |
|---|---|
| | *activities* |
| is accepted | |
| is registered | |
| medical operation | |
| internal transfer | |
| transfer | |
| release | |
| death | |
| | *collaborators* |
| Doctor | |
| Medical records | |
| Insurance account | |
| Release report | |

**Fig. 2.** Patient

| Doctor | |
|---|---|
| | *activities* |
| acceptance | |
| registration | |
| performs surgery | |
| transfers | |
| requests for material | |
| writes record | |
| ends therapy | |
| | *collaborators* |
| Patient | |
| Medical records | |
| Insurance account | |
| Release report | |

**Fig. 3.** Doctor

cards technique. Process diagram consists of participants, their states and transitions and their mutual communications. Each participant is composed of a set of states, activities and transitions (communications). Formally, it is a Mealy-type FSM. [12] Conceptual link within one participant can be considered as a transition between states, it contains no data, because it is only behavioral concept. On the other side communication between more participants may contain the data and therefore can be considered as data flows between activities of these participants making together some concrete process. Therefore a whole process diagram can be seen as a set of several finite state machines where each FSM represents just one participant.

If we consider the basic concept of the FSM, each $i$-th participant will be represented as a unique entity, defined as 5-tuple $P_i(S_i, I_i, \delta_i, s_i^0, s_i^e)$, where:

- $S_i$ is a finite non-empty set of states which the participant may be in it.
- $I_i$ is a finite non-empty set of all possible inputs
- $\delta_i$ represents the activities carried out, i.e. transitions between states, $\delta_i : I_i \times S_i \rightarrow S_i$.
- $s_i^0$ is the initial state of the process, $s_i^0 \in S_i$
- $s_i^e$ is the final state of the process, $s_i^e \in S_i$

The participant starts from the state $s_i^0$ and according user input $I_i$ and actual state transfers itself into a next state. In case the participant ends in the state $s_i^e$ we say that $P_i$ accepts user word from input $I_i^*$. We allow reading an empty symbol X so the participant can continue to the next state even without any user input.

So far we have considered a model with only one participant. Let's extend out model by $N$ not communicating participants $P_1 \ldots P_N$ simulated together. Let's suppose that user input symbols differs for each participant.

$$\bigcap_{i=1}^{N} I_i \subseteq \{\varepsilon\} \tag{1}$$

We can define a finite state machine $P_\Sigma$, which will be composition of the partial automata representing individual participants. That machine will simulate all participants together.

$$S = S_1 \times \ldots \times S_N, \quad s_0 = \left(s_1^0, s_2^0, \ldots, s_N^0\right), \quad s_e = \left(s_1^e, s_2^e, \ldots, s_N^e\right) \tag{2}$$

$$I = \bigcup_{i=1}^{N} I_i \tag{3}$$

Therefore inner states of $P_\Sigma$ are tuples of length $N$ composed of individual participant's inner states. Same can be said about start state and end state. We suppose that user input symbols are different for each automata thus we can easily define action function for compound FSM with the help of individual action function X.

$$\delta : I \times S \rightarrow S \tag{4}$$

$$\delta(i, s_1, \ldots, s_N) = \left(s_1, \ldots, s_{j-1}, s_j', s_{j+1}, \ldots, s_N\right) | \exists j \in \hat{N}, \delta_j(i, s_j) = s_j' \tag{5}$$

*If we didn't need to capture the participants communications, we considered above for a full description. So far we are using finite automata to describe participants of the process and introduced a model, which is made up of one finite state machine composed of sub-machines. Each sub-machine corresponds to a just one participant in the process. Business processes are not made up of isolated participants. They also contain communication between participants and there can be also communications across processes. Communication is realized by sending or receiving messages. Messages are sent during the execution of activities, i.e. within participants Activities. Communication model used in BORM process diagrams assumes that communication operation is atomic and is done just between two participants [9]. In case any listening participant is not in the appropriate listening state the action which will lead to sending the message cannot be performed. Thus the communication can be viewed as a action which can be performed only when each participant is in the appropriate state and leads to transition of all communicating participants to the new states. Unfortunately this approach using only basic concept of finite state machine has not been enough. There is concept of communicating finite state machines (CFSM) which allows describe that kind of communications. The presence of communications requires a significant change from the above definition of the participants using basic concept of FSM, but allows us to describe the process diagram as a whole. The following process description is based on the basic concept of a finite automaton, but it enhances the part of the model of communicating finite state machines that are necessary to capture the mutual communication participants.*

Business-process diagram representing a particular process can be defined as a finite set of participants.

$$BP = \{P^i\} \tag{6}$$

Each participant then can be described as an ordered 6-tuple

$$P^i = (S^i, -M^i, +M^i, f^i, g^i, s_1^i)$$

where:

- $S^i$ is a finite set of all possible states which the participant may be in it
- $-M^i$ is a finite set of all outgoing messages
- $+M^i$ is a finite set of all received messages
- $f^i$ represents the activities carried out, i.e. transition between states. The transition function can be defined as $f^i : S^i \times +M^i \to S^i$
- $g^i$ is output function that can be defined as $g^i : S^i \times +M^i \to -M^i$
- $s_1^i$ is the initial state of participant $P^i$, if $s_1^i \in S^i$

Without loss of generality, we assume that the participant will not send the message to itself

$$-M^i \cap +M^i = \varnothing \tag{7}$$

The set of all messages $P^i$ participant will be the union of the set of all outgoing and incoming messages

$$M^i = -M \cup +M \tag{8}$$

Without loss of generality, assume that within the entire communications of a system is just one identical $m_i$. Each message has only one recipient and one sender.

$$\forall m_1 \in \mathrm{M}^1, m_2 \in \mathrm{M}^1 : m_1 \neq m_2 \tag{9}$$

The set of all messages $\mathrm{M}^i$ consists of an ordered triple $\langle \sigma^i, in^i, out^i \rangle$

$$\mathrm{M}^i = \{\langle \sigma^i, in^i, out^i \rangle\} = \{m\}^i, \tag{10}$$

where:
$\sigma^i$ is representing the transition
$in^i, out^i$ are data

Each message has its sender and recipient

$$\forall \mathrm{P}^i : \bigcup_i -\mathrm{M}^i = \bigcup_i +\mathrm{M}^i \tag{11}$$

We can define functions $data(\mathrm{P}^i)$ and $in(m^i)$ for recipient where

$$data(\mathrm{P}^i); in(m^i) = in^i; m^i = \langle \sigma^i, in^i, out^i \rangle \tag{13}$$

$$in(m^i) = in(\langle \sigma^i, in^i, out^i \rangle) = m^i \tag{14}$$

Analogously we define functions $data(\mathrm{P}^j)$ and $out(m^i)$ for sender:

$$data(\mathrm{P}^j); out(m^i) = out^i; m^i = \langle \sigma^i, in^i, out^i \rangle \tag{15}$$

$$out(m^i) = out(\langle \sigma^i, in^i, out^i \rangle) = m^i \tag{16}$$

Although the exchange of messages carried out from the perspective of BORM semantics at the same time, if we apply the theory of finite automata, we must distinguish the state before the transition and the new state after transition. Sent or received message at time t +1 will depend on the state at time t.

Data interchange between participants we can define for recipient as:

$$data^{t+1}(\mathrm{P}^i) = data^t(\mathrm{P}^i) \cup in(m^{ij}) \wedge in(m^{ij}) \subseteq data^t(\mathrm{P}^j) \tag{17}$$

And for sender:

$$data^{t+1}(\mathrm{P}^j) = data^t(\mathrm{P}^j) \cup out(m^{ij}) \wedge out(m^{ij}) \subseteq data^t(\mathrm{P}^i) \tag{18}$$

Using the formal description based on the theory of finite state machines we have defined process participant which can communicate with other participants by sending messages. Process diagram consists of a set of participants obtaining partial composition of finite state machines into a single comprehensive machine. Such a complex machine will represent a whole process diagram. Chance composing machines, thereby reducing the complexity of the resulting process has been known for decades [12]. In detail, the issue of composition, minimization and generalization of finite state machines deals such as [3], which describes the specific algorithms for their composition.

Based on the derived definition of communicating participants, we can describe any process diagram in BORM as a finite state machine. This composed machine will consist of a set of finite state machines each of which will represent just one participant. If we apply the algorithm for the composition of finite state machines described in [12] on a set of participants, we get

$$\text{FSM}^{BP} = (\text{Æ}, \dot{\text{E}}, \hat{\text{E}}, \varphi, \gamma, \sigma_1) = \{P^i\} = \{(S^i, -M^i, +M^i, f^i, g^i, s_1^i)\} \text{ where:}$$

The transition function $\varphi$ for the composed finite state machine obtained using the transition functions of each automaton represents participants.

The output function $\gamma$ for the composed finite state machine obtained using the transition functions of each automaton represents participants.

As we have shown above with we can be able to describe any process model in BORM using FSM theory. The practical impact is the ability to use all the theoretical assumptions and practices that are known from the theory of FSM for process models in BORM. Therefore it can verify that all states of participants of the process are reachable and that all activities performed. It is also possible to automatically identify the state in which could lead to deadlock the process and evaluate the consistency of the model. Formal description also opens up opportunities for better implementation of the method BORM in CASE tools, especially in the construction process simulators.

# 4  The Project

Our project was the analysis and subsequent reorganization process in one of the largest hospital complexes in the Czech Republic - General University Hospital in Prague. Our task was to map all processes related to the system of patient care and to connect this bio-technological process-based system with management and financial systems of the hospital.

Together, we identified 37 different types of participants in 16 different top-level processes. These process models have had an average of four participants for each process and the total number of states and activities (transitions) was around 70 for each process after its decomposition.

The resulting analysis was the basis for business-process re-engineering. After subsequent organizational change, this matter was also a basis for a selection procedure for the requirement description for a management information system in the hospital.

There is an example of BORM business process diagram at Fig. 4. It shows a general process of a patient in hospital. There are four participating subjects in this process: Patient, Doctor, Medical record and Insurance account. The small rectangles within these subjects are their states. The ovals within the same subjects are their activities, which are conceivable as the transitions between the states as well. This example shows mutually connected the FSM of a Patient and the FSM of a Doctor. The

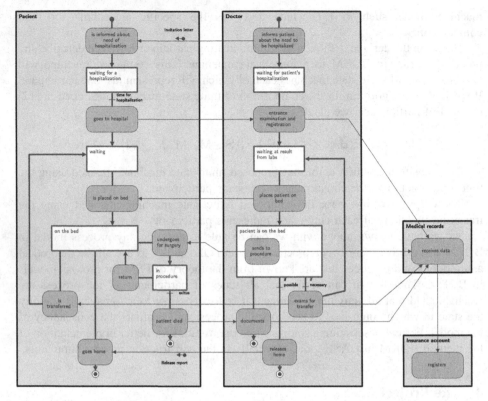

**Fig. 4.** Hospital care general process example (simplified)

thin arrows between these subjects are the mutual communications, and the very small arrows are the data flows being performed during these communications. If a line is crossed, it contains a condition that makes its force.

## 5   Conclusion

Based on our long-year experience, we decided to apply the BORM method [8, 9]. Business Object Relation Modeling (BORM) is a complex method for systems analysis and design that utilizes an object oriented paradigm in combination with business process modeling. It originated at the Loughborough University, UK in 1993. Successful BORM experience has been reported and published ever since, mostly for orchestration-intensive systems of several socio-technical projects related to the work-flow systems, industrial business processes, governmental processes, self-administration and law. BORM provides process workflow formalization that is similar to BPMN [6], however it is theoretically better founded. The basic idea of BORM approach is the combination of the object-oriented paradigm and theory of finite-state machines (theory of automata) [12]. BORM process decomposition is based on a set of more mutually communicating Mealy-type automata representing independent process participants in their states and activities.

## 5.1 Future Work

We are building the project coordination support system based on the BORM orchestration. The system will be built on a client-server architecture. The server will be hosting BORM diagrams, users and other data, while a thin web client application will provide a portal solution where participants will be able to log in and operate in the workflow. Individual process diagrams are graphically animated during the simulation. Individual users have different access rights from the full process control to simple viewing. The portal will provide the following features to users according to their specific role and rights:

1. General process overview (diagrams)
2. Activities timing overview (calendar)
3. Tasks inbox
4. Process instances spawning
5. Graphical simulation
6. Audit trail (log)
7. Document storage

**Acknowledgments.** The authors would like to acknowledge the support of the research grant SGS14/209/OHK4/3T/14.

# References

1. van der Aalst, W.M.: Business process simulation revisited. In: Barjis, J. (ed.) EOMAS 2010. LNBIP, vol. 63, pp. 1–14. Springer, Heidelberg (2010)
2. Allweyer, T.: BPMN 2.0, Books on Demand GmbH, Norderstedt (2010). ISBN 978–3-8391-4985-0
3. Barjis, J.: Developing executable models of business systems. In: Proceedings of the ICEIS - International Conference on Enterprise Information Systems, pp. 5–13. INSTICC Press (2007)
4. Eriksson, H., Penker, M.: Business Modeling with UML. Wiley, New York (2000). ISBN 0-471-29551-5
5. Figl, K., Laue, R.: Cognitive complexity in business process modeling. In: Mouratidis, H., Rolland, C. (eds.) CAiSE 2011. LNCS, vol. 6741, pp. 452–466. Springer, Heidelberg (2011)
6. Grosskopf, A., Decker, G., Weske, M.: Business Process Modeling Using BPMN. Meghan Kiffer Press, Cambridge (2006). ISBN 978-0-929652-26-9
7. Igen, D., Hulin, C.L.: Computational Modeling of Behavior in Organizations - The Third Scientific Discipline. American Psychological Association, Washington DC (2000). ISBN 1-55798-639-8
8. Knott, R.P., Merunka, V., Polak, J.: The BORM methodology: a third-generation fully object-oriented methodology. Knowl.-Based Syst. 16, 77–89 (2003). ISSN 0950-7051

9. Knott, R.P., Merunka, V., Polak, J.: Process modeling for object oriented analysis using BORM object behavioral analysis. In: Proceedings of 4th International Conference on Requirements Engineering, N.p., 2000, pp. 7−16. IEEE Xplore. Web (2000)
10. MDA − The Model Driven Architecture, OMG − The Object Management Group. http://www.omg.org
11. Rubin, K., Goldberg, A.: Object behavioral analysis. Commun. ACM - Special Issue on Analysis and Modeling in Software Development CACM **35**(9)(1992)
12. Shlaer, S., Mellor, S.: Object Lifecycles: Modeling the World in States. Yourdon Press, Upper Saddle River (1992). 0136299407
13. Scheldbauer, M.: The Art of Business Process Modeling - The business Analyst Guide to Process Modeling with UML and BPMN. Cartris Group, Sudbury MA (2010). ISBN 1-450-54166-6
14. Schach, S.: Object-Oriented Software Engineering. McGraw Hill, Singapore (2008). ISBN 978-007-125941-5
15. Silver, B.: BPMN Method and Style: with BPMN Implementer's Guide. A Structured Approach for Business Process Modeling and Implementation Using BPMN 2.0, 2nd edn. Cody-Cassidy Press, Aptos (2011)
16. Taylor, D.A.: Business Engineering with Object Technology. John Wiley, New York (1995). ISBN 0-471-04521-7
17. The UML standard, OMG − The Object Management Group, http://www.omg.org, ISO/IEC 19501

# Big Data Analytics for Supply Chain Management: A Literature Review and Research Agenda

Samuel Fosso Wamba[1](✉) and Shahriar Akter

[1] NEOMA Business School,
1 Rue du Maréchal Juin, BP 215, 76825 Mont Saint Aignan Cedex, France
samuel.fosso.wamba@neoma-bs.fr
[2] Faculty of Business, University of Wollongong,
Northfields Ave, Wollongong, NSW 2522, Australia
sakter@uow.edu.au

**Abstract.** The main objective of this study is to provide a literature review of big data analytics for supply chain management. A review of articles related to the topics was done within SCOPUS, the largest abstract and citation database of peer-reviewed literature. Our search found 17 articles. The distribution of articles per year of publication, subject area, and affiliation, as well as a summary of each paper are presented. We conclude by highlighting future research directions where the deployment of big data analytics is likely to transform supply chain management practices.

**Keywords:** Big data analytics · Value · Adoption and use · Supply chain management · Review

## 1 Introduction

Big data analytics (BDA) is defined as a holistic approach to manage, process and analyze the "5 Vs" data-related dimensions (i.e., volume, variety, velocity, veracity and value) in order to create actionable insights for sustained value delivery, measuring performance and establishing competitive advantages [1]. It has recently emerged as "the next big thing" in management. Some scholars and practitioners even suggest that BDA is the "fourth paradigm of science" [2, p. 34], or even "the next frontier for innovation, competition, and productivity" [3, p. 1], or the "new paradigm of knowledge assets" [4, p. 2]. These statements are mainly driven by the pervasive adoption and use of various tools and technologies, including social media (e.g., Facebook, Twitter), mobile devices (e.g., laptops, smartphones), automatic identification technologies enabling the Internet of Things (IoT) (e.g., radio frequency identification (RFID), Bluetooth), and cloud-enabled platforms to support intra- and inter-organizational business processes and achieve a competitive advantage. Some analysts estimate that Twitter users generate more than 250 million tweets per day, while about 50 h of video are uploaded each minute on YouTube from around the world. The same analysts estimate that Facebook now holds more than 90 billion photos, with over 200 million photos uploaded per day [5].

© Springer International Publishing Switzerland 2015
J. Barjis et al. (Eds.): EOMAS 2015, LNBIP 231, pp. 61–72, 2015.
DOI: 10.1007/978-3-319-24626-0_5

For example, the consulting firm IDC predicts that 2015 will see accelerating disruption, based on expanding adoption of the 3rd Platform's cloud, mobile, social, big data, and IoT technologies [6]. In addition, worldwide IT and telecommunications spending is expected to grow by 3.8 % in 2015 to more than $3.8 trillion. Virtually all of this growth in expenditures and one third of total spending will be absorbed by new technologies such as mobile, cloud, BDA and IoT. With regard to big data spending, IDC believes that spending on big-data-related software, hardware, and services worldwide will reach $125 billion in 2015 [6].

The pervasive diffusion of these tools and technologies is expected to transform the way we currently conduct business. This is particularly true of supply chain management (SCM). Prior studies of SCM have highlighted the importance of achieving a high level of integration of inter- and intra-organizational processes and information systems in order to attain a greater level of seamless coordination and reduce repeated efforts and related inefficiencies. For example, the combination of RFID-enabled intelligent products and intelligent services with the existing information and communication technologies in supply chains (SCs) should play a facilitating role – thus making products and services more visible to SC members – and in parallel should offer more opportunities for quick and efficient SC activities [7]. SC members will therefore face greater strain as they will be expected to manage not only their own activities in relation to those products and services but also the integration of upstream and downstream core business processes and inter- and intra-organizational information systems. In this context, the access to critical information for informed decision-making becomes not only a prerequisite but also a major challenge. The main objective of this paper is to contribute to this debate by examining the following research questions:

1. What is the potential of BDA in the SC?
2. Where should future development effort be directed to accelerate the adoption and use of BDA in the SC?

To address these questions, this research draws on the emerging literature on BDA and SCM, as well as an in-depth analysis of articles on BDA-enabled SC identified in SCOPUS, the largest abstract and citation database of peer-reviewed literature.

The rest of this paper is structured as follows. Section 2 reviews BDA in the SC. Section 3 describes the research methodology. Section 4 presents the results and discusses the key findings. Finally, Sect. 5 provides the conclusion including future research directions.

## 2 BDA-Enabled Supply Chain

A supply chain has been defined as "a bidirectional flow of information, products and money between the initial suppliers and final customers through different organizations"; SCM includes planning, implementing and controlling this flow [8]. In the current digital economy, SCs have been viewed as key levers for competitive advantage. That is probably why some scholars argue that competition within the market space [9] has evolved from "firm versus firm" towards "supply chain versus supply chain" [10]. In this context, the adoption and use of innovative IT has been considered as a critical resource for SC optimization. For example, SCM plays an important role in minimizing a company's overall risk of fraud, bribery, and corruption [11]. Prior studies identified numerous benefits related to IT-enabled SC optimization, including end-to-end information sharing among SC stakeholders [12–15]; intra- and inter-organizational business process transformation (e.g., cancellation, redesign, automation) [7, 16]; improved decision-making within the SC [17]; improved operational efficiency [18, 19]; and increased revenue [14].

BDA is expected to take SC transformation to a level of transformation never before achieved. For example, BDA represents a critical source of meaningful information that may help SC stakeholders to gain improved insights they can use for competitive advantage [4, 11]. In addition, BDA could help SC stakeholders to reduce their exposure to various risks including the risk of fraud and other malfeasance [11]. In the context of SC execution, BDA could lead to increased efficiency and profitability in the SC by maximizing speed and visibility, improving SC stakeholders' relationships, and enhancing SC agility [20]. BDA could result in faster time to market and the potential for superior revenue recognition [5]. However, some analysts argue that the deluge of data threatens to "break the existing data supply chain" [5, p. 3].

## 3 Methodology

For this study, a hybrid approach derived from work by Ngai and Wat [22] and Fosso Wamba et al. [21, 22] was used. This approach consisted in a search using the following keywords: "Big data" AND "supply chain" within the SCOPUS database. SCOPUS is the largest abstract and citation database of peer-reviewed literature. This bibliographic database holds more than 19,000 peer-reviewed journals, over 1,800 "open access" journals, more than 600 trade publications, 350 book series, and content from over 435 million web pages. The search was conducted on Friday 30 January 2015, and we found 17 articles on the topic [23–36, 38–40].

## 4 Results and Discussion

The section below presents and discusses the findings of big-data-related SC articles identified in SCOPUS [23–36, 38–40], with the summary presented in the Appendix A.

Table 1 presents the distribution of articles by the year of publication. We can see a jump in big-data-related SC publications in 2013 (7 articles or 41 %), with a small increase in 2014 (8 articles or 47 %). On 30 January 2015, we already had 1 article (or 6 %) on big-data-related SC topics in 2015, which is the equivalent of the whole year's publication on the same topic in 2012.

The distribution of articles by subject area is presented in Table 2. It is clearly appears that the vast majority of articles identified in our review are from "Business, Management and Accounting" (8 articles, 25.8 %), and "Computer Science" (7 articles, 22.6 %), followed by "Decision Sciences" and "Engineering" with 6 articles each (or 19.4 % of all publications). Surprisingly, no article was identified for the "Multidisciplinary" and "Psychology" subject areas. Clearly, more studies are needed in these two subject areas.

**Table 1.** Distribution of publications by year

|       | Number of papers | %     |
|-------|------------------|-------|
| 2015  | 1                | 6 %   |
| 2014  | 8                | 47 %  |
| 2013  | 7                | 41 %  |
| 2012  | 1                | 6 %   |
| Total | 17               | 100 % |

**Table 2.** Distribution of publications by subject area

|                                        | Number of papers | %      |
|----------------------------------------|------------------|--------|
| Business, Management and Accounting     | 8                | 25.8 % |
| Computer Science                        | 7                | 22.6 % |
| Decision Sciences                       | 6                | 19.4 % |
| Engineering                             | 6                | 19.4 % |
| Agricultural and Biological Sciences    | 1                | 3.2 %  |
| Arts and Humanities                     | 1                | 3.2 %  |
| Economics, Econometrics and Finance     | 1                | 3.2 %  |
| Materials Science                       | 1                | 3.2 %  |
| Multidisciplinary                       | 0                | 0 %    |
| Psychology                              | 0                | 0 %    |
| Total[a]                                | 31               | 100 %  |

[a]Some articles are counted more than once because they cover more than one subject area.

Table 3 shows the classification of articles by country. So far, most published articles on BDA in the SC come from the United States (12 articles, 63.2 %), trailed by China (4 articles, 21.1 %), and Germany, Latvia and Netherlands with 1 article each (5.3 %). Clearly, the United States is leading in research on BDA in the SC. The impact of BDA in emerging economies and less developed countries should be part of future research directions.

**Table 3.** Distribution of publications by country

|               | Number of papers | %      |
|---------------|------------------|--------|
| United States | 12               | 63.2 % |
| China         | 4                | 21.1 % |
| Germany       | 1                | 5.3 %  |
| Latvia        | 1                | 5.3 %  |
| Netherlands   | 1                | 5.3 %  |
| Total[a]      | 19               | 100 %  |

[a]Some articles are counted more than once because their authors come from more than one country.

With regard to authors, the ones with the largest number of publications are S.E. Fawcett and M.A. Waller, with 4 articles each on BDA-related SC topics.

## 5 Conclusion and Future Research Directions

In this paper, we used a hybrid approach derived from two earlier studies [21, 22] to conduct a review of articles on big data in the SC in SCOPUS. Our review found 17 articles on the topic. Distributions of articles by year of publication, subject area, and country, as well as the summary of each article were presented. Our review showed that the vast majority of articles appeared in the fields of "Business, Management and Accounting," "Computer Science," "Decision Sciences" and "Engineering." Therefore, more research needs to be done to assess the impact of big data on others subject areas including "Agricultural and Biological Sciences," "Arts and Humanities," "Economics, Econometrics and Finance," "Materials Science," "Multidisciplinary," and "Psychology."

How we deploy new tools and technologies to support BDA projects for high-level business value realization at the firm and SC levels is another interesting avenue for future research. Indeed, early studies on BDA argue that, in order to close the "gap between what the data knows and what we know as individuals," organizations must develop and deploy new technologies that integrate the impressive amount of data collected across the organization as well as "provide smarter tools for analysis, visualization and access" [4, p. 2]. In addition, Hagstrom [4] identifies the collection and storage of data in silos as a problem, which may make analysis quite difficult. Thus, the impact of BDA technologies on the firm and the SC level when these technologies are used only in a localized portion of the SC should be a focus of future research. In addition, it would be interesting to examine the impact of BDA on overall firm IT spending. Indeed, some scholars posit that BDA may create a data deluge "that further accelerates IT expenditures and hinders rather than helps. (...) [as] Adding to data is not so important; it is what you take away from the data that matters" [4, p. 3]. Furthermore, future research must be conducted to assess BDA's ability to enhance intra- and inter-firm efficiency and effectiveness (e.g., identification of bottlenecks, improved predictive maintenance, and scenario building for improved quality control). What is the cost of the complementary resources (e.g., IT, HR, trust) needed to capture the value from BDA at the firm and SC levels? For example, analysts estimate that big data drove $34 billion in IT spending in 2013 [40]. Also, how easily will data become a valuable asset within the SC? If it does, how can we develop a new business monetization model with data as an asset [5]? Assessing the cost related to the digitization of big data should be included in future research programs. Developing new strategies, tools and technologies that will foster data quality and the cleaning of big data represents an interesting challenge. Indeed, analysts estimate that the cost of poor data quality within a typical firm is between 8 % and 12 % of revenues [5]. What will be the best big data management strategy at the firm and SC levels? Should we develop internal data centers at the firm level or move toward a cloud-based architecture at the firm and SC levels for data storage? In the latter case, who owns the data? The answers to these questions should be included in future research avenues. Evaluating the impact of big data on the structure of traditional SCs and various industries should also be a future research topic. Consequently, it would be useful to investigate the potential of big-data-enabled new business models and new industry structures.

## Appendix A. Summary of Articles

| Study | Context | Key findings |
|-------|---------|--------------|
| [29] | ERP selection and implementation. | • ERP users are more mature than non-ERP users in three key indicators: strategic sourcing, category management, and supplier relationship management.<br>• SAP ERP users are more mature than non-ERP users in strategic sourcing, category management, and supplier relationship management |
| [35] | Exploration of opportunities for research where SCM intersects with data science, predictive analytics, and big data. | • BDA has significant implications for operations and SCM, and presents an opportunity and a challenge to our research and teaching approach.<br>• It is easy to see how data science and predictive analytics apply to SCM but sometimes more difficult to see the direct connection of big data to SCM.<br>• Call for more research on BDA including for *Journal of Business Logistics*. |
| [36] | Discussion about big data, predictive analytics, and theory development in the era of a maker movement SC. | • Predictive analytics can be part of the theory building process, even when a given study does not produce or test a specific theory.<br>• Points to the need for strong predictive analytics applications and theory because the disintermediation of the traditional supply chain channels means that consumer behavior has become an integral part of both production and demand.<br>• Call for more research on BDA including for *Journal of Business Logistics*. |
| [26] | Discussion of the impact of emerging concepts and technologies (e.g., 3D printing, BDA) on future of SCM. | • All these new concepts and technologies are changing the SCM world.<br>• However, very few firms are proactively managing renewal well. The authors argued that "Paradoxically, past successes often stand in the way, undermining rejuvenation" (p. 21).<br>• Call for more research on these concepts and technologies including for *Journal of Business Logistics*. |

*(Continued)*

*(Continued)*

| Study | Context | Key findings |
|-------|---------|--------------|
| [25] | Exploration of SC game changers. | • Exploration of five emerging "game changers" that represent potential supply chain design inflection points: (1) big data and predictive analytics, (2) additive manufacturing, (3) autonomous vehicles, (4) materials science, and (5) borderless supply chains. <br> • Consideration of four forces that impede transformation to higher levels of value co-creation: (1) supply chain security, (2) failed change management, (3) lack of trust as a governance mechanism, and (4) poor understanding of the "luxury" nature of corporate social responsibility initiatives. <br> • Conclusions: how well managers address sociostructural and sociotechnical issues will determine firm survivability and success (p. 157). |
| [31] | Exploration of the potential of big data with the latest statistical and machine-learning techniques via the discussion of the Hazy project. | • The high-profile success of many recent BDA-driven systems, also called trained systems, has generated great interest in bringing such technological capabilities to a wider variety of domains. A key challenge in converting this potential to reality is making these trained systems easier to build and maintain. |
| [33] | Examination of the potential for BDA application in the agricultural sector. | • Integration of data and analysis across business and government entities will be needed for successful implementation (p. 1). <br> • The eventual impact of BDA within the agricultural sector will likely require both organizational and technological innovation (p. 1). |
| [27] | Exploration of BDA analysis in the context of SCM, followed by a proposal for the use of agent-based competitive simulation as a tool to develop complex decision-making strategies and to stress test them under a variety of market conditions. The authors also propose an extensive set of key performance indicators and apply them to analyze market dynamics. | • When automating business processes, designers should be concerned with business agility and particularly with how the automated process will respond to situations where the standard assumptions of the market may be violated (p. 283). <br> • The use of KPIs may facilitate the process by providing characteristics to measure across the automated SC, and realistic simulation techniques provide rich data sets with which to accurately measure behavior in different situations (p. 283). |

*(Continued)*

(Continued)

| Study | Context | Key findings |
|---|---|---|
| [39] | A case study of sensor data collection and analysis in smart city with a focus on smart food supply chain. | • One of the important application areas of the IoT in cities is the food industry.<br>• IoT systems help to monitor, analyze, and manage the food industry in cities.<br>• The proposed smart sensor data collection strategy for IoT has the ability to improve the efficiency and accuracy of provenance (e.g., tracing contamination source and back-tracking potentially infected food in the markets) and minimize the size of the data set at the same time. |
| [38] | Review of the current research on OI that uses streaming data and proposes an approach to design intelligent operational dashboards for SCM systems. | • With the BDA advantage, live streaming data can be processed to build intelligent dashboards providing insights for management teams (p. 9). |
| [34] | Discussion of the third industrial revolution. | • The Third Industrial Revolution (TIR) is based on the confluence of three major technological enablers: big data analytics, adaptive services and digital manufacturing (p. 257).<br>• These three major technological enablers underpin the integration or mass customization of services and/or goods.<br>• The TIR potential:<br>- is about the integration of services and goods into "servgoods";<br>- is about the integration of demand and supply chains;<br>- requires more big data analytics, adaptive services, digital manufacturing, mass customization and other white-collar professionals;<br>- minimizes the need for outsourcing and offshoring; and<br>- can subsume mass production within its broader mass customization framework.<br>• As for concerns, TIR:<br>- makes uneducated or undereducated men and women jobless;<br>- aggravates cybersecurity, privacy and confidentiality problems;<br>- aggravates the economic and social divide between the rich and poor within a country; and<br>- aggravates the economic and social divide between the have and have-not countries (p. 293). |

(Continued)

(*Continued*)

| Study | Context | Key findings |
|---|---|---|
| [37] | An ontology-driven approach for distributed information processing in SC environments. | • Using supply chain event ontology based on the ABC and SCOR models, the study shows that automatic access rules on local ontology and the use of ontology mapping could facilitate the realization of heterogeneous data integration, and thus foster facilitate distributed decision-making. |
| [24] | Analysis of the extended analytics ecosystem. | • The extended analytics ecosystem includes individuals and groups who use analytics functions, and involves several key roles and elements including: executive sponsors (e.g., chief marketing officer (CMO), chief financial officer (CFO), or chief operating officer (COO)), data owners, subject-matter experts, business users, external analytics ecosystem places the organization within the wider data supply chain (e.g., incorporate data from the SC network to multiply the value generated or provide focal firm data and analytics to other firms in the SC network), customers, external data providers, external data consumers, cloud analytics platform and business analytics as services, and big data analytics vendors and consultants. |
| | | • Analytics is a game changer that will revolutionize how individuals, businesses, and society can use technology. However, the full value of analytics can be realized only when applied to integrated data from multiple sources and when insights are immediate and actionable. |
| | | • Analytics should be explored gradually to understand what value can be gained from it, but this exploration should be done in a way that enables it to grow so more value can be obtained. |
| | | • "Viewing big data analytics as an ecosystem provides the understanding of how to chart the way to start small while enabling growth to achieve advanced levels of maturity and value. By observing the success or failure in building a big data analytics capability in small and large organizations, several recommendations can be adopted" (p. 5). |
| [32] | Work breakdown structure method based on information SC. | • Using the guiding ideology of the MapReduce programming model, historical data, maps and reduce operations, the authors argue that it is possible to trace the source of an SC's unstable link. |

(*Continued*)

(Continued)

| Study | Context | Key findings |
|---|---|---|
| [30] | Selection strategies related to the problem of partnership choice of SC in the context of 3D printing and BDA based on analytic hierarchy process and fuzzy synthetic evaluation. | • Analytic hierarchy process and fuzzy synthetic evaluation may reduce the influence of subjective factors on partner choice, enhance the accuracy and reliability of partner choice and strengthen the competitiveness of SC enterprises. |
| [23] | Introduction to a general concept to model and analyze logistical state data, in order to find irregularities and their causes and dependences within SCs. | • To perfectly manage an efficient and effective supply chain with a continuous and undisturbed flow of goods, it is possible to use data mining methods on logistical state data to filter irregularities and their causes. |
| [41] | Introduction to problems and benefits of data quality for data science, predictive analytics, and big data in SCM. | • The growing importance of data to SC managers should lead to an amplified awareness and sensitivity to their need for high-quality data products.<br>• The results of decisions based on poor quality data could be costly.<br>- SC managers should begin to view the quality of the data products they depend upon for decisions in much the same way they view the quality of the products their SC delivers.<br>- Managers who appreciate the value of data products that are accurate, consistent, complete, and timely should consider the potential for using control methods to improve the quality of data products, much as these methods improved the quality of manufactured products (p. 78). |

# References

1. Wamba, F.S., et al.: How big data can make big impact: findings from a systematic review and a longitudinal case study. Int. J. Prod. Econ. **165**, 234–246 (2015)
2. Strawn, G.O.: Scientific research: how many paradigms?. EDUCAUSE Rev. **47**(3), 26 (2012)
3. Manyika, J., et al.: Big Data: the Next Frontier for Innovation, Competition and Productivity. McKinsey Global Institute, New York (2011)
4. Hagstrom, M.: High-performance analytics fuels innovation and inclusive growth: use big data, hyperconnectivity and speed to intelligence to get true value in the digital economy. J. Adv. Anal. **2**, 3–4 (2012)
5. Sethuraman, M.S.: Big Data's Impact on the Data Supply Chain, in Cognizant 20–20 Insights Cognizant, New Jersey (2012)
6. IDC, IDC Predictions 2015: Accelerating Innovation — and Growth — on the 3rd Platform (2015)
7. Wamba, F.S., et al.: Exploring the impact of RFID technology and the EPC network on mobile B2B ecommerce: a case study in the retail industry. Int. J. Prod. Econ. **112**(2), 614–629 (2008)

8. Nurmilaakso, J.-M.: Adoption of e-business functions and migration from EDI-based to XML-based e-business frameworks in supply chain integration. Int. J. Prod. Econ. **113**(2), 721–733 (2008)
9. Gunasekaran, A., Ngai, E.W.T.: Information systems in supply chain integration and management. Eur. J. Oper. Res. **159**, 269–295 (2004)
10. Ketchen, D.J.J., Hult, G.T.M.: Bridging organization theory and supply chain management: the case of best value supply chains. J. Oper. Manage. **25**, 573–580 (2007)
11. Kenny, J.: Big data can have big impact on supply chain management: The use of data analytics is underused in supply chain management to minimize risk exposure. IC Inside Counsel (2014). Accessed on 17 February 2015 http://www.insidecounsel.com/2014/04/23/big-data-can-have-big-impact-on-supply-chain-manag
12. Sahin, F., Robinson, E.P.: Flow coordination and information sharing in supply chains: review, implications, and directions for future research. Decis. Sci. **33**(4), 505–536 (2002)
13. Saeed, K.A., Malhotra, M.K., Grover, V.: Examining the impact of interorganizational systems on process efficiency and sourcing leverage in buyer-supplier dyads. Decis. Sci. **36**(3), 365–396 (2005)
14. Rai, A., Patnayakuni, R., Seth, N.: Firm performance impacts of digitally enabled supply chain integration capabilities. MIS Q. **30**(2), 225–246 (2006)
15. Eric, T.G.W., Hsiao-Lan, W.: Interorganizational Governance Value Creation: Coordinating for Information Visibility and Flexibility in Supply Chains*. Decis. Sci. **38**(4), 647–674 (2007)
16. Wamba, F.S.: Achieving supply chain integration using RFID Technology: the case of emerging intelligent B-to-B e-commerce processes in a living laboratory. Bus. Process Manage. J. **18**(1), 58–81 (2012)
17. Asoo, J.V.: e-business and supply chain management. Decis. Sci. **33**(4), 495–504 (2002)
18. Johnston, H.R., Vitale, M.R.: Creating competitive advantage with inter-organizational information systems. MIS Q. **12**(2), 153–165 (1988)
19. Devaraj, S., Krajewski, L., Wei, J.C.: Impact of eBusiness technologies on operational performance: the role of production information integration in the supply chain. J. Oper. Manage. **25**(6), 1199–1216 (2007)
20. Vasan, S.: Impact of Big Data and Analytics in supply chain execution. Supply Chain Digital (2014). Accessed on 13 February 2015 http://www.supplychaindigital.com/logistics/3382/Impact-of-Big-Data-and-Analytics-in-supply-chain-execution
21. Ngai, E.W.T., Wat, F.K.T.: A literature review and classification of electronic commerce research. Inf. Manag. **39**(5), 415–429 (2002)
22. Wamba, F.S., Anand, A., Carter, L.: A literature review of RFID-enabled healthcare applications and issues. Int. J. Inf. Manage. **33**(5), 875–891 (2013)
23. Brandau, A., Tolujevs, J.: Modelling and analysis of logistical state data. Transp. Telecommun. **14**(2), 102–115 (2013)
24. Fattah, A.: Going beyond data science toward an analytics ecosystem: Part 3. IBM Data Manage. Mag. **3**, 8–11 (2014)
25. Fawcett, S.E., Waller, M.A.: Supply chain game changers-mega, nano, and virtual trends-and forces that impede supply chain design (i.e., building a winning team). J. Bus. Logistics **35**(3), 157–164 (2014)
26. Fawcett, S.E., Waller, M.A.: Can we stay ahead of the obsolescence curve? on inflection points, proactive preemption, and the future of supply chain management. J. Bus. Logistics **35**(1), 17–22 (2014)
27. Groves, W., et al.: Agent-assisted supply chain management: analysis and lessons learned. Decis. Support Syst. **57**(1), 274–284 (2014)

72 S. Fosso Wamba and S. Akter

28. Hazen, B.T., et al.: Data quality for data science, predictive analytics, and big data in supply chain management: an introduction to the problem and suggestions for research and applications. Int. J. Prod. Econ. **154**, 72–80 (2014)
29. Huang, Y.Y., Handfield, R.B.: Measuring the benefits of erp on supply management maturity model: a big data method. Int. J. Oper. Prod. Manage. **35**(1), 2–25 (2015)
30. Jin, Y., Ji, S.: Partner choice of supply chain based on 3D printing and big data. Inf. Technol. J. **12**(22), 6822–6826 (2013)
31. Kumar, A., Niu, F., RÉ, C.: Hazy: making it easier to build and maintain big-data analytics. Commun. ACM **56**(3), 40–49 (2013)
32. Li, Y., Ren, N., Cao, M.: WBS data analysis method based on information supply Chain. J. Appl. Sci. **13**(12), 2355–2358 (2013)
33. Sonka, S.: Big data and the ag sector: more than lots of numbers. Int. Food Agribusiness Manage. Rev. **17**(1), 1–20 (2014)
34. Tien, J.M.: The next industrial revolution: integrated services and goods. J. Syst. Sci. Syst. Eng. **21**(3), 257–296 (2012)
35. Waller, M.A., Fawcett, S.E.: Data science, predictive analytics, and big data: A revolution that will transform supply chain design and management. J. Bus. Logistics **34**(2), 77–84 (2013)
36. Waller, M.A., Fawcett, S.E.: Click here for a data scientist: big data, predictive analytics, and theory development in the era of a maker movement supply chain. J. Bus. Logistics **34**(4), 249–252 (2013)
37. Wu, J., Ni, Y.H., Lv, Y.: Ontology-driven approach for distributed information processing in supply chain environment. Zhejiang Daxue Xuebao (Gongxue Ban)/Journal of Zhejiang University (Engineering Science) **48**(11), 2017–2024 (2014)
38. Yesudas, M., Menon, G., Ramamurthy, V.: Intelligent operational dashboards for smarter commerce using big data. IBM Journal of Research and Development **58**(5–6), 6:1–6:12 (2014)
39. Zhang, Q., et al.,: A case study of sensor data collection and analysis in smart city: Provenance in smart food supply chain. Int. J. of Distrib. Sens. Netw. Article ID 382132, 12 p. (2013). doi:10.1155/2013/382132
40. Brock, J., et al.: Big Data's Five Routes to Value: Opportunity Unlocked, In: FOCUS, The Boston Consulting Group, London (2013)
41. Hazen, B.T., et al.: Data quality for data science, predictive analytics, and big data in supply chain management: an introduction to the problem and suggestions for research and applications. Int. J. Prod. Econ. **154**, 72–80 (2014)

# Enterprise Modelling
# Formal Foundation

# One Solution for Semantic Data Integration in Logistics

Elena Andreeva[1(✉)], Tatiana Poletaeva[1(✉)], Habib Abdulrab[2(✉)],
and Eduard Babkin[1(✉)]

[1] National Research University Higher School of Economics,
Nizhny Novgorod, Russia
{eandreeva,eababkin}@hse.ru, ta.poletaeva@gmail.com
[2] INSA de Rouen, LITIS Laboratory, Rouen, France
abdulrab@insa-rouen.fr

**Abstract.** This paper proposes a logistics ontology based on both the theory of organizational ontology and the consistent methodology of semantic data modeling applied towards the supply chain operations reference model. Codification of the proposed ontology is aimed to facilitate meta-data and data integration of autonomous parties of supply networks. Using a simulated business case, we exemplify the use of the created ontology for knowledge integration in a supply network.

**Keywords:** Domain ontology · Knowledge management · Semantic data modeling · Semantic interoperability · Supply network

## 1 Introduction

Seamless information exchange between information systems of supply network participants is vitally important for their efficient interactions. However, heterogeneity of autonomous data stores along with the dynamics of information flows impedes information processing in open supply networks. As an attempt to standardize business valuable data in the domain of logistics many e-business standards were developed such as Universal Business Language UBL (OASIS project)[1], UN/CEFACT[2] logistics module, GS1[3] Logistics Interoperability Model to name just a few of them. However, even being integrated, data stores may still not provide end-to-end data exchange between parties of complex business processes. Moreover, the declaration of one universal standard puts too much of a constraint on open supply networks. On the other hand, data stores built upon different standards are not smoothly integrable [1]. Existence of additional non-standardized (but meaningful for participants) data for exchange enlarges the problem of data integration.

The most successful approaches to data integration are based on domain ontologies [2–4]. Formal domain ontology facilitates communication people's assumptions

---

[1] OASIS: https://www.oasis-open.org/.
[2] UN/CEFACT: http://www.unece.org/CEFACT/.
[3] GS1: http://www.gs1.org/.

© Springer International Publishing Switzerland 2015
J. Barjis et al. (Eds.): EOMAS 2015, LNBIP 231, pp. 75–86, 2015.
DOI: 10.1007/978-3-319-24626-0_6

about the nature and structure of a particular domain, and provides a theory of formal distinctions and connections within the categories people use to think about this domain. Data metamodels created upon the codification [5] of formal domain ontologies allow use of formal logic and world semantics in automated data analysis. Moreover, since the meaning of ontological concepts can be extracted from their interrelations and ontology axioms, automated data interpretation and mapping between ontology-based autonomous data metamodels becomes feasible. Creation of underlying domain ontology is propagated by many standards in different domains (ISO 15926, IDEAS, OMG FIBO, etc.).

Our research is aimed at the ontologization of knowledge prescribed by the Supply Chain Operations Reference (SCOR) model [6]. This model is the source of unambiguously defined concepts that participants of supply networks may operate. As opposed to known logistics ontologies built upon the SCOR model [7, 8], we propose an ontology that incorporates (1) a thorough *ontological* analysis of logistics business processes by means of Design and Engineering Methodology for Organizations (DEMO) [9], and (2) the real-world semantics[4] of the logistics domain resulted the application of BORO (Business Objects Reference Ontology) methodology [10] to the analysis of SCOR model.

Moreover, in the presented research we extend a domain independent Formal Enterprise Ontology (FEO) proposed in [11], which in turn is derived from a synthesis of foundational ontologies[5] and the DEMO enterprise ontology [9]. FEO ontology facilitates integration of concise ontological abstractions of business processes (with respect to DEMO) with their infological perspective.

Hereafter, for making a distinction between terms borrowed from different vocabularies, we use the XML namespace prefix syntax and write, for example, "SCOR:Transferring", "DEMO:Actor", and "BORO:ProcessState".

The rest of this paper is organized as follows. First, brief description of exploited DEMO and BORO methodologies, as well as the FEO ontology is summarized in Sect. 2. Our approach to ontology codification is described in Sect. 3. The proposed logistics ontology and the basic information patterns applicable for modeling of supply networks are explained in Sect. 4. In Sect. 5 we demonstrate a semantic power of the created ontology by the set of complex queries executable for a network of autonomous data stores. Finally, Sect. 6 provides conclusions and directions for further research.

## 2   Our Approach to Ontology Engineering

In this section we describe the background of the proposed logistics ontology. Thus, we present some important aspects of DEMO [9] and BORO [10] methodologies, as well as the core part of the FEO ontology [11].

---

[4] Real-world semantics is the nature and structure of real world entities that define the meaning of ontological concepts and relations between them.

[5] *Foundational ontologies* are theoretically well-founded domain independent systems of categories, which form a general foundation for domain-specific ontologies.

## 2.1 DEMO Theory and Methodology of Enterprise Ontology

In our research, we apply the DEMO methodology [9] to conceptualize common logistics business processes prescribed by the SCOR model. Based on the strong theoretical basis, the DEMO methodology describes the function and construction of social organizations by their ontological models that are essential, complete, logical and free from contradictions, compact and succinct, independent of their realization and implementation issues.

The interpretive and intersubjective world view of the methodology results in considering an enterprise as a discrete dynamic system, of which the elements are social individuals or *actors*, capable to communicate with others by performing *coordination acts* and to contribute to bringing about the goods and/or services by performing *production acts*. By performing coordination acts actors express their intensions and comply with commitments towards each other regarding the performance of production acts [9]. For example, they *request, promise, state*, and *accept* the result of some production act. By performing production acts actors take a *responsibility* for changes in a production world. By performing both kinds of acts, actors transfer the world into the new states characterized by resulted *coordination* and (if any) *production facts*. Thus, the changes that are brought about in the course of acts performed by actors are discrete.

The core concept in DEMO is the notion of the uniform communication patterns between autonomic actors involved in a business deal. These patterns, also called *transactions*, always involve two *actor roles* (the initiator and the executor) and consist of certain coordination acts related to one production act of a particular type. The actor, who starts the transaction and eventually accepts the results, is called the initiator, the other one, who actually brings changes in a production world, is called the executor. A transaction consists of three phases: the order phase, the execution phase, and the result phase. During each of the phases new transactions may be initiated, the result of which new one is needed to proceed with the original transaction. In this way transactions constitute chained intersubjective reality.

DEMO transaction concept distinguishes between intersubjective and objective world. According to DEMO, when engaged into communication, social individuals are trying to influence each other's behavior, in other words, an act of saying is an act of doing [12]. Thus, the coordination acts and their results (coordination facts) relate to the intersubjective world. By performing production acts actors of enterprises change the states of products or services related to the objective world. The distinction of these two worlds at the conceptual level gives an opportunity for coherent modeling of business processes and product lifecycles of enterprises.

Finally, the methodology builds a comprehensive view on the interaction and management processes of an enterprise in four Aspect Models [9]. Through these conceptual models expressed in an enterprise-specific modeling language, it is possible to achieve a solid understanding of business agent roles, their potential communications and fulfilled changes in a production world, the types of transactions taking place in an organization and relations between them, as well as the information that is processed and created in the course of transactions execution. Application of the BORO methodology to the Aspect Models makes it easier to get the true set of the business objects and their interrelations.

## 2.2 BORO Object Paradigm for Data Modeling

The matching of semantically heterogeneous data focuses on identifying the entities that the data describes (at the analysis stage). In theory and practice, this identification currently relies mostly on experience and intuition [13]. However, ontologies provide a framework and suggest a process for the analysis needed for semantic matching. Domain ontologies are built upon the set of foundational ontological commitments articulated implicitly or explicitly. In the presented research we explicitly exploit the ontological commitments of the Object paradigm (OP) [10] to perceive the real-world semantics within the logistics domain and to create data modeling constructs.

The Object paradigm expressed in the BORO methodology [10] (i) clearly and precisely represents reality based on unambiguous identification of spatial-temporal (4D) objects; (ii) preserves changes of objects over time in stable modeling constructs; (iii) provides a substantial view on processes; and (iv) enables the conceptualization of processes via philosophically grounded set of information patterns.

The first ontological assumption – the spatio-temporal (4D) world view – is aimed at grounding modeling constructs on objects that have a spatial extension and persist over time. From Descartes [10] it is recognized that objects are unambiguously identified and separated from each other by their spatial extensions. Focusing on dimensional objects alleviates modelling errors and biases.

Secondly, as other perdurantist approaches, the OP assumes that all objects have a temporal dimension in addition to spatial ones. Objects are considered as partly existent within each period of time through their life span, i.e. objects are timeless. A consideration of temporality allows ascribing different characteristics to objects' states while preserving objects' identity over time. This, in turn, allows modelling of objects as the sequence of their 4D-states.

The Object Paradigm proposes to identify a production process by the *set* of 4D-objects involved into this process. Consequently, a process is also considered as a spatio-temporal object. In terms of DEMO, the extension of a simple process may be constituted by the extension of some actor and the extension of some resource that have a state changed by this actor. State changes of constituent objects drive a process over time.

Finally, in the Object Paradigm, C. Partridge proposed philosophically grounded, essential and comprehensive information patterns for the modelling of production processes, to wit: *whole-part, before-after* and *pre-condition* patterns. Consideration of at least two *ordered states* of a *whole* product, along with *an actor purposefully caused* this state change matches with the Aristotle's system of causes.

## 2.3 Formal Enterprise Ontology (FEO)

The FEO ontology [11] was derived from a synthesis of two foundational ontologies (1) the Unified Foundational Ontology (UFO) [14] and (2) the Object Paradigm [10] with (3) the enterprise ontology DEMO [9].

A complete description of UFO falls completely outside the scope of this paper. However, in the sequel we give a brief explanation of the UFO elements which appear in the fragment of FEO presented in Fig. 1. Moreover, an ontologically well-founded

UML modeling profile proposed by G. Guizzardi in [14] is used for the representation of the FEO ontology and its domain-specific extensions.

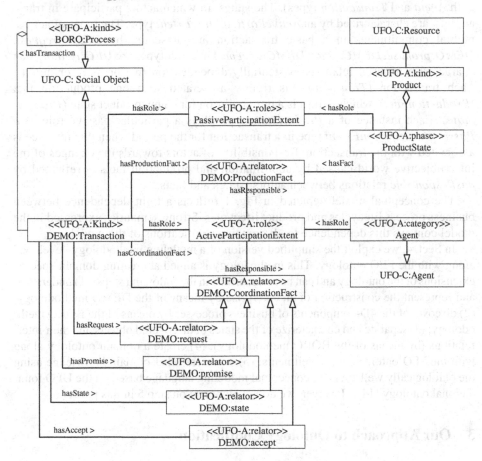

**Fig. 1.** Conceptual model of the basic transaction pattern in FEO 0.1

The ontological interpretation of the UML class meta-construct is that of a type (universal). The ontological interpretation of the UML association meta-construct is that of a formal relation between types. The UML ontological profile employed here makes explicit ontological distinctions among types (kinds, roles, phases, relators, etc.) and the categories of formal relations (mediation, derivation, characterization, etc.). Type names are written in *italics* wherever they are referred throughout this paper.

Conceptual model of the basic transaction pattern based on the DEMO theory of enterprise ontology is shown in Fig. 1. Both *DEMO:Transaction* and *BORO:Process* types are specified by *UFO:kind*. Each type which is of a *UFO:kind* necessarily applies to its instances in every possible world and supplies a principle of identity for substantial individuals that instantiate it. Processes and transactions are associated with actors (e.g. persons or organizations) which are individuals of an *Agent* type.

In some of their states, actors participate in a transaction by playing a particular social role (this aspect of the world-semantics is reflected by *hasRole* relations of both *Agent* and *Transaction* types). The states, in which actors participate in transactions, are characterized by an *ActiveParticipationExtent* type. The types of actors' mutual commitments in a basic transaction are presented by *DEMO:request*, *DEMO:promise*, *DEMO:state*, *DEMO:accept*. The latter types are *UFO:relators* that characterize material relations existentially dependent on two or more endurants. Each transaction (*Transaction*) is rigidly associated with one production fact (*ProductionFact*), which in turn is a pre-condition for a new product state (*Product-State*). Each instance of a *ProductState* type plays a particular passive role of *a PassiveParticipationExtent* type in a transaction for the period when this instance is associated with the transaction. Responsibility of actors towards the changes of the intersubjective world caused by coordination and production facts is reflected by *hasResponsible* relations between actors' states and facts.

The conceptual model depicted in Fig. 1 reflects a tight dependence between business process lifecycles and product lifecycles. Strong semantics expressed in the model conveys this dependence to all domain specifications of the model.

In Sect. 4, we exploit the simplified version of a modeling methodology developed along with the FEO ontology. This methodology is aimed at creating domain-specific extensions of the ontology and can be summarized in the following steps: (1) understand and represent the construction of an enterprise by means of the DEMO methodology; (2) discover of the 4D-components of business processes by means of the BORO methodology; (3) separate and characterize of the states of discovered objects and their inter-relations (by means of the BORO methodology); (4) create a domain ontology along with the FEO ontological commitments; (5) represent other domain knowledge using the ontologically well-founded conceptual modeling language based on the UFO foundational ontology [14]. However, we do not elaborate on step 5 in this paper.

## 3   Our Approach to Ontology Codification

Mapping of the created logistics ontology onto the constructs of Web Ontology Language (OWL) results in a core data metamodel for logistic networks. This ontology-based data metamodel is a reusable computational artefact.

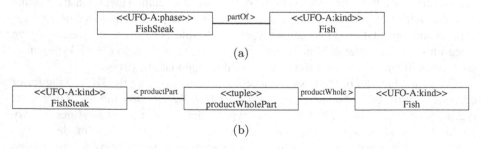

**Fig. 2.** a. Non-reified relation between *Fish* and *FishSteak* types. b. Reified relation between *Fish* and *FishSteak* types

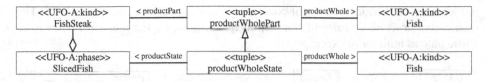

**Fig. 3.** Tuple-types hierarchy

Following the BORO methodology at the codification stage, we reified the relations between the types of substantial individuals by representing the relations as types (so-called *tuple-types*) of artificial instances – *tuples*. A tuple is composed by a pair of 4D-objects. All tuples of the same tuple-type are ascribed with the same meaning of relations between objects in tuples. For example, the *partOf* relation between types *Fish* and *FishSteak* (Fig. 2a) can be represented by a *productWholePart* tuple-type (Fig. 2b). Though a tuple-type is shown as an element of conceptual model in Fig. 2b, we do not visualize tuple-types for the ontology proposed in Sect. 4. However, we implement tuple-types in particular OWL structures for all appropriate relations.

Reified relations can be organized into hierarchies using a common understanding of inheritance, bun on circularity, and deducing descendants. From the example in Fig. 3 we can deduce that *productWholeState* tuple-type is a sub-type of *productWholePart* tuple-type.

The semantics of tuple-type hierarchies reinforces considerably analysability of a data metamodel. For example, the codification of the hierarchy shown in Fig. 3 allows finding all spatial as well as temporal parts of *Fish* individuals in case the information about individual parts was inquired. A separate request about the states of individuals is implicitly deduced from the original one. In our research, we exploit the created hierarchy of tuple-types for a semantic search on our codified ontology. Also a prototype of knowledge extraction tool was implemented on Apache Jena[6] platform.

## 4   The Logistics Ontology

In this section, we demonstrate the ontologization of two processes of the SCOR model: the Source Stocked Product and Deliver Stocked Products processes.

The SCOR model describes the Source Stocked Product process as one aimed at maintenance of pre-determined level of inventory [6]. The process includes several stages: scheduling product deliveries, receiving products to contract requirements and the determination of product conformance to requirements and criteria. As soon as a product is transferred to the destination, the initiator of the process pays for the order. However, the sequence of activities within the source process is not strictly prescribed by the standard. For instance, a product may be paid before or after its transportation.

The first step towards the ontologization of the source process is the process analysis by means of the DEMO methodology. At this stage, we extracted transactions, actor roles, coordination and production facts from the process description in the SCOR

---

[6] Jena Ontology API: http://jena.apache.org/documentation/ontology/.

model. The interaction structure of considered source process is shown in Fig. 4. The interaction structure consists of transaction types in which the identified actor roles participate as initiator or executor.

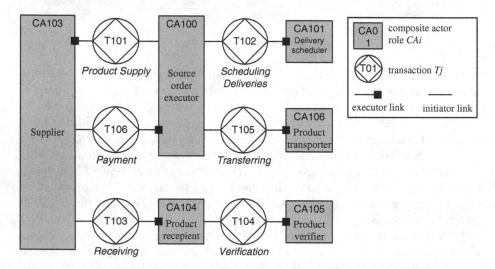

**Fig. 4.** Interaction structure of the Source Stocked Product process expressed in the Actor Transaction Diagram notation [9]

At the second step we analyzed the Source Stocked Product process from BORO perspective. Particularly, we focused on the modeling of product lifecycle. The following sequence of product states within the Source Stocked Product process is recommended by the standard: *ProductTransferred*, *ProductReceived* and *Product-Verified*. Taking into account the results of the previous stage, we modeled the production facts of *Transferring*, *ReceivingProduct* and *ProductVerification* transactions as preconditions for required product states. According to the Object Paradigm, a product (*Product*) and its states (*ProductReceived*, *ProductTransferred* and *ProductVerified*) are associated via a whole-part pattern. In addition, the standard requires product receiving (*Receiving*) precedes product verification (*Verification*), which in turn precedes product transferring (*Transferring*). Therefore, we ordered product state types as follows: *ProductReceived* precedes *ProductVerified*, and *ProductVerified* precedes *Product-Transferred*.

Finally, we associated the concepts found at previous steps with the concepts of the Formal Enterprise Ontology [11]. Some examples of this generalization are shown in Figs. 5, 6 and 7. In Fig. 5, *SCOR:Transferring* is a sub-type of *DEMO:Transaction*. In Fig. 6, *SCOR:SourceOrderExecutor* is a sub-type of *FEO:ActiveParticipationExtent*; individuals of a *SCOR:SourceOrderExecutor* type are responsible for production facts of a & *ProductTransferred* type; these facts occur in transactions of a *Transferring* type. In Fig. 7, *ProductTransferred* is a subtype of *ProductState*; production facts of a &*ProductTransferred* type are preconditions of product states of a *ProductTransferred* type.

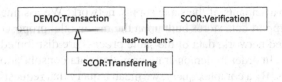

**Fig. 5.** *Verification* transaction precedes *transferring* transaction

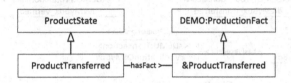

**Fig. 6.** Responsibility for a production fact occurred in *transferring* transactions

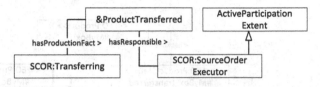

**Fig. 7.** Pre-condition relation between production facts and product states in *transferring* transactions

In future, both *ProductState* and *ProductionFact* types will be associated with additional characteristics extracted from the SCOR model. Additional associations will provide unambiguous definitions of particular product states in the metamodel.

Following the same modelling methodology, we ontologized the Deliver Stocked Products process. The intention of this process is to provide the availability of products when a customer order arrives (to prevent the customer from looking elsewhere) [6]. Created conceptual model of the process includes the following transaction types: *InventoryReservation*, *OrderConsolidation*, *LoadsBuilding*, *ShipmentsRouting*, *CarrierSelection*, *Receiving*, *Pick*, *Pack* and *Payment*; and the recommended product state types: *ProductReceived*, *ProductPicked* and *ProductPacked*.

## 5   Our Solution for Data Consolidation

In this section we demonstrate the use of the proposed data metamodel for data consolidation within a supply network with autonomous participants. For this purpose we consider a simulated business-case of the Italian company General Ricambi S.p.A.

General Ricambi S.p.A. owns a chain of stores selling a wide range of auto parts. One of the key business processes of the company is managed in accordance with Source Stocked Product of the SCOR model. This process is aimed at replenishment stores with pre-determined level of inventory. The verification of products, the determination of their conformance to requirements, standards and criteria is outsourced to a survey company EBF (Engineering Bureau Franke). Therefore, both General Ricambi S.p.A and EBF are the participants of the same supply network. We assume that their information systems support data stores built upon the metamodel proposed in this paper.

In this simulated network, data of the same process are distributed between autonomous data stores. In order to demonstrate provided data consolidation we build a set of complex queries. By a complex query, we mean a query that requests the information from other participants. The structure of complex queries includes the sequence of information items; each of them is formed by a pair of interconnected concepts.

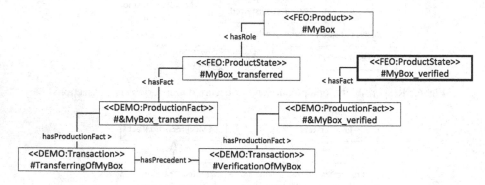

**Fig. 8.** Complex query execution

For example, a customer of General Recambi S.p.A. wants to know if his product *#MyBox* was verified or not (Fig. 8), considering that only name and identifications of the product are available. In the metamodel products and their states are related via a particular case of 'whole-part' pattern – *hasRole* association. Therefore, an information system finds all the states of the product using *hasRole* association and takes the last one. The last state (*#MyBox_transferred*) is the current state of the product. Product state is associated with a production fact (via *hasFact* relation). So, *#MyBox_transferred* state is associated with *#&MyBox_transferred* production fact. Using the extracted production fact, related transaction (*#TransferringOfMyBox*) may be inquired (via *hasProductionFact* association). Then, the metamodel allows inquiring for a previous transaction (*#VerificationOf-MyBox*) (via *hasPrecedent* relation) and its production fact (*#&MyBox_verified*) (via *hasProductionFact* relation). Finally, having the information about *#&MyBox_verified* production fact, the metamodel allows obtaining the information about *#MyBox_verified* product state. Thus, the customer obtains the required information about his box. Foregoing complex query execution demonstrates the possibility of data consolidation between autonomous data stores.

Usually, the quality of domain ontology is evaluated by the set of competency questions that the ontology can answer. In the presented research we used the set of competency questions formulated by A. Scheuermann in [15]. The following questions are executable for a simulated data store built upon the codification of our ontology:

- CQ1: What is the role of an agent in a process?
- CQ2: What are the resources/products involved into a process?
- CQ3: What types of logistics services are offered by an agent?
- CQ4: What activities are involved into a process?

- CQ5: What are required resources (inputs) of a process?
- CQ6: What is the result (outputs) of a process?
- CQ7: What is the detailed lifecycle of a product?
- CQ8: Who is responsible for a transaction?

At this moment, the list of competency questions executable for the created meta-model does not include ones about process metrics. Conceptualization of the metrics and practices recommended by the SCOR model is planned for the future research.

# 6 Conclusions

In this paper we present the top-level logistics ontology built upon the SCOR model by means of the DEMO methodology and the BORO methodology. The ontology comprises 26 types and 31 associations.

The data metamodel resulted the codification of the created ontology may facilitate data consolidation within supply networks. This ability of the metamodel was demonstrated on a simulated business case. In addition, we listed the competency questions executable for the created metamodel.

In the nearest future, after the conceptualization of other parts of the SCOR model, the ontology will be extended by the additional characteristics of process and product states.

**Acknowledgments.** This research is partially supported by LATNA Laboratory, NRU HSE, RF government grant 11.G34.31.0057, and by the CLASSE ("Les Corridors Logistiques: Application a la Vallee de la Seine et son Environnement") project of the Grand Research Network of in Upper Normandy (Grand Réseaux de Recherche de Haute-Normandie).

# References

1. Magdalenić, I., Vrdoljak, B., Schatten, M.: Mapping of core components based e-business standards into ontology. In: Sánchez-Alonso, S., Athanasiadis, I.N. (eds.) MTSR 2010. CCIS, vol. 108, pp. 95–106. Springer, Heidelberg (2010)
2. Guarino, N.: Formal Ontology and Information Systems. In: Guarino, N. (ed.) Formal Ontology in Information Systems: Proceedings of the 1st International Conference, 6-8 June 1998, Trento, Italy, pp. 3–15. IOS Press, Amsterdam (1998)
3. Partridge, C.: The role of ontology in semantic integration. In: Second International Workshop on Semantics of Enterprise Integration at OOPSLA 2002, Seatle (2002)
4. West, M.: Developing high quality data models. Elsevier Inc., USA (2011)
5. de Almeida Falbo, R.: SABiO: systematic approach for building ontologies. In: Guizzardi, G., Pastor, O., Wand, Y., de Cesare, S., Gailly, F., Lycett, M., Partridge, C. (eds.) Proceedings of 1st Joint Workshop Onto.Com/ODISE on Ontologies in Conceptual Modeling and Information Systems Engineering, Rio de Janeiro, Brazil 22–25 September 2014, vol. 1301. CEUR-WS (2014)
6. Supply Chain Operations Reference (SCOR) Model Version 9.0. Supply Chain Council (2008)

7. Zdravkovic, M., Panetto, H., Trajanovic, M., Aubry, A.: An approach for formalizing the supply chain operations. J. Enterp. Inf. Syst. **5**, 401–421 (2011)
8. Bjeladinovic, S., Marjanovic, Z.: A comparison and integration of ontologies suitable for interoperability extension of SCOR model. In: Bogdanova, A.M., Gjorgjevikj, D. (eds.) ICT Innovations 2014. AISC, vol. 311, pp. 75–84. Springer, Heidelberg (2015)
9. Dietz, J.: Enterprise Ontology – Theory and Methodology. Springer-Verlag, Berlin Heidelberg (2006)
10. Partridge, C.: Business Objects: Re-Engineering For Re-Use (2000). http://www. brunel.ac.uk/~cssrcsp/BusObj.pdf
11. Poletaeva, T., Babkin, E., Abdulrab, H.: Ontological framework aimed to facilitate business transformations. In: Guizzardi, G., Pastor, O., Wand, Y., de Cesare, S., Gailly, F., Lycett, M., Partridge, C. (eds.) Proceedings of the 1st Joint Workshop Onto.Com/ODISE on Ontologies in Conceptual Modeling and Information Systems Engineering, Rio de Janeiro, Brazil, 22–25 September 2014, vol. 1301. CEUR-WS (2014)
12. Barjis, J., Dietz, J.L.G., Liu, K.: Combining the DEMO methodology with semiotic methods in business process modeling. In: Liu, K., Clarke, R.J., Andersen, P.B., Stamper, R.K. (eds.) Information, Organisation and Technology: Studies in Organisational Semiotics, pp. 213–246. Kluwer Academic Publishers, Boston (2001). ISBN 0-7923-7258-1
13. Partridge, C.: The role of ontology in semantic integration. In: Second International Workshop on Semantics of Enterprise Integration at OOPSLA (2002)
14. Guizzardi, G.: Ontological foundations for structural conceptual models. Telematics Instituut Fundamental Research Series, ISSN 1388–1795, No. 015, The Netherlands (2005)
15. Scheuermann, A., Hoxha, J.: Ontologies for intelligent provision of logistics services. In: Proceedings of the 7th International Conference on Internet and Web Applications and Services (ICIW 2012), pp. 106–111 (2012)

# A Wide-Spectrum Approach to Modelling and Analysis of Organisation for Machine-Assisted Decision-Making

Vinay Kulkarni[1(✉)], Souvik Barat[1], Tony Clark[2], and Balbir Barn[2]

[1] Tata Consultancy Services, 54B, Industrial Estate, Hadapsar, Pune, India
{vinay.vkulkarni, souvik.barat}@tcs.com
[2] Middlesex University, The Burroughs, Hendon NW4 4BT, UK
{T.N.Clark, B.Barn}@mdx.ac.uk

**Abstract.** This paper describes a modeling approach that helps to represent necessary aspects of complex socio-technical systems, such as organization, in an integrated form and provides a simulation technique for analyzing these organisations. An actor-based language is introduced and compared to a conventional simulation approach (Stock-and-Flow) by simulating aspects of a software services company.

## 1 Introduction

Modern enterprises are complex systems involving multiple stakeholders that need to respond to a variety of changes within a highly constrained setting. The cost of an erroneous response is prohibitively high and may possibly reduce options for subsequent changes in direction. Large enterprises adopt an organisational structure best suited for ease of management and control; this can lead to undesirable side-effects such as scattered and fractured knowledge about goals, operational processes, IT systems, design rationale, IT infrastructure and best practices. Analysis of such an organisation relies almost exclusively on human experts who are expected to keep track of current and historical phenomena or traces (possibly using large collection of spreadsheets), and interpret them with respect to the problem under consideration; this is a huge challenge considering the size and complexity of modern enterprises [21].

Current practice advocates the use of multi-dimensional view-decomposition techniques to address complexity and size of an organization [1–7, 10, 16]. For instance, the Zachman Framework [1] recommends a two dimensional classification matrix describing six interrogative aspects that include *what, where, when, why, who* and *how* with five levels of perspectives (*i.e., Scope, Business Model, System Model, Technology Model* and *Detailed Representation*) to represent an enterprise as set of interrelated views. This structured representation helps to improve documentation quality and visual navigability of enterprise artefacts to a large extent. However, the analysis support for one or limited views(s) results into view integration issue in practice [18, 19]. The existing machineries for organizational decision making are mostly limited to one specific aspect only. For example, an organizational decision making process that involves goal, strategy, and business processes of an organization

© Springer International Publishing Switzerland 2015
J. Barjis et al. (Eds.): EOMAS 2015, LNBIP 231, pp. 87–101, 2015.
DOI: 10.1007/978-3-319-24626-0_7

can only be addressed by integrating i*[1] (for goal aspects), iThink[2] (for strategic aspects) and BPMN tools[3] judiciously. The paradigmatically diverse nature of languages for goal modelling, Stock-and-Flow (SnF) modelling, and business process modelling means it is difficult to come up with a single meta language in terms of which the three modeling languages can be expressed. As a result, one is left with no recourse but to establish suitable mapping relationships between the relevant model elements across different models for co-simulation [25]. Clearly, such a method has to rely heavily on human expertise for correctness of execution. Moreover, being at model-level and models being purposive, the mapping relationships are rarely reusable across different contexts let alone different problems thus making the modelling endeavour both effort and cost intensive. All in all, current state of practice suffers from several limitations as regards comprehensive and efficient support for organizational decsion making.

Our claim is that the problem of organizational analysis and support for decision making that involves multiple aspects, such as goal, strategy and operational aspects, can be addressed by simulation using a single language. Importantly, a single language for representing an organization in the context of decision making solves the view integration issue; and simulation can be used to support various forms of what-if and if-what analysis for organizational decision making.

This paper introduces Enterprise Simulation Language (ESL) for organisational analysis and simulation. To validate our claim that ESL based approach is more appropriate than existing analysis and simulation machineries that support a single organizational view (or subset of views) we define a simple real-world case study and represent it using both, a representative leading current approach Stock `n` Flow (SnF) and ESL. We carried out analyses that predict likely impact of modifying control variables onto the observable variables of the system at steady state. We show that the ESL approach is at least as good as SnF in terms of producing analytical results for operational strategy in organizational decision making, and that the SnF model exhibits problems that are not present in the ESL specification.

## 2    State of the Art

Enterprise decision making is a complex process and it requires precise understanding of enterprise in terms of goals, strategies, operational process, organizational structures, constraints, etc., and ability to analyse and predict them in dynamic environment. Traditional domains like engineering, manufacturing, military, traffic and control industry use computer aided decision making to reduce the human dependency and increase precision. Several projects those are based on CIMOSA [2], TOVE [3], PERA [4], GERAM [5], GRAI [6], DoDAF [7], MoDAF[4] have benefited significantly by

---

[1] http://www.cs.toronto.edu/km/istar.

[2] http://www.iseesystems.com/Softwares/Business/ithinkSoftware.aspx.

[3] http://www.softwareag.com/corporate/products/aris/default.asp.

[4] https://www.gov.uk/mod-architecture-framework.

adopting methods that supports quantitative and qualitative simulation. While simulation has evolved into a mature discipline in traditional domains, its application to complex socio-technical systems such as organisations is relatively new [8, 9]. The challenges in this domain are, in part, posed by the informality of the specification and dominance of symbolic and qualitative approaches in practice.

The current state-of-the-art of enterprise specifications in information system are broadly classified into two: those focusing on operational aspect that includes *what*, *how* and *who*, [10, 11] and those focusing more on the goal aspect that includes *i.e.*, *why* and *who* [12–14]. Supporting machinery for the former is best seen as a means to create high level descriptions that are meant for human experts to interpret in the light of synthesis of their past experience. The stock-n-flow model [15] provides an altogether different paradigm for modeling high-level *operational strategy* (the *what* plus abstract specification of *how*) and comes with a rich simulation machinery (iThink) for quantitative analysis using averaging out models and formulae. Several BPMN tools, such as ARIS and Bizagi[5], providing simulation capability exist but they are limited to the *how* and *who* aspects only. Supporting infrastructure for goal aspects is comparatively more advanced in terms of automated deduction. However, they are largely removed from operational aspects. There are limited specifications, such as Archimate [17] and EEML [16], that balances goal and operational aspects but they are lacking in precise execution/simulation semantics. Hence they solve the integration and interoperability issues [18, 19] but are not capable of promoting machine assisted techniques, such as simulation, in decision making.

At present, the only recourse available is the use of a method to construct a tool-chain of the relevant set of analysis and simulation tools with the objective of answering the desired questions. The projects based on TOGAF and Zachman adopt a standardized method but the use of analysis and simulation tools is still a challenge.

## 3 Our Approach

An enterprise can be understood well by understanding *what* an enterprise is, *how* it operates and *why* it is so. It further provides clarity on organizational responsibilities by understanding the *who* (*i.e.,* responsible stakeholders for *what*, *how*, and *why*) aspect of the organization. We argue that the information about *what*, *how* and *why*, augmented with *who*, aspects of an enterprise is necessary and sufficient for organizational decision making activities under various operating conditions. The further proposition of our work is the need for a language to specify these aspects as a single integrated model. A single unified specification is believed to be a viable option to overcome present problems due to multiple partial views that need to be integrated for deriving insights obtainable from their analysis and simulation. An executable model can enable what-if and if-what scenario playing thus leading to a priori, data-driven, and informed decision making. Naturally, such a specification language needs to be close to execution infrastructure and therefore quite a distance away from the end-user decision-maker.

---

[5] www.bizagi.com.

This abstraction gap is best bridged by developing domain specific language(s) (DSLs) each describing the *why*, *what* and *how* aspects for all relevant stakeholders or the *who* aspect in a localized relatable 'business facing' form specific for an analysis use-case. As both languages express the same aspects albeit at different levels of abstraction, it is possible to automatically transform a DSL specification to the simulatable closer-to-machine lan-

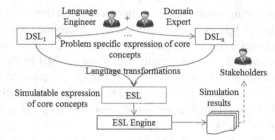

**Fig. 1.** High Level Approach for organizational decision making

guage (ESL). We propose model based engineering to address these practical issues. Figure 1 presents a pictorial description of this approach.

## 4   ESL

From an external stakeholder perspective, an organisation can be viewed as something that raises and responds to a set of events as it goes about achieving its stated goals. Organisations consist of many autonomous units, organised into dynamically changing hierarchical groups, operating concurrently, and managing goals that affect their behaviour. We describe structure and behaviour of an organization using a small set of concepts and their relationships as depicted in Fig. 2. An *Abstraction Unit* is the core conceptual element that can represent organization unit, people as well as IT systems. It interacts with the environment through *inEvents* and *outEvents*. It exposes a set of *Goals* as its intent, *Levers* as possible configuration parameters and *Measures* that describe qualitative and/or quantitative evaluation of its state to the external stakeholders. An *Abstraction Unit* is defined in terms of *Data* as a set of state variables/state variables, *History* as a set of past states, *Behaviour* as what the unit "does", and sub-units that it may compose of. Our hypothesis is that these concepts are necessary and sufficient for specifying *why*, *what*, *how* aspects from the perspectives of the relevant stakeholders (*i.e.*, the *who* aspect) of an organization. The structural elements *Abstraction Unit, In Event, Out Event, Data* and nesting capability of *Abstraction Unit* specify the *What* aspect, *Goal* specifies the *Why* aspect, *Behaviour* specifies the *how* aspect and *Abstraction Unit*, as individual, defines the *who* aspect of an organization.

In addition, we argue that *Abstraction Unit* must support a set

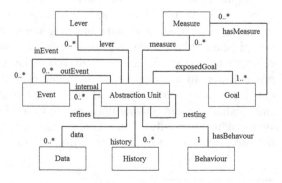

**Fig. 2.** High level conceptual meta model

of characteristics of organization theory [20] as essential requirements for modeling basic elements of organizations, *i.e.,* organizational units, human elements and IT system components [21]. These charateristics are as follows: **reactive** *i.e.,* Abstraction Unit must respond appropriately to its Environment; **adaptable** *i.e.,* Abstraction Unit may construct and reconstruct its structure in its life cycle [20]; **modular** *i.e.,* Abstraction Unit must encapsulate structure and behaviour of organisation; **autonomous** *i.e.,* Abstraction Unit is a standalone entity; **intentional** *i.e.,* Abstraction Unit has its own goals; and **compositional** *i.e.,* an Abstraction Unit can be an assembly of Abstraction Unit. The *In Event* and *Out Event* concepts help to capture reactive nature of Abstraction Unit, the intent is captured using *Goal*, modularity is achieved through *Abstraction Unit*, autonomy is possible due to the concept of *Internal Event*, and composition can be specified using nesting relation. We use these concepts as the basis for ESL language definition where adaptability is incoporated using the operational semantics of ESL.

We aim for the ESL to reflect these core concepts by having an operational semantics based on the Actor Model of Computation (AMC) [22] and its relation to organisations, *i.e.,* iOrgs [23]. Computationally, an Actor has an address and manages an internal state that is private and cannot be shared with other actors in the system. Execution proceeds by sending asynchronous messages from a source actor to the address of a target actor. Each message is handled in a separate execution thread associated with the target of the message and the message itself (collectively referred to as a task). During task-execution an actor may choose to change its state and behaviour (becoming a new actor) that is immediately available to process the next message sent to the target address. AMC is also appropriate to support the key characteristics listed such as:- **reactive**: Actor interacts with other Actors; **adaptability**: An actor changes behaviour as a result of handling each message; **modularity**: Access to an actor's hidden implementation is provided by a message interface; **automomy**: The AMC is highly concurrent with each actor being able to spawn multiple threads and over which other actors have no control; **intent**: Actors can form the basis for Multi-Agent Systems [24]; **composition**: Actors can be nested.

We are implementing a robust execution engine for ESL as part of a larger initiative for developing pragmatic framework for organizational decision making[6]. A prototype of ESL execution engine has been implemented in the programming language Racket[7] and all results in this paper are generated by our implementation.

### 4.1  Decsion Making Using DSL

ESL supports decision making through *what-if* (what would be the consequence in terms of *Measures* if *Levers* and *Organization Unit* definition are specified) and *if-what* (what *Levers* and *Organization Unit* would have led to a consequence) scenario playing. Organization under consideration can be modelled as an instance of the meta

---

[6] www.tcs.com/about/research/research_areas/software/Pages/Model-Driven-Organization.aspx.
[7] http://docs.racket-lang.org/drracket/.

model in Fig. 2, behaviour and conditions describing the impacts of goals in a behaviour can be encoded using ESL. In a *what-if* simulation, if the *Measures* are not within expected range then error could either be with the model (*i.e.,* organization definition) or with values supplied to the *Levers*. The *if-what* simulation requires sophisticated guidance to arrive at meaningful organizational structure and values to the *levers*. Current ESL execution engine implementation is capable of *what-if* simulation.

# 5   Case Study

In this section, we consider a software provisioning organization to illustrate simulation of organizational aspects in the context of organizational decision making. For space reason, we limit our discussion to operational strategy or the *what* aspect in this paper. The organization under consideration bids for software development projects in response to requests for proposals (RFPs) based on customer profile and price considerations. Once acquired, a project is resourced and executed using tried-and-tested development processes, finally delivering to the customer and releasing resources. This business as usual (BAU) scenario involves operational strategies including skill-matching, dealing with unforeseen demand, staff attrition, resource utilisation, accounting for operational delays, while ensuring business targets are met.

In addition to maintaining its BAU state, the organisation needs to decide upon strategies to improve its BAU state. An increase in similar projects should improve the maturity of the workforce with consequent improvements in productivity, quality and track-record. Project costs can be reduced by employing fewer resources or less experienced resources, but this might increase the pressure on the workforce inducing undesirable delays. Investment in training and productivity tools might mitigate the delays but incur their own costs and delays, however this might be balanced by the future profit margins that are supported by better quality processes. The decision to adopt a tool-centric approach hinges upon being able to compute return on investment in tools and the break-even point at which productivity and quality gains start to outweigh costs.

## 5.1   Description and Implementation

Figure 3 shows such a software provisioning organization, which operate in an environment that comprises of a *Demand* and *Supply*. In this case study, the Demand is characterized by four kinds of software development projects: low margin low risk (LMLR), medium margin low risk (MMLR), medium margin high risk (MMHR) and high margin high risk (HMHR). The characteristics of these projects, *i.e.,* typical project arrival rate, standard chargeable rate and size of the projects, are specified in a table that associated with Demand in Fig. 3. We consider *Resources* are the primary element that forms the Supply of this organization. The case study considers four kinds of workforce resources: junior (J), skilled junior (SJ), senior (S) and expert (E). Individual characteristics of resources are also depicted in Fig. 3. The software provisioning organization has a goal to improve profit margin without compromising service qualities (*i.e.*, on time delivery of the software with desired quality). The organization measures three metrics: revenue, expense and timely delivery, to keep track of the BAU state.

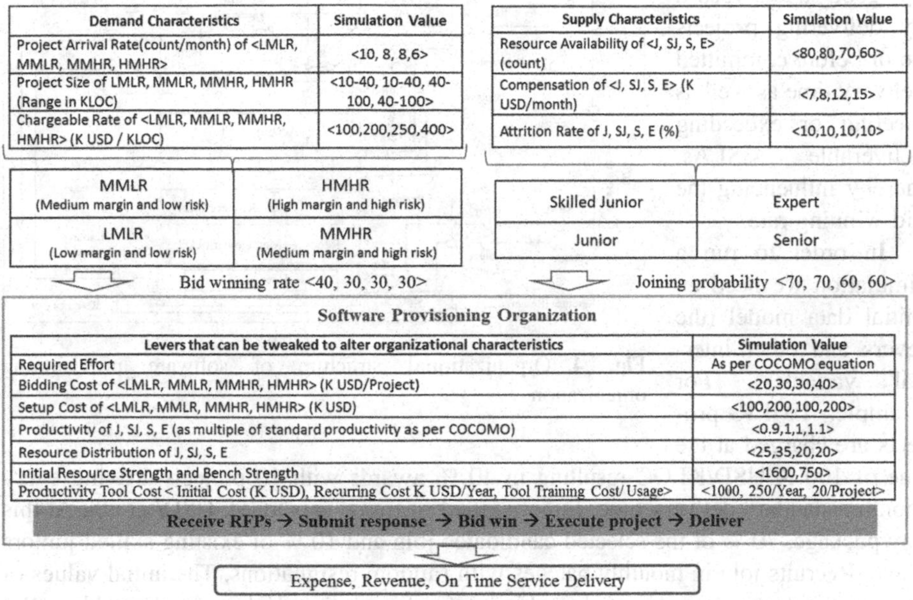

| Demand Characteristics | Simulation Value |
|---|---|
| Project Arrival Rate(count/month) of <LMLR, MMLR, MMHR, HMHR> | <10, 8, 8,6> |
| Project Size of LMLR, MMLR, MMHR, HMHR (Range in KLOC) | <10-40, 10-40, 40-100, 40-100> |
| Chargeable Rate of <LMLR, MMLR, MMHR, HMHR> (K USD / KLOC) | <100,200,250,400> |

| Supply Characteristics | Simulation Value |
|---|---|
| Resource Availability of <J, SJ, S, E> (count) | <80,80,70,60> |
| Compensation of <J, SJ, S, E> (K USD/month) | <7,8,12,15> |
| Attrition Rate of J, SJ, S, E (%) | <10,10,10,10> |

| MMLR (Medium margin and low risk) | HMHR (High margin and high risk) |
|---|---|
| LMLR (Low margin and low risk) | MMHR (Medium margin and high risk) |

| Skilled Junior | Expert |
|---|---|
| Junior | Senior |

Bid winning rate <40, 30, 30, 30>          Joining probability <70, 70, 60, 60>

| Software Provisioning Organization | |
|---|---|
| Levers that can be tweaked to alter organizational characteristics | Simulation Value |
| Required Effort | As per COCOMO equation |
| Bidding Cost of <LMLR, MMLR, MMHR, HMHR> (K USD/Project) | <20,30,30,40> |
| Setup Cost of <LMLR, MMLR, MMHR, HMHR> (K USD) | <100,200,100,200> |
| Productivity of J, SJ, S, E (as multiple of standard productivity as per COCOMO) | <0.9,1,1,1.1> |
| Resource Distribution of J, SJ, S, E | <25,35,20,20> |
| Initial Resource Strength and Bench Strength | <1600,750> |
| Productivity Tool Cost < Initial Cost (K USD), Recurring Cost K USD/Year, Tool Training Cost/ Usage> | <1000, 250/Year, 20/Project> |

Receive RFPs → Submit response → Bid win → Execute project → Deliver

Expense, Revenue, On Time Service Delivery

**Fig. 3.** Case study description

Internally, organization adopts different strategies, by defining best possible values to the levers and organizational structure, to fulfil desired goals. The internal levers of software provisioning organization are depicted in a table within organization in Fig. 3. The *Bid Winning Rate* and *Joining Probability* of Fig. 3 are also considered as levers of software provisioning organization but they are not completely controlled by the organization, rather they have influence on external factors as well. For example, the efficacies of internal sales strategies determine the initial *Bid Winning Rate*, but in a long run it is largely influenced by track record and market perception of the ability to deliver a project with increased service quality. The internal structure of the organization in terms of abstraction units is depicted in Fig. 4. Each unit is implemented as an ESL actor. The Customer Unit and External Resources interact with Service Provisioning Organization Unit. The Service Provisioning Organization Unit is realized as four interacting Units – Sales, Delivery, Resource Management and Account Units. The bidding process and project execution processes are encoded within Sales Unit and Delivery Unit respectively. The recruitment strategy and current resources are managed by the Resource Management Unit. The resources are also modeled as an abstraction unit (or actor) where each resource managing its own productivity, leaving strategy, *etc.* and they move between Resource Management Unit and Project Unit based on allocation and deallocation requests. The Account Unit coordinates with all other internal units and updates the state of Revenue and Expenses. The organization builds up good track record by delivering projects on or before committed delivery time as well as meeting or exceeding deliverable SLAs, thereby influencing the bid winning rate.

In order to run a simulation we need an initial data model (the levers and other internal variables). For example, LMLR projects are charged at the

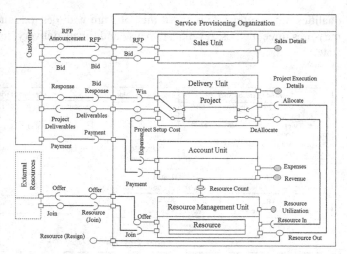

**Fig. 4.** Organizational structure of software provisioning organization

rate of 100 K USD/KLOC resulting in 40 % awards with 10 projects arriving every month a standard delivery time. Junior skilled resource is paid 8 k USD/month. At this pay package, 70 % of the selected candidates join and 10 % of existing skilled juniors leave. Recruits join in monthly batches with random resignations. The initial values of rest of the levers are depicted in Fig. 3 as *Simulation Values* in the tables. We implemented a Racket based GUI for setting *Levers* values and observing *Measures* of a simulation run. Customized GUI interacts with generic ESL execution engine to supply input data and get Meassures values from a simulation run.

## 5.2   Simulation & Results

The organization is faced with several business-critical decisions such as: Are resources optimally loaded or is there some slack? Will quoting a reduced price or delivery time be more effective at winning more bids? Will staff training or the use of productivity tools reduce delivery time? When would the benefits start outweighing the costs? What J:SJ:S:E configuration delivers optimal KPIs? What would be the impact of scarcity of Expert resources on KPIs? What would be the result of focusing on high margin projects only?

We consider a goal of increased revenue without compromising the service quality. Management would like to have as precise answers as possible to the following kind of questions: Q1: Are we operating in a comfort zone? If so, how far can one go by removing existing slack (without compromising desired service quality)? Q2: How far can one go with existing workforce distribution (J:SJ:S:E)? Q3: For this organization setting, what is the best workforce distribution possible *i.e.*, a local optimal situation? Many other questions are associated with the decision making that may lead to global optimum solution. In this paper, we limit our discussion to first two questions due to the space limitation.

**Simulation Result of Q1.**
Figure 5 shows the *Measures* of a simulation run when *Lever* values are as depicted in Fig. 3. The horizontal histograms depict the number of RFP Received, RFP Responded, RFP Won, Projects completed on time, Projects completed with delay and Project Pipeline (from to bottom to top),

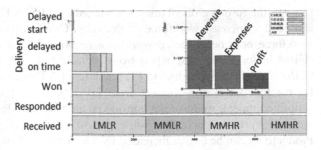

**Fig. 5.** Measures of a simulation run with initial values

where four colors of each histogram (except project pipeline histogram) represent the metrics related to LMLR, MMLR, MMHR and HMHR respectively. The vertical histograms depict the Revenue, Expenditure, Profit and Saving due to productivity tool respectively (from left to right). The organization is winning about 33 % of bids all of which are being executed within the expected time. Also, there is hardly any project that is not able to start due to non-availability of resources. Clearly, the organization seems to be operating in a comfort zone; how much more can the existing workforce deliver? The organization needs to win more bids. Delivery time and cost are the variables influencing bid winning percentage. We change the chargeable rates for LMLR, MMLR, MMHR and HMHR projects from {100, 200, 250, 400 (all in \$K per KLOC)} to {90, 180, 225, 350} thus improving their bid winning percentage from {40, 30, 30, 30 (all in percentage)} to {90, 70, 70, 70}. Figure 6a shows the effect of this modification on measures. Bid winning percentage improves to 76 % from 33 %. The number of projects completed on time remains more or less the same but there is significant increase in the number of projects delivered late. Also, a significant number of projects witness delayed start due to non-availability of resources. Significant increase in bids won results in significantly high revenues even when chargeable price is reduced. With expenses remaining more or less the same (linked largely to number of resources on board) profits increase significantly.

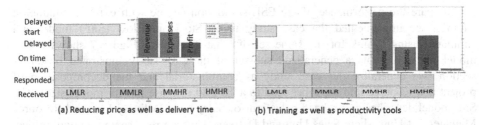

**Fig. 6.** Modifying simulation parameters

**Simulation Result of Q2.** As seen from Fig. 6a, delayed delivery and project kick-off queue build-up are critical concerns. How can these concerns be effectively addressed keeping the resource distribution unchanged *i.e.,* J:SJ:S:E::25:35:20:20? Clearly there is a need to increase workforce productivity. One can think of having a better trained workforce or a better-tooled workforce or both. We change productivity of junior, skilled junior, senior and expert from {0.9, 1, 1, 1} (all as a factor of standard CO-COMO[8] productivity metric) to {1, 1.1, 1.1, 1.1}. This comes at increased training cost for the four kinds of workforce from {10, 10, 10, 15} to {20, 20, 20, 25}. In this simplified model, we have not considered an adverse side effect namely, revenue loss incurred by the organization while part of its workforce was undergoing training. Productivity can be further increased by a factor of 1.25 by using tools. This too comes at tool license and training costs. Figure 6b shows the effect of these changes on the measures. There is increase in the number of projects delivered on time. More significantly, no HMHR project is delivered late thus saving on delayed delivery penalties. Also, there is a significant increase in proportion of HMHR projects delivered on time. The sum total of all is a significant increase in revenue as well as profits. However, the delayed start for projects remains a cause for concern.

**Simulation Results of Other Questions.** Essentially, the management would like to have an idea of the possible outcomes (*Measures* – revenue, expenses, on time deliveries, resource utilization) for given set of operating parameters (*i.e., Lever* values), and prediction on operating parameters (possible *Lever* values and organization structure) for a specific set of *Measures* as part of what-if and if-what analysis. We demonstrated two scenarios where *Measures* are observed by setting values to the *Levers* using what-if simulation runs. The rest of the analyses are not very different than above two. However, a complex decision making process involves an iterative scenario playing process that involves both kinds of simulations (*i.e.,* what-if and if-what) till a satisfactory result is observed. While reaching a satisfaction level an organization can be altered in many ways that include the change in lever values, reconstruction of organization structure (by adding new unit, refining existing units and/or both), refinement of sub-unit goals. Thus a method (simulation method) supported by ESL simulation engine is better suited for complex organizational decision making process.

# 6    Comparative Study

To compare the performance of the ESL simulation engine with existing simulation engines, we implemented the case study using Stock-and-Flow (SnF) model and simulated using iThink for the same set of what-if analysis. Figure 7 shows a SnF model that represents a generalized sub-set of the case study illustrated in earlier section (we generalize our case study as combinatorial and the decomposition of project and resource into the types lead to a 16-fold increase in SnF model size). The SnF model describes generalized behaviour of Sales Unit, Delivery Unit and Resource Management Unit where Sales Unit and Delivery Unit are represented without project specialization (LMLR, MMLR, MMHR and HMHR projects), and Resource Management Unit is represented without resource specialization (*i.e.,* junior, skilled junior,

---

[8] Barry W Boehm. Software Engineering Economics. Prentice Hall, 1981 ISBN:0138221227.

senior and expert resources). Lever values with ranges, *e.g.*, *Project Size* and *Project Duration*, are simplified into fixed values to fit formulation using SnF model. The variable *Bid Rate* is dependent on the project pipeline, and *Bid Winning Rate* is dependent on the project delivery track record. Bid Rate is implemented using SnF equations but a fixed Bid Winning Rate is considered in SnF model as individual behaviour cannot be recorded in a generalized formation. For space reasons, we do not discuss Resource Management Unit, Account Unit and their interactions here. We specified an equivalent ESL model with Bid Winning Rate as dependent variable (instead of fixed value in SnF model) and observed the following results.

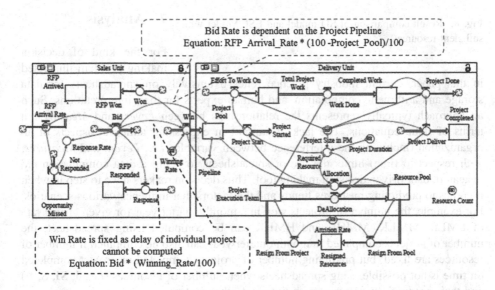

**Fig. 7.** Stock-and-flow model

We simulated SnF and ESL models with input values < TotalResource-Count = 1000, AttritionRate = 10, ProjectArrivalRate = 10/month, Project-Size = 100PM, ProjectDuration = 6 months, InitialWinningRate = 80 % > with the simulation results shown in Fig. 8. The top row describes an overview (*i.e.*, number of RFP arrived, number of RFP responded, number of projects won, number of project started, and completed) and the bottom row describes resource trends (*i.e.*, free resource, allocated resources and number of resource resigned from organization). Simulation results are almost similar for SnF and ESL simulation engines. Steady state values of simulation results for resource trends are also similar. However, simulation output of ESL model is closer to reality with clear indication of resources joining a project in batches whereas resignations do not necessarily happen in chunks or specific interval.

We changed the operating environment by reducing available resources to half while keeping rest of the levers unchanged and observed results as shown in Fig. 9. The SnF simulation can only say that, within the stipulated time period of simulation, how many projects got initiated and how many were completed. It is silent regarding project

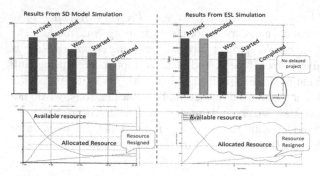

delays, whereas the ESL simulation clearly depicts the details of projects that got delayed and can provide additional important information regarding non-availability of resources and how they influence project delays.

**Fig. 8.** Result comparison of SD model and ESl. Model with sufficient resources

## 7  Analysis

For the kind of decision making problem illustrated in this paper, current industry practice relies extensively on spreadsheets for data storage and arithmetic computation, and human experts for their interpretations. Such an approach typically represents the relationships between *Levers* and *Measures* in terms of static equations. The lack of support in expressing temporal aspects of an organization (including the interference between variables *i.e.*, *Levers* and *Measures,* with respect to time) limits the use of spreadsheets to being a data computation aid instead of data-driven decision making tool. Thus decision makers have to step in when it comes to predicting measures trends and the factors that influence various scenarios. For example, the number of projects won in a month/quarter/year for given arrival rate of LMLR, MMLR, MMHR and HMHR can be computed using spreadsheet; the number of projects completed in month/quarter/year can also be computed if number of resources are fixed; but predicting number of projects completed or project completed on time is not possible using spreadsheets when number of resources (*i.e.*, J, SJ, S, E) and their productivity changes with time and other factors.

SnF models are also used for this kind of decision making. In this approach, the system is specified in terms of stocks, flows of stocks, and equations over levers and variables that control the flows. The quantitative nature of SnF models and sophisticated simulation support enables decision making through what-if scenario playing. Expressing relationships between influencing factors or system variables over time is possible in such a dynamic model. However, it is best suited for an aggregated and generalized view of a system where individual details are abstracted out through averaging, and the sequences of events are grouped as continuous flows. This generalized approach and ignorance of individual characteristics that significantly influence the system over time often leads to a model that is somewhat removed from reality. For example, consider a policy that junior resource becomes a senior resource after working for 3 years. It is possible to capture this policy in a SnF model but the impact of improved productivity and additional cost for this junior-to-senior transition in a specific project cannot be detected in a model that uses averaging. Similarly, it is possible to determine the number of projects completed over time given a certain joining and resigning characteristics, but determining the number of projects delayed due to attrition is not possible. Since a resource is an individual actor in ESL and a set

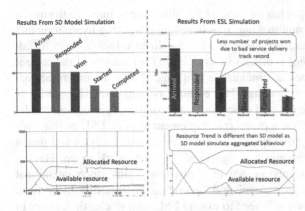

**Fig. 9.** Simulation run with reduced resources

of individual actors participate in a project (instead of set average junior resources), it is possible to determine which specific project will be impacted. Similarly ESL can detect individual projects that are impacted due to resignations of allocated resources and junior-to-senior transition.

Though a SnF model is not intended for specialized behaviour, it is possible to argue that it can be specialized for such detailed analyses. But the effort required to specialize such models at the level of types leads to model size explosion *e.g.*, specialization of the notion of project into LMLR, MMLR, MMHR and HMHR projects and of the notion of resource into Junior, Skilled Junior, Senior and Expert resources leads to 16-fold increase in model size. Moreover, since SnF models offer poor support for modularity and change isolation, they are ineffective in dealing with industry-scale problems. For example, incorporating a minor change in the bidding strategy of a specific kind of project (*e.g.*, the decision not to bid HMHR projects when significant project pipeline is built up) may impact many flows and equations of SnF model.

We conducted a series of experiments to evaluate the desired characteristics of organizational decision making. We found that ESL scores better with respect to SnF in terms of modularity, compositionality, adaptability and intentionality. In different experiments, we also found ESL to be better than BPMN (and associated simulation engines) in terms of autonomicity, adaptability, intentionality; and better than intentional models, such as i*, in terms of autonomicity and compositionality. Moreover, ESL is capable of specifying the *why*, *what* and *how* aspects from the perspectives of a stakeholder (*i.e.*, *who* aspect) in a localized and relatable form, which we believe is a significant advance if industry practice is to take to simulation as a decision making aid for socio-technical systems.

## 8 Conclusion

This research is being undertaken by research lab of organization in the business of offering software, processes and technology consultancy[9]. It is becoming increasingly apparent that coming up with the right solution and demonstrating its likely efficacy is lot more important and harder than implementing the solution. We believe formal modeling of relevant aspects of enterprise in a manner that supports what-if and if-what

---

[9] www.tcs.com/about/research/research_areas/software/Pages/Model-Driven-Organization.aspx.

simulation holds the key. This paper has introduced an initial step to improve the use of simulation in organizational decision making. It is based on a working hypothesis that specification of the *why, what* and *how* aspects in a localized relatable form for all relevant stakeholders (*i.e.,* the *who*) is critical in overcoming limitations of the current state of practice. We have defined a simulatable language (ESL) for organisational analysis and support for decision making. The essence of simulation capability is demonstrated with a simplified real-world case study and compared simulation results with traditional simulation (SnF) on a prototype implementation of ESL engine. We conclude that our approach is highly promising for organisational analysis and that it offers advantages over existing approaches, but there is much work to do. Having added structure to simulation models we are in a position to introduce intentional behaviour in the form of both system-level and individual goals, using ideas from multi-agent systems. In addition, we will need to extend ESL with stochastic features in order to capture uncertainty in real life that leads to variability in the simulation. In longer term, we are working towards to a general purpose framework for organizational decision making where ESL based simulation engine will be used in coordination with business facing DSLs to enable business experts to pose their questions using business facing language and get their answers back in business terms. We think ideas from Fact Based Modelling (FBM) [26] could be useful especially as regards semantics.

**Acknowledgements.** We would like to thank Arun Bahulkar for his help in defining the case study.

# References

1. Zachman, J.A.: A framework for information systems architecture. IBM Sys. J. **26**(3), 276–292 (1987)
2. Kosanke, K.: CIMOSA—overview and status. Comput. Ind. **27**(2), 101–109 (1995)
3. Fox, M.S.: The TOVE Project: Towards A Common-sense Model of the Enterprise, Enterprise Integration Laboratory Technical report (1992)
4. Williams, T.J., Rathwell, G.A., Li, H.: A Handbook on Master Planning and Implementation for Enterprise Integration Programs. North Holland Publishing, Amsterdam (2001)
5. Bernus, P., Noran, O., Molina, A.: Enterprise architecture: twenty years of the GERAM framework. In: The International Federation of Automatic Control, pp. 24–29, Cape Town, August 2014
6. Doumeingts, G., Chen, D., Vallespir, B.P., Marcotte, F.F.: GIM (GRAI integrated methodology) and its evolutions - a methodology to design and specify advanced manufacturing systems. In: DIISM, pp. 101–120 (1993)
7. Wisnosky, D.E., Vogel, J.: In Managing and Executing Projects to Build Enterprise Architectures Using the Department of Defense Architecture Framework (DoDAF) (2004)
8. Barjis, J.: Enterprise, organization, modeling, simulation: putting pieces together. In: Proceeding of EOMAS (2008)
9. Barjis, J., Verbraeck, A.: The relevance of modeling and simulation in enterprise and organizational study. In: Barjis, J. (ed.) EOMAS 2010. LNBIP, vol. 63, pp. 15–26. Springer, Heidelberg (2010)
10. Vernadat, F.: UEML towards a unified enterprise modelling language. Int. J. Prod. Res. **40**(17), 4309–4321 (2002)

11. OMG Document, Business Process Model and Notation, formal/2011–01-03, January 2011. http://www.omg.org/spec/BPMN/2.0/
12. van Lamsweerde, A., Letier, E.: From object orientation to goal orientation: a paradigm shift for requirements engineering. In: Wirsing, M., Knapp, A., Balsamo, S. (eds.) RISSEF 2002. LNCS, vol. 2941, pp. 325–340. Springer, Heidelberg (2004)
13. Yu, E., Strohmaier, M., Deng. X.: Exploring intentional modeling and analysis for enterprise architecture. In: 10th IEEE International Enterprise Distributed Object Computing Conference Workshops (EDOCW 2006), IEEE (2006)
14. Object Management Group. Business Motivation Model v. 1.1 (2010). www.omg.org/spec/BMM/1.1/
15. Meadows, D.H.: Thinking in systems: A primer. Chelsea Green Publishing, Amsterdam (2008)
16. Krogstie, J.: Using EEML for combined goal and process oriented modeling: a case study. IDI, NTNU. In: Proceedings of EMMSAD, Trondheim (2008)
17. Iacob, M., et al.: State of the art in architecture support, ArchiMate deliverable D3.1. Enschede, The Netherlands: Telematica Instituut (2003)
18. Chen, D., Doumeingts, G., Vernadat, F.B.: Architectures for enterprise integration and interoperability: Past, present and future. Comput. Ind. **59**(7), 647–659 (2008)
19. Fox, M.S.: Issues in Enterprise Modelling. In: Proceedings of the IEEE Conference on Systems, Man and Cybernetics, Le Toquet, IEEE (1993)
20. Parsons, T., Jones, I.: Structure and Process in Modern Societies, vol. 3. Free Press, New York (1960)
21. Barn, B.S., Clark, T., Kulkarni, V.: Next generation enterprise modelling - the role of organizational theory and multi-agent systems. In: ICSOFT EA, pp. 482–487 (2014)
22. Hewitt, C.: Actor model of computation: scalable robust information systems. arXiv preprint arXiv:1008.1459 (2010)
23. Hewitt, C.: Norms and commitment for iorgs (tm) information systems: Direct logic (tm) and participatory grounding checking. arXiv preprint arXiv:0906.2756 (2009)
24. Van Harmelen, F., Lifschitz, V., Porter, B.: Handbook of Knowledge Representation, vol. 1. Elsevier, Melbourne (2008)
25. Camus, B., Bourjot, C., Chevrier, V.: Combining DEVS with Multi-agent Concepts to Design and Simulate Multi-models of Complex Systems (2015)
26. Bollen, P.: Using fact-based modeling for business simulation. In: Barjis, J. (ed.) EOMAS 2010. LNBIP, vol. 63, pp. 59–78. Springer, Heidelberg (2010)

# Revisiting the BORM OR Diagram Composition Pattern

Martin Podloucký[✉], Robert Pergl, and Petr Kroha

Department of Software Engineering, Faculty of Information Technology,
Czech Technical University, Prague, Czech Republic
{martin.podloucky,robert.pergl,petr.kroha}@fit.cvut.cz

**Abstract.** This paper addresses the notion of process decomposition as a tool for managing process complexity in BORM Object Relation Diagram. It investigates the composition principle already present in ORD and shows it as ambiguous and mostly unsuitable for that purpose. Substantial changes to the original meta-model of ORD are proposed by introducing a new concept called tasks. The implications of introducing this new concept are then investigated, especially concerning decomposition of communications in a BORM process.

**Keywords:** Process composition · BORM · BOBA · OR diagrams

## 1 Introduction

The *Business Object Relation Modelling (BORM)* has been developed at the Loughborough University since 1993 [6] and later have became a practically-applied method with scientific interest, becoming a tradtitional topic of EOMAS [7–9,11]. BORM is an elaborate method for systems analysis and design utilising object-oriented paradigm in combination with business process modelling. Since we are mostly interested in the business process modelling, the primary focus of our research is on the initial phase of the BORM called Object Behaviour Analysis (BOBA) [6].

### 1.1 Motivation

We have been using BOBA and other BPM methods successfully in practice for several years in management consulting practice, research projects and software development. Throughout the time, we began to greatly appreciate the BOBA approach to business process modelling, and we see many strengths and qualities in this approach. On the other hand, however, we also ran across several problems in the original BOBA, one of which is the concept of process decomposition.

It is probably not necessary to explain that real-life business processes are seldom clear and simple. In many cases, the processes are very complicated, and the resulting model is very difficult to comprehend. We believe that the most effective concept for managing such complexity in processes is the idea of composition. Unfortunately, the principle of composition in the BOBA's ORD (Object Relationship Diagram) is defined quite vaguely, and we see significant inconsistencies and limitations in its usage.

© Springer International Publishing Switzerland 2015
J. Barjis et al. (Eds.): EOMAS 2015, LNBIP 231, pp. 102–113, 2015.
DOI: 10.1007/978-3-319-24626-0_8

## 1.2   The Goal

The intention behind this paper is to address the issues of process composition in ORD. Our goal is to identify problematic spots in this original concept and eventually present a new approach and new definition of process composition which, once incorporated into ORD, would bring the BOBA to a next level of practical usefulness.

# 2   The BORM Method

In this paper, we use a version of ORD which is slightly different then the original concept described in [6]. In our previous work [12], we introduced some minor changes to the original syntax of the diagram to make it more compliant with the definition of Mealy's machine and to make it more useful in practice. We always point out these differences throughout the paper when in danger of confusion.

The original concept of BORM was inspired by experience in the area of software engineering. There is often a significant discord in the communication of ideas about particular problem domain between different stakeholders such as software developers and analysts on one hand, and business people on the other. This observation is supported be the original authors of BORM, who say that there is a problem to

> "... find a common language for the developers to express their understanding of the problem space that is both sufficiently rich for the developers to fully articulate their ideas, while also being comprehensible to users from all areas of discourse." [6]

We agree with this experience and, in unison with the authors, we believe BORM may be such a common language. As we explained in the motivation, we cherish the fundamental principles upon which BOBA is built. In our view, the most important of them is *simplicity*. The BOBA process model is based upon communicating finite-state machines which makes ORD especially clear in structure and appearance (see Fig. 1). This truly allows people with varying technical and business backgrounds to easily understand the process diagrams even at the very first sight. The properties that contribute most to the high comprehensibility of ORD are in our view:

1. a small set of simple and easy-to-understand building blocks with clear intentions behind them,
2. a straightforward depiction of participants of the process and
3. a very transparent depiction of communication amongst participants similar to that of UML sequence diagrams.

On the contrary, however, there are also several weaknesses in the original BOBA framework. Over the time we came into disagreement with some of the fundamental notions upon which the BOBA process diagram stands. Since we still believe that BOBA has a big potential especially regarding rigorous process analysis, our overall and long-term goal is to elevate BOBA to a next level by addressing its shortcomings and proposing appropriate enhancements to overcome them.

Our objections towards ORD are essentially twofold. Firstly, it is the lack of sound formal foundations of ORD meta-model and secondly, it is the unsatisfying definition of the composition.

## 2.1 The Formal Foundations

We agree completely with van der Aalst that solid formal foundations are very valuable since they allow for exact reasoning about the properties of the whole process, they do not leave any scope for ambiguity, and they increase the potential for analysis [1].

The original authors of BORM claim that ORD is based upon communicating finite-state machines (FSMs), namely Mealy's machines [3]. However, the proposed ORD behaviour diverges significantly from the execution semantics of the FSMs. This leaves a big scope for ambiguity in the execution and simulation of the modelled processes. In our previous work [11,12], we explored these problems to a great extent, and we observed that ORD *structure* is based upon Mealy's machines but the *behaviour* corresponds more to Petri nets. This led us to a formulation of a new formal model of ORD execution called the Prefix Machine [11], which is to some extent a combination of

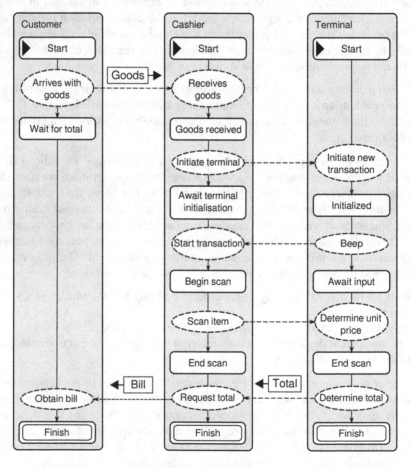

**Fig. 1.** A sample BORM Object Relation Diagram taken from [11]. Each participant is a Mealy finite-state machine. States are represented as rounded rectangles and activities as dashed ovals. Transitions are depicted as solid lines and communications as dashed lines.

Mealy's machines and Petri nets. That work introduced a precise formal grounding of ORD and BOBA. The relation between ORD, Mealy's machines, and Petri nets is discussed in our previous paper [12] in detail. Some open questions still remain, though. One of such open topics is process composition that we intend to explore in this paper.

## 2.2    The Process Composition

We believe that one of the most important tasks in process modelling is managing process complexity. Processes in the business reality are seldom simple and neat, the very opposite is quite often the case. As we explained in the beginning of this section, the primary aim of BORM and BOBA in particular is to serve as a communication language bridging the areas of discourse of software engineers and business stakeholders. As such, it strives for greatest simplicity and abstraction to suit the business people, yet still maintaining sufficient technical detail for the engineers. This is hard to achieve without a powerful system for managing the process complexity.

The human mind certainly has a limited capacity for processing visual information. A process diagram with hundreds of elements is difficult to comprehend even for a skilled person. A famous work by George Miller [10] in the field of cognitive psychology suggests that the number of objects an average human can hold in working memory is $7 \pm 2$. Having this argument in mind, we would like to have a well-defined concept of process composition in BOBA allowing us to decompose a process diagram into different levels of abstraction each of which contaning as few elements or concepts as possible.

Object relation diagram in BOBA already has a construct to express process composition, however, we find it mostly unsuitable. In order to describe this construct and to support the further discussion, we are using a simplified version of the waterfall software development process as an illustrative example.

Figure 2 depicts this process in both collapsed and expanded form. Notice how the state `Develops the software` on the left side of the diagram is marked with a plus sign signalling that the state is composite. Composite states in ORD are used to encapsulate a sub-process and to hide it when a reader wants to abstract from too much detail. The sub-process can be revealed by expanding the composite state as seen on the right side of Fig. 2.

The waterfall example in Fig. 2 shows a standard way of using composition in BOBA. At the first sight, this concept may seem useful and straightforward. Though, under a more thorough look, serious doubts arise.

Imagine at first, that the software company is unable to create the product on its own and it needs an external supplier to develop a specialised library. As a result, the sub-process in the composite state now contains a communication, as depicted in Fig. 3.

Now the important question is, what to do with this communication when the composite state is collapsed. Since the ORD meta-model is based upon communicating finite-state machines, states cannot communicate, only the activities can. It seems, therefore, that states should not allow composition, and they should rather be atomic elements. Actually, this issue points to a more fundamental ontological problem in the BOBA method.

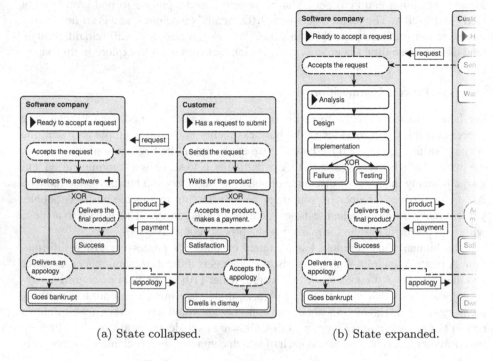

(a) State collapsed.                    (b) State expanded.

**Fig. 2.** Example of a simple composite state.

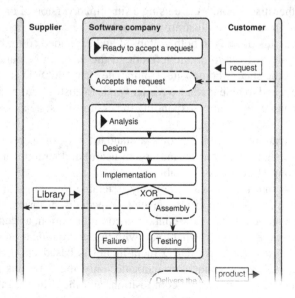

**Fig. 3.** Composite state with a communication.

Many a time, we see that processes modelled using BOBA contain states that represent some non-trivial work being done. Let us look again at Fig. 3 and at states such as `Analysis`, `Design` or `Testing`. In our view, this approach overloads the concept of a state too much. It is contradiction with the fundamental concepts of state machines and computation theory in general. There, a state is understood as a kind of milestone and not as a unit of work. By allowing composite states, BOBA itself goes against this very principle.

> To make BOBA compliant with the theory of FSM, we propose that states should be only milestones or named points in time. The only allowed activity in a state ought to be waiting. The only way how some actual work can be done in a process is by transitioning from one state to another.

### 2.3  New Composition in BOBA

From the above paragraphs, it seems that BOBA and ORD require some polishing and redefinition of some basic terms to make it more consistent. In fact, though, the problem of composition goes much deeper and revels broader area of ideas and problems to deal with.

In the following two sections, we elaborate on these challenges.

> First, we propose that ORD would benefit from more then a single principle of process decomposition. In fact, we see two orthogonal decomposition principles which can be incorporated into ORD to better manage the complexity of BOBA processes. We call them the *horizontal* and the *vertical* decomposition.

## 3   Vertical Decomposition

The term *vertical decomposition*[1] covers the principle of the composite states described in the previous section. Beware, however, that we had already dismissed the construct of composite states as contradictory. Yet, we still find the concept of vertical decomposition very useful. The question is, then, how to express this concept in a proper way.

The obvious first choice might be to use composite activities. As they represent transitions between states, they ought to represent the actual units of work in the process. This concept can be, however, dismissed just as promptly as the previous one using states. Let us look again at the right side of Fig. 2. The sub-process in the expanded state `Develops the software` has two mutually exclusive outcomes. These have to be mapped to corresponding distinct branches in the super-process. Yet, when we change the composite state to a composite activity, this is no longer possible since the control flow cannot branch at an activity[2].

---

[1] The name of the notion comes from the visual appearance of ORD. When the composite states are collapsing, the diagram is shrinking vertically.

[2] The original version of ORD actually allows branching at an activity. The modified version we are working with now does not. It became necessary to restrict activities in such a way to get a better alignment with the definition of Mealy's machine [12].

Since only a state can be used to fork and join the control flow, we can use neither states nor activities as elements of composition without completely violating their fundamental semantics. It seems we need to keep states and activities atomic and introduce a completely new kind of element used as means of composition.

## 3.1 Tasks

We call the new composition element *a task*. Figure 4 shows the original composite state transformed into a task. In the diagram, we use a wide border to depict a task to distinguish it from the states and activities. As Fig. 4 shows, a task can be expanded and collapsed to show or hide the inner content.

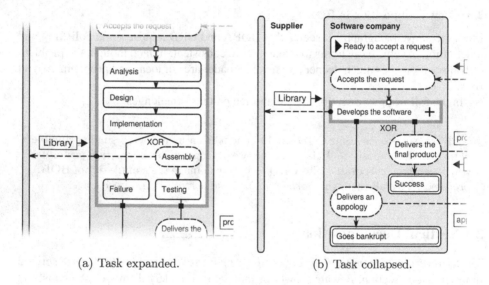

(a) Task expanded.                    (b) Task collapsed.

**Fig. 4.** Example of a task.

A fundamental new concept coming with the tasks are so-called *ports*. They appear as symbols on the border of a task and they are used to define an *interface* of the task with the outer world. We distinguish two kinds of task interfaces, the *transition interface* and the *communication interface*.

The transition interface is used to specify the branching of the process flow. The interface uses the so-called *entry ports* (depicted as empty squares □) and *exit ports* (depicted as filled squares ■). Entry ports specify where a branch of the process may enter the task. Each task must have at least one entry port. When it has two entry ports for example, two distinct branches of the process need to enter the task. The number of exit ports specifies how many branches exit from the task when it is completed (see Fig. 4). The task has no exit ports if the process terminates in it.

The communication interface is used to specify communications of a task and it is based upon exactly the same principles as the transition interface. The interface uses *inputs ports* (depicted as empty circles ◯) and *output ports* (depicted as filled circles ●). Each input port represents a target of one communication and a task may have any number of such ports (including zero). Similarly, each task can have any number of output ports representing sources of communication.

Thanks to the ports, the transition and communication interface of a task remain exposed even when the task is collapsed. This is not the case in the original concept of composition using states or activities.

We can say that introducing our concept of tasks and interfaces in business process modelling corresponds to the concept of separation of interface and implementation in software engineering. This successful concept lead to the possibility of implementation evolution without changing the interface. In this case, the old, well-known method of stepwise decomposition may be viewed as corresponding.

## 4   Horizontal Decomposition

In fact, we have already been silently using the horizontal decomposition in ORD diagrams throughout the paper. See for example Fig. 3 where two of the participants are collapsed horizontally to omit unnecessary detail in their structure. Using this second kind of decomposition, any participant can be collapsed to a vertical line representing just its communication interface. This is another convenient way to hide a large amount of possibly insubstantial detail in the process diagram.

An interesting observation (though, without further elaboration in this paper) is the fact that we get a diagram very similar to the UML sequence diagram [4] (Fig. 5a) by

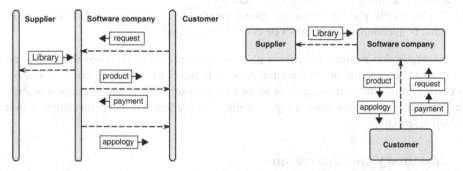

(a) A horizontally collapsed ORD reminds of a UML Sequence Diagram

(b) A totally collapsed ORD reminds of a UML Communication Diagram.

**Fig. 5.** UML-like diagrams of the waterfall model.

horizontally collapsing all of the participants. To bring this idea even further, we can at first collapse all the participants vertically as far as possible arriving at participants containing only the top-most task or tasks. Second, we can do complete horizontal collapse, eventually arriving at something similar to the UML Communication diagram [4] (Fig. 5b). In order to do this, however, we need to also collapse all the communications between participants to a single connection. This option opens a non-trivial discussion we touch in the next section.

Nevertheless, the horizontal decomposition does not seem to pose such challenges as the vertical one and it seems fairly consistent in its simplicity. Therefore, we leave it now and focus on the issue of vertical decomposition of communications.

## 5    The Challenge of Communication Decomposition

The above illustration suggests that the idea of collapsing communications to a single connection is rather straightforward. Yet, it is so only when we do not want to retain any structure of the communication interface among the respective participants. In this simple case, one cannot take one of the aggregated connections and connect it to an input port of some task, since the connection represents several single communications.

Eventually, we would like to be able to collapse the communication interface of a participant (or a task) as much as possible, while still retaining enough information about the structure of this interface, so it can be used to connect the participant to communication ports of other tasks in the process. Figure 6 shows a simple situation of this kind. The expanded version of the task on the left has four output communications. When this task is collapsed (on the right), there are several possibilities how to deal with the communications:

1. To leave them as they are. In that case, each communication can be connected to some input port right away, but we lose all the information about the structure of the interface.
2. To collapse all communications into one connection. This time, however, we cannot connect these connections to input ports right away since the only thing we know about the communication is its existence.
3. To group only parallel communications together. Yet, still are we left with aggregated connections which cannot be connected to input ports.

We argue that neither of the three proposed approaches is fully suitable. Some do not reflect the structure of the communication interface, whilst the others do not allow to connect the communications right away to input ports. The issue of communication decomposition seems to open a bigger topic, and we leave it to be investigated in a further research.

## 6    Summary and Discussion

Throughout the previous sections, we argued that the composition principle already present in ORD is not suitable as means for managing process complexity. The concepts of composite states or activities result in ambiguities and even contradictions

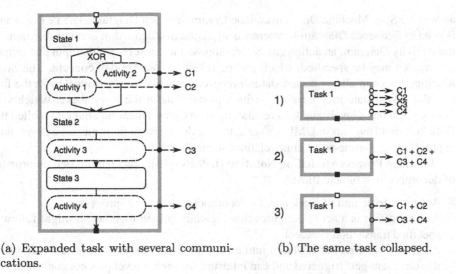

(a) Expanded task with several communi-       (b) The same task collapsed.
cations.

**Fig. 6.** Collapsing communications of a task.

(Sect. 2.2) with the basic notion of state in the finite-state machines. Having realised that, we strived to introduce a proper concept of composition into ORD. Our concept of tasks addresses the composition issues and brings flexible ways of composition result-ing in new forms of ORD diagrams that resemble certain UML diagrams. However, the topic of composition is not totally solved, mostly due to challenges concerning decomposition of communications. The structure of communications of a task seems to contain an inherent complexity in it which is difficult to abstract from.

# 7   Related Work

Decomposition is an established concept in process-modelling methods and notations, as the goal of model comprehensibility is a natural driver, as we described in Sect. 2.2. Let us here briefly elaborate on most notable related efforts in other process-modelling approaches and their features.

Let us start with Yourdon's **Data-flow diagrams** (DFD) [14]. *Processes* are the holders of activities. Activities may be decomposed into a larger detail, i.e. DFD dia-grams are generally recursive. We like the way decomposition is solved in DFDs, as it exhibits pure recursive behaviour and maintains consistency between the various decomposition levels: everything that goes into an activity on the level up needs to go into the decomposed diagram and so on. We adopt this approach of consistency handling, however it is impossible to maintain purely recursive composition in more complex approaches like BORM.

In the family of **Unified Modeling Language** (UML) diagrams [2,4], there are sev-eral behaviour-related diagrams that may be used to model certain aspects of processes. The basic ones are the Sequence Diagram and the Activity Diagram we already touched above, the State Machine Diagram and the Communication Diagram. The `ref` operator is used in Sequence Diagram to reference an interaction defined in another diagram. In the Activity Diagram, an action can be decomposed into a subactivity. Input and output parametres may be specified, which can be related to our "ports" concept. The State Machine Diagram allows nested states, however, we perceive a serious flaw in the fact that the nested state may have a transition to the state in the level above, which violates separation of levels and kills recursivity. The Communication Diagram (called the Collaboration Diagram in UML 1.x) enables the decomposition of message flows, thus expressing the routine-subroutine relations in an algorithm.

**Business Process Modelling Notation** (BPMN) [13] offers a quite rich assortment of decomposition of activities:

- A *Task*, a basic unit of work may be decomposed into a sub-process.
- A *Transaction* is a set of activities that logically belong together; it might follow a specified transaction protocol.
- An *Event Sub-Process* is placed into a Process or Sub-Process. It is activated when its start event gets triggered and can interrupt the higher level process context or run in parallel (non-interrupting) depending on the start event.
- A *Call Activity* is a wrapper for a globally defined Task or Process reused in the current Process.

Moreover, various activity markers may be used to refine the behaviour of decomposed activities: the Loop Marker, the Parallel Marker, the Sequential Marker, the Ad Hoc Marker. The broad offer of decomposition concepts in BPMN may be a benefit for executable BPMN models, however, we find them too complex and hardly comprehensible for business users.

The last related work, we mention here, is the **Hierarchical Coloured Petri Net** (HCPN) extension [5], which brings the concept of *modules* into the standard Petri Net. Modules have ports similar to our approach, apart from input and output ports, input-output ports are supported. HCPN introduces also a new type of model, the Hierarchical Protocol Model, which shows the decomposition relations. The decomposition in HCPN is clean and recursive, which is possible mostly due to the simple nature of Petri Net concepts.

## 8   Conclusion and Future Work

We proposed a new model of decomposition for the BORM OR Diagrams. The new model addresses ontological and formal flaws of the original "naive" way of decomposition and offers interesting new concepts like vertical and horizontal decomposition. At the same time, new challenges arise, mostly in the topic of communication (de)composition, which would support further abstraction and detail hiding. Also, by introducing the concept of tasks, we substantially changed the structure of ORD and its execution semantics which needs to be reflected in its formal meta-model. The Prefix Machine mentioned at the beginning of this paper needs to be revisited to accommodate these new concepts.

Last but not least, the new decomposition concepts need thorough testing in practice to show possible ontological or practical flaws in special situations.

# References

1. van der Aalst, W.M.P., ter Hofstede, A.H.M., Weske, M.: Business process management: a survey. In: van der Aalst, W.M.P., ter Hofstede, A.H.M., Weske, M. (eds.) BPM 2003. LNCS, vol. 2678, pp. 1–12. Springer, Heidelberg (2003)
2. Arlow, J., Neustadt, I.: UML 2.0 and The Unified Process: Practical Object-Oriented Analysis and Design, 2nd edn. Addison-Wesley Professional, Boston (2005)
3. Brožek, J., Merunka, V., Merunková, I.: Organization modeling and simulation using BORM approach. In: Barjis, J. (ed.) EOMAS 2010. LNBIP, vol. 63, pp. 27–40. Springer, Heidelberg (2010)
4. Fowler, M.: UML Distilled: A Brief Guide to the Standard Object Modeling Language. Addison-Wesley Professional, Reading (2003)
5. Jensen, K., Kristensen, L.M.: Coloured Petri Nets. Springer, Berlin (2009)
6. Knott, R., Merunka, V., Polák, J.: Process Modeling for Object Oriented Analysis using BORM Object Behavioral Analysis. In: 4th International Conference on Requirements engineering, 2000. Proceedings. pp. 7–16. IEEE (2000)
7. Merunka, V.: Instance-level modeling and simulation using lambda-calculus and object-oriented environments. In: Barjis, J., Eldabi, T., Gupta, A. (eds.) EOMAS 2011. LNBIP, vol. 88, pp. 145–158. Springer, Heidelberg (2011)
8. Merunka, V., Merunková, I.: Role of OBA approach in object-oriented process modelling and simulation. In: Barjis, J., Gupta, A., Meshkat, A. (eds.) EOMAS 2013. LNBIP, vol. 153, pp. 74–84. Springer, Heidelberg (2013)
9. Merunka, V., Nouza, O., Brožek, J.: Automated model transformations using the C.C language. In: Dietz, J.L.G., Albani, A., Barjis, J. (eds.) Advances in Enterprise Engineering I. Lecture Notes in Business Information Processing, vol. 10, pp. 137–151. Springer, Berlin (2008)
10. Miller, G.A.: The magical number seven, plus or minus two: some limits on our capacity for processing information. Psychol. Rev. **63**(2), 81–97 (1956)
11. Podloucký, M., Pergl, R.: The prefix machine – a formal foundation for the BORM OR diagrams validation and simulation. In: Barjis, J., Pergl, R. (eds.) EOMAS 2014. LNBIP, vol. 191, pp. 113–131. Springer, Heidelberg (2014)
12. Podloucký, M., Pergl, R.: Towards formal foundations for BORM ORD validation and simulation. In: Proceedings of the 17th International Conference on Enterprise Information Systems, pp. 315–322, April 2014
13. Silver, B.: BPMN method and style with BPMN implementer's guide: a structured approach for business process modeling and implementation using BPMN 2.0. Cody-Cassidy Press, Aptos (2011)
14. Yourdon, E.: Modern Structured Analysis. Yourdon Press, Englewood Cliffs (1989)

# Formal Grammar Approach to the Virtual Enterprise Synthesis as Web-Services Composition by Parsing Algorithm

Victor Romanov$^{(\boxtimes)}$, Ekaterina Yudakova, and Svetlana Efimova

Information Systems in Economics and Management Department,
Russian Plekhanov University, 117997 Moscow, Russia
victorromanovl@gmail.com, {kat-youdakova, marta266}
@yandex.ru

**Abstract.** The fast changing world around dictates need for the same speed to change structure of the enterprise to save clients and compliance to world around. The virtual enterprises provide such opportunity. Existence of a large number of various services in the Cloud does potentially possible both fast changing of the enterprise, and assembly of the new enterprises of atomic services. It is known that algorithms of automated planning are important part of such synthesis.

In this paper it is proposed to apply the theory of the formal grammar and the appropriate procedures as means of support of automated planning for composition of web services.

**Keywords:** Virtual enterprise synthesis · Web services composition · Automated planning · Formal grammar · Hierarchical Task Network (HTN) · Parsing

## 1 Introduction

From one side nowadays users' queries are changing very fast. To create a stable set of ERP services for provider imply to lose significant part of potential users. Modern ERP structure must be dynamic for satisfying needs demand of different categories of users. From other side in the Internet is developed and posted a wide quantity of services that may serve as elements for building ERP system.

Virtual Enterprise (VE) Concept is becoming more important in this situation. A virtual enterprise [1] is a temporary alliance of cooperating enterprises that acts as a single organization to share skills, core competencies and resources in order to react quickly to changes in the market conditions and become agile enterprises.

The virtual enterprise is useful for both the small and large organizations at the same time.

Collaboration of small enterprises gives them the chance to provide effective and individual customer service, which they couldn't provide separately. Moreover, they get access to the bigger capital and various technologies due to cooperation with large organizations.

J. Barjis et al. (Eds.): EOMAS 2015, LNBIP 231, pp. 114–124, 2015.
DOI: 10.1007/978-3-319-24626-0_9

In return large organizations become more flexible. Thereby they can quicker react to changes in the market and can develop their business more effectively.

Virtual enterprises serve customers faster and more flexible, because their interaction is based on an electronic selection of partners. As an example of the virtual enterprise it is possible to consider travel agency as this type of VE is widespread most widely.

The remainder of this paper is organized as follows. Section 2 describes stages of web-service development and involved elements. The formal grammar approach is presented in Sect. 3. Section 4 explains how to apply Hierarchical Task Network Planning to virtual enterprise composition. Finally, we present our performance results, related work and conclusions.

## 2  Web-Service Composition

Different books and different organizations provide different definitions to Web Services [2]. To summarize, a complete web service is, therefore, any service that:

- Is available over the Internet or private (intranet) networks
- Uses a standardized XML messaging system
- Is not tied to anyone operating system or programming language
- Is self-describing via a common XML grammar
- Is discoverable via a simple find mechanism

A web service enables communication among various applications by using open standards such as HTML, XML, WSDL, and SOAP. The steps to perform this operation are presented below.

As we can see from Fig. 1, process of VE development includes the following stages:

Stage 1: First of all, it is necessary to answer some questions: for what the web service will be used? Who will use it? How it will be used? Thus, user elaborates requirements to the developed system and its architecture.

Stage 2: On the following step it is necessary to translate the received requirements of the formal language. Ontologies are used for this purpose. A standard ontology consists of a set of basic classes and properties. It is used to declare and describe services.

Stage 3: Further the set of requests for search of a web service is worked out. Several technologies, such as SOAP, WSDL, are being developed to provide a standard way of describing Web Services:

(a) WSDL – syntactic description

WSDL definitions describe how to access a web service and what operations it will perform [14]. Thus, functionality of a web service is determined by types of messages, which it receives and sends in WSDL interface. An operation associates a message exchange pattern with one or more messages. A message exchange pattern identifies the sequence and cardinality of messages sent and/or received as well as who they are logically sent to and/or received from. An interface groups together operations without any commitment to transport or wire format [13]. WSDL is often used in combination

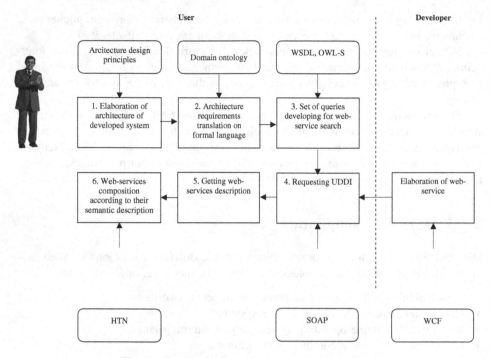

**Fig. 1.** Stages of information system development

with SOAP and XML Schema to provide web services over the Internet [14]. The abstract interfaces are associated to concrete message formats and transmission protocols with binding descriptions.

(b) OWL – semantic description

OWL-S ontology - standard language for the description of web services. OWL-S includes opportunities which are used for automatic service discovery. The functional description of service is based on those changes which it makes. Moreover, this ontology describes preconditions and the expected effects and results. So on the example of travel agency, which is used in this paper, a precondition will be the valid credit card, and the expected result - number of the armor in hotel.

Stages 4–5: UDDI [15] is an XML-based standard for describing, publishing, and finding web services. UDDI allows businesses to promote their services by publishing their description in the global registry. The Registry consists of three main parts: the white pages with contact information, yellow pages describing service belonging to different categories and green pages which directly contain WSDL description. Thereby, user sends a query containing WSDL description to UDDI by means of the special protocol of communication SOAP developed for message exchange between applications on a network. Having automatically carried out comparing of the description made by the user with the description provided on yellow pages at the fifth stage the user receives a web service and its description.

Stage 6: Finally, we propose to use HTN planning to compose VE from obtained web-services. HTN planning is similar to classical planning in that each state is provided by a set of literals, and each action attracts state transition. However, unlike classical planning, The objective of an HTN planner is to produce a sequence of actions that perform some activity or task [3]. Descriptions of planning domain consists of a set of operators, and also a set of methods. Each method defines how it is necessary to decompose the task into subtasks. HTN planning proceeds until primitive tasks, which can't be executed, are reached. For example, the task "reach the airport" can be broken into primitive subtasks "to take a taxi" and "to use public transport". Application of planning in relation to VE will be covered more detailed in the 4th chapter.

All above-mentioned is preceded by creation of service and its registration in UDDI. This can be made by various means, for example by WCF. WCF stands for Windows Communication Foundation. The elementary feature of WCF is interoperability. It is one of the latest technologies of Microsoft that is used to build service-oriented applications. Based on the concept of message-based communication, in which an HTTP request is represented uniformly, WCF makes it possible to have a unified API irrespective of diverse transport mechanisms. WCF platform is also known as the Service Model [4].

Complex or 'composite' services are composed of multiple more primitive services, and may require an extended interaction or conversation between the requester and the set of services that are being utilized [5].

Among the most important Web resources are those that provide services. By "service" we mean Web sites that do not merely provide static information but allow one to effect some action or change in the world, such as the sale of a product or the control of a physical device. The Semantic Web should enable users to locate, select, employ, compose, and monitor Web-based services automatically. That is why we propose to apply the theory of the formal grammar to support the automated planning for composition of web services.

The dynamic composition of services primarily requires understanding the capabilities of the available services (i.e., what they can do) and the compatibility of those services. Several technologies, such as SOAP, WSDL, are being developed to provide a standard way of describing Web Services.

Web Service descriptions can be extended to include information such as preconditions and effects. OWL-S description language uses these constructs give more information about what the service does. It is possible to map such descriptions to planning operators and exploit AI planning techniques for automatic service composition by treating service composition as a planning problem. Ideally, given a user's objective and a set of Web services, a planner would find a collection of Web Services that achieves the objective.

The available OWL-S web service descriptions are used to obtain the available actions in the planning domain. More specifically, each web service description WSDi is translated to a domain action Ai, using the information provided by the corresponding profile instance (each web service description is actually an instance of the OWL-S Profile class). More specifically [6]:

The name of the action is the *rdf:ID* of the profile instance:

$$name(Ai) = WSD_i.ID \tag{1}$$

The preconditions are based on the service input and precondition definitions (concepts):

$$prec(A_i) \equiv \bigcup_{k=1}^{n}\{WSD_i.hasInput_k\} \cup \bigcup_{k=1}^{m}\{WSD_i.hasPrecondition_k\} \tag{2}$$

The add effects consists of the service output and positive effect definitions (concepts):

$$add(A_i) \equiv \bigcup_{k=1}^{n}\{WSD_i.hasOutput_k\} \cup \bigcup_{k=1}^{m}\{WSD_i.hasEffect_k^{+}\} \tag{3}$$

The delete list is formed by the negative effect definitions (concepts). The SWRL language [7] was used in order to model the preconditions and effects of the web services. Preconditions are modeled by SWRL rule conditions, while positive effects are modeled as SWRL atomic expressions that are true in the world after the execution of the web service. Since SWRL does not directly support negation and negated atomic expressions, which would model negative (delete) effects, the negation element of RuleML [8] was employed. The < neg > element is used by the transformation process in order to dis-criminate between add and delete effects. The delete list of the action is formulated as follows:

$$del(A_i) \equiv \bigcup_{k=1}^{n}\{WSD_i.hasEffect_k^{-}\} \tag{4}$$

Invocation of planning algorithms over the newly formulated planning problem produces plans, representing the description of the desired composite web service.

## 3 Formal Grammar

A formal grammar [9] is a system for defining the syntax of a language by specifying the strings of symbols or sentences that are considered grammatical.

A grammar G is a quadruple $G = (\Sigma, V, S, P)$ where $\Sigma$ is a finite set called the terminal alphabet. The elements of $\Sigma$ are called the terminals. V is a finite nonempty set disjoint from $\Sigma$. The elements of V are called the nonterminals or variables.

$S \in V$ is a distinguished nonterminal called the start symbol. P is a finite set of productions (or rules) of the form

$\alpha \rightarrow \beta$ where $\alpha(\Sigma \cup V)^*V(\Sigma \cup V)$ and $\beta \in (\Sigma \cup V)^*$, i.e. $\alpha$ is a string of terminals and nonterminals containing at least one nonterminal and $\beta$ is a string of terminals and nonterminals.

Let $G = (\Sigma, V, S, P)$ be a grammar. G is also called a Type-0 grammar or an unrestricted grammar. G is a Type-1 or context-sensitive grammar if each production in

P satisfies $|\alpha| \leq |\beta|$. By "special dispensation", we also allow a Type-1 grammar to have the production $S \rightarrow \varepsilon$, provided S does not appear on the right-hand side of any production. The symbol $\varepsilon$ is a regular expression, and represents the language whose only member is the empty string, namely $\{\varepsilon\}$.

G is a Type-2 or context-free grammar if each production $\alpha \rightarrow \beta$ in P satisfies $|\alpha| = 1$; i.g., $\alpha$ is a single nonterminal.

# 4 Parsing Algorithm

We suppose that HTN-like parsing should be applied to synthesis of VE because decomposition of tasks in planning HTN is similar to decomposition of composite processes, which are used in case of formal grammar parsing tree of VE. Moreover, HTN encourages the modular principle which will well be coordinated with web services. There are many advantages of application of this algorithm. For example, author can be focused on the certain level of decomposition, and methods can be written without considering how its subtasks will decompose or what compound tasks it decomposes. Methods correspond to recursively composable workflows. These workflows [10] can come from diverse independent sources and then integrated by the planner to produce situation specific, instantiated workflows.

We suppose that special knowledge discovery program tool is used for extracting from natural language description of web-service profile, formed with Web Services Modeling Ontology, the set of formal concepts [12]. Values and attributes detected by this algorithm, form a formal context [11]. Formal context K: = (G, M, I) consists of sets G, M and a binary relation $I \subseteq G \times M$, M –attribute set, G –objects sets, $(g, m) \in I$ - object g has attribute m. Let us define the mapping: $\phi: 2^G \rightarrow 2^M$ and $\psi: 2^M \rightarrow 2^G$, $\phi$ (A) = def $\{m \in M \mid g Im \, \forall g \in A\}$, $\psi(B)$ = def $\{g \in G \mid g Im \, \forall m \in B\}$, $A \subseteq G, B \subseteq M$. If $A \subseteq G, B \subseteq M$, then (A,B)- formal concept of context K, if $\phi(A) = B$, $\psi(B) = A$.

The correspondence between query and web-service description is based on the concepts' coincidences and implications. Let M – attribute set and G objects set. The rules are defined as the implication $X \Rightarrow Y$, where $X, Y \subseteq M$, $X \cap Y = \emptyset$. Then confidence criteria is defined as conf($X \Rightarrow Y$) = supp($X \cap Y$)/supp(X). The implication means that all objects of context which contain attributes X also contain attribute Y. The attribute Y may be web-service class number or just ID. The sub- and super concepts relations are used in case of approximate matching. Subconcept - superconcept relationship: is expressed as; $A1, A2 \subseteq G, B1, B2 \subseteq M$:

1. $(A1, B1) \leq (A2, B2) \Leftrightarrow (A1 \subseteq A2) \wedge (B2 \subseteq B1)$
2. $(A1, B1)$ – subconcept,
3. $(A2, B2)$ – superconcept.

Using HTN-like parsing we can decompose non-primitive tasks recursively until primitive tasks are reached and present them according to formal grammar rules (Fig. 2).

We have introduced several logical operations in this modified parsing tree, which define different kinds of web-services connections for VE composition.

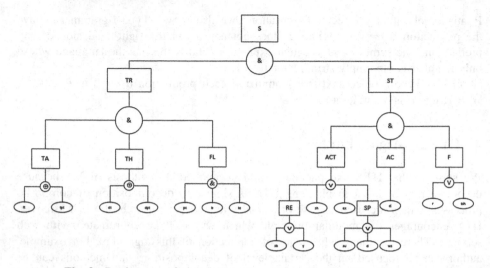

**Fig. 2.** Parsing tree of virtual enterprise on the example of travel agency

The atomic services (terminal symbols) are introduced by lowercase letters:
"lt" is for local taxi atomic service;
"lpt" is for local public transport atomic service;
"dt" is for destination taxi atomic service;
"dpt" is for destination public transport atomic service;
"pc" is for passport control atomic service;
"b" is for boarding atomic service;
"le" is for luggage examination atomic service;
"sh" is for shopping atomic service;
"ex" is for excursions atomic service;
"su" is for surfing atomic service;
"sb" is for sunbathing;
"y" is for "yoga";
"d" is for diving atomic service;
"ws" is for water skis atomic service;
"ci" is for check-in atomic service;
"r" is for restaurant atomic service;
"bih" is for breakfast in the hotel atomic service.
The composite services (nonterminal symbols) are introduced by uppercase letters:
"S" is for tour package composite services;
"TR" is for transportation composite services;
"TA" is for transportation to the airport composite services;
"TH" is for transportation to the hotel composite services;
"FL" is for flight composite services;
"ST" is for stay composite services;
"F" is for food composite services;
"AC" is for accommodation composite services;

"ACT" is for activity composite services;

"RE" is for relaxation;

"SP" sport composite services;

If "&" means "AND", "∨" means "OR", "⊕" means "EXLUSIVE OR", the formal grammar of the parsing tree can be described in the following way:

S → TR & ST

TR → TA & TH & FL

TA → lt ⊕ lpt

TH → dt ⊕ dpt

FL → pc & b & le

ST → ACT & AC & F

F → r ∨ bih

AC → ci

ACT → sh ∨ ex ∨ SP

SP → su ∨ d ∨ ws

RE → sb ∨ y

So as formal grammar describes the operation of concatenation of symbols and is monoid. Describing the parsing tree, we used extra symbols &, ⊕ , ∨ but that doesn't mean that we try to change the algebraic properties of Formal grammar. We use these symbols to simplify the writing Formal grammar rules and parsing tree. These symbols are used in the following meanings:

& – all symbols belong to concatenation.

⊕ – only one symbol belongs concatenation.

∨ – supposes including of one or more symbols of the previous level.

We suggest a HTN-like algorithm of composition of web-services. The algorithm is based on the idea of representation of the structure of a VE as a syntax tree where web-services are represented as nonterminal symbols.

Parsing algorithm is pushdown automaton-based.

The automaton consists of the stack and several groups of recognizers.

1. Terminal symbols appear on the input tape.
2. Terminal symbols are read by the stack automaton and placed in the stack for subsequent analysis and recognition.

The string of terminal symbols begins and ends with the symbol "#".

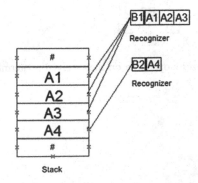

**Fig. 3.** Memory structure of terminal symbols recognizer

3. The stack is connected with recognizers of terminal symbols and recognizers of nonterminal symbols.
4. The recognizers of terminal symbols associate every terminal symbol with one of the finite number of the categories of nonterminal symbols.
5. Every recognizer of terminal symbols has memory in the form of the list of terminal symbols that belong to the certain category. Every recognizer compares a terminal symbol in the stack with every terminal symbol stored in its list. At the same time the recogniser checks correspondence the IOPEs (input, output, postcondition, effect) of the current and next concatenated services to provide outputs, post conditions (results) of the current service satisfies the inputs, preconditions of the next service (Fig. 3)
   B1 → A1&A2&A3
   B2 → A4
6. The defined categories that include existing terminal symbols are placed in the stack.
7. When every terminal symbol is associated with one of the categories, the string of nonterminal symbols is considered to be formed.
   The string of nontermal symbols also begins and ends with the symbol "#".
   The analysis of the string of nonterminal symbols begins.
8. The recognizers of nonterminal symbols operate on the received nonterminal symbols (Fig. 4).
   S → B1&B2
   Every nonterminal symbol has a counter denoting its valency (n) – the number of inferior symbols (e.g. valency of S = 2). When the counter is reset to zero, the string of the nonterminal symbols of the next level begins to form.
   The algorithm ends when the upper-level symbol S is defined.

   1 – number of not defined nonterminal symbols of the next level
   The result of the algorithm: the set of web-services, that entered the algorithm, satisfies the parsing rules and can be used for VE composition (Fig. 5).

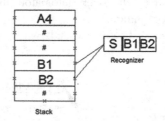

**Fig. 4.** Recognizer's operation on the received nonterminal symbols

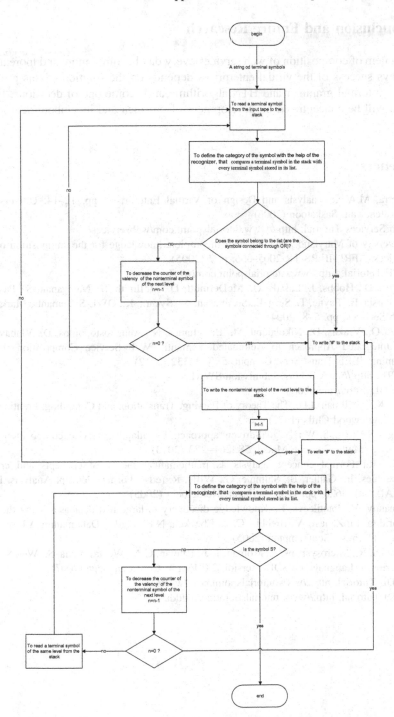

**Fig. 5.** VE Web services composition algorithm

## 5 Conclusion and Future Research

The problem of composition of web services every day becomes more and more actual. Nowadays success of the virtual enterprises depends on the solution of this problem. Use of the formal grammar and HTN algorithm can become one of decisions. Future research will be concentrated on development of our idea and its embodiment in life.

## References

1. Guerra, M.A.P.: Analysis and Design of Virtual Enterprises, pp. 12–14. University of Saskatchewan, Saskatoon (2006)
2. Web Services Tutorial. http://www.tutorialspoint.com/webservices/
3. University of Maryland. Planning with incomplete knowledge for the composition of web services. AFRL-IF-RS-TR-2005–306, p. 7 (2005)
4. WCF Tutorial, http://www.tutorialspoint.com/wcf/
5. Martin, D., Hobbs, J., Lassila, O., McDermott, D., McIlraith, S., Narayanan, S., Paolucci, M., Parsia, B., Payne, T., Sirin, E., Srinivasan, N., Sycara, K.: OWL-S: Semantic Markup for Web Services, pp. 5–8 (2004)
6. Hatzi, O., Vrakas, D., Nikolaidou, M., Bassiliades, N., Anagnostopoulos, D., Vlahavas, I.: An Integrated Approach to Automated Semantic Web Service Composition through Planning. IEEE Trans. Serv. Comput. **5**, 319–332 (2012)
7. SWRL, http://www.w3.org/Submission/SWRL/
8. RuleML, http://ruleml.org/
9. Aho, A.V., Ullman, J.D.: The Theory of Parsing, Translation, and Compiling. Prentice-Hall, Inc., Englewood Cliffs (1972)
10. Songa, S., Lee, S.-W.: A goal-driven approach for adaptive service composition using planning. Math. Comput. Model. **58**, 261–273 (2013)
11. Wille, R.: Formal concept analysis as mathematical theory of concepts and concept hierarchies. In: Ganter, B., Stumme, G., Wille, R. (eds.) Formal Concept Analysis. LNCS (LNAI), vol. 3626, pp. 1–33. Springer, Heidelberg (2005)
12. Romanov, V., Pantileeva, E.: Knowledge discovery in large text databases using the MST algorithm. In: Zanasi, A., Brebbia, C.A., Ebecken, N.F.F. (eds.) Data maning VI, pp. 153–163. WIT Press, Southampton (2005)
13. Chinnici, R., Microsystems, S., Moreau, J.-J., Ryman, C.A., Weerawarana, S.: Web Services Description Language (WSDL) Version 2.0 Part 1: Core Language (2007)
14. WSDL Tutorial, http://www.tutorialspoint.com/wsdl/
15. UDDI Tutorial, http://www.tutorialspoint.com/uddi/

# Formalising Responsibility Modelling for Automatic Analysis

Robbie Simpson(✉) and Tim Storer

University of Glasgow, Glasgow, UK
r.simpson.3@research.gla.ac.uk

**Abstract.** Modelling the structure of social-technical systems as a basis for informing software system design is a difficult compromise. Formal methods struggle to capture the scale and complexity of the heterogeneous organisations that use technical systems. Conversely, informal approaches lack the rigour needed to inform the software design and construction process or enable automated analysis.

We revisit the concept of responsibility modelling, which models social technical systems as a collection of actors who discharge their responsibilities, whilst using and producing resources in the process. Responsibility modelling is formalised as a structured approach for socio-technical system requirements specification and modelling, with well-defined semantics and support for automated structure and validity analysis. The effectiveness of the approach is demonstrated by two case studies of software engineering methodologies.

## 1 Introduction

A range of research efforts have highlighted the importance of understanding the social context that a technical software system is developed for [24]. Baxter and Sommerville [2] argues that a common cause of failure in software development is the focus on the functional requirements for the system at hand, to the exclusion of an understanding of the wider organisation(s) in which the system is to be employed. Besnard and Baxter [3] observes that this focus can limit the ability of users to recover a system when technical components fail. Even when the importance of the wider organisational context is understood, the methods available to development teams are inadequate in the face of the scale of modern systems engineering challenges [10].

As a consequence, a variety of research efforts have been undertaken to develop methods that enable the modelling, analysis and construction of large scale systems comprised of human, organisational and technical components. Such systems are often referred to as *socio-technical* systems [31]. In particular, *responsibilities* have been proposed by a variety of research efforts as a suitable abstraction for capturing the structure of socio-technical systems [4,8,9,11]. Sommerville et al. [29] provided a working definition of a responsibility as:

> "A duty, held by some agent, to achieve, maintain or avoid some given state, subject to conformance with organisational, social and cultural norms."

© Springer International Publishing Switzerland 2015
J. Barjis et al. (Eds.): EOMAS 2015, LNBIP 231, pp. 125–140, 2015.
DOI: 10.1007/978-3-319-24626-0_10

Responsibilities therefore provide a different type of abstraction from other approaches that have been proposed for modelling socio-technical-systems, such as goal [18] or activity [1] oriented approaches. Describing a socio-technical system in terms of responsibilities is concerned with monitoring and managing some part of the state of a socio-technical system, rather than the performance of specific task or activity. Similar to goal-oriented approaches, responsibilities can be discharged (achieved) in a variety of different ways by a variety of different actors (whether human, technical, or organisational).

However, responsibilities are distinct from goals, because of the incorporation of the notion of *duty* or *commitment* by the agent to discharge the responsibility. Goal oriented approaches assume that if an agent has the necessary capabilities to achieve a goal then it will succeed. However, a responsibility oriented approach acknowledges the greater complexities of socio-technical systems that may mean a responsibility is not discharged, even if an actor has the capability to do so. In this situation, it is possible to model fall back mechanisms, such as consequences for the agent, or 'backup' responsibilities held by other agents.

In addition, Sommerville et al. [27] argues that responsibilities are easier to elicit from a problem domain through discussion with stakeholders than other abstractions, such as goals. Stakeholders working within a system may struggle to explain the goals associated with their work without the description sounding somewhat artificial: "My goal is to secure the building at night." Describing the same work in terms of responsibilities is more intuitive: "I am responsible for securing the building at night."

Responsibility modelling has been shown to be effective as a basis for analysing a variety of socio-technical systems engineering activities, including analysing organisational roles [9]; risk analysis [22]; capturing security policies [30]; and requirements engineering [28]. However, much of this work depends on manual intervention and analysis by the engineer. As a consequence, it is difficult to use these methods for the construction of proposed systems. They may also be prove too costly when used for more complex systems involving many responsibilities.

This paper introduces an extension to the current state of the art in responsibility modelling. The novel contribution is a formalisation of the graphical responsibility notation adopted by Lock and Sommerville [21], Sommerville et al. [27–29]. The paper demonstrates how a formalisation of the notation as a language can enhance the automation of analytical techniques and aid in the construction of socio-technical system designs.

Section 2 reviews previous work employing responsibility modelling for analysing socio-technical systems, as well as other approaches, in greater detail. Section 3 presents our formalisation of the responsibility modelling notation used in previous research. The notation is formalised as a declarative language about the responsibilities held in a socio-technical system; the agents that hold those responsibilities; and the resources required or produced as a result of responsibility discharge.

Section 4 presents and analyses two example responsibility models, based on standard models of software development team organisation. The example illustrates how the application of a formal approach to responsibility modelling can automatically elicit system level vulnerabilities without requiring expert analysis.

Section 5 examines the current tool support for formalised responsibility modelling. A prototype responsibility modelling software tool is introduced, as well as several different techniques for automated model analysis.

Finally, Sect. 6 summarises the paper, emphasising difficulties of effectively modelling social-technical systems and highlighting the strengths of formalised responsibility modelling as a semi-formal approach that combines flexibility with sufficient rigour for automation.

## 2    Modelling Socio-Technical Systems

Developing modelling techniques for socio-technical systems requires a difficult trade-off between formal notations that support automated analysis and provide input for construction techniques such as refinement or static verification; and notations that enable validation by end-users and other stakeholders of a proposed system. An additional challenge is provide techniques and notations that are scalable so that a system can be described consistently at several different levels of granularity, while also managing the complexity and nuances that are often encountered when modelling socio-technical systems.

Systems modelling techniques such as SysML [16], the Department of Defense Architecture Framework (DoDAF) [17] and The Open Group Architecture Framework (TOGAF) [14] have been developed to support larger scale systems engineering. SysML is an extension of the Unified Modelling Language (UML) that is intended for capturing larger scale concerns and support wider systems engineering efforts that are not addressed by the UML. A particular example is closer integration of non-functional requirements into design concerns.

Leveson [19], Leveson and Dulac [20] describe an alternative methodology, STAMP, for analysing interactions between heterogeneous systems components. In addition to providing a modelling notation based on systems dynamics, the technique also incorporates a methodology for identifying potential instabilities in system behaviour that may eventually lead to failure. Leveson illustrates the technique by re-constructing the causes of the failure of the MilStar Satellite launch in 1999 [19]. A disadvantage is the need for expert application of the method to identify weaknesses.

Deontic logic provides a formal basis for reasoning about *norms* in socio-technical systems, employing operators such as *commitments* [23]. Several authors have proposed methods for capturing different aspects of socio-technical system specification and design based on deontic logic. For example: Garion and van der Torre [13] proposed a design-by-contract style language for multi-agent systems based on deontic logic; Padmanabhan et al. [25] proposed the integration of deontic logic concepts into business process modelling methods and

Cholvy et al. [6] proposed the use of deontic logic as means of formalising concepts of responsibility. However, we are unaware of work that bridges the gap between formal expressions of system specifications in a deontic logic and notations that can be comprehended by non-expert domain stakeholders.

Goal oriented approaches [18], such as KAOS [7] and i* [32] employ a graphical notation to capture the goal seeking behaviours of agents in a system. These techniques provide a means for decomposing high level system goals into sub-goal structures to be pursued by actors within a socio-technical system.

Responsibility modelling has been proposed as a means of understanding a variety of different concerns in socio-technical systems design. Blyth et al. [4] first proposed the modelling and analysis of responsibilities in the Ordit methodology. The aim was to identify and understand organisational requirements for socio-technical systems. Later, Harper and Newman [15] proposed employing a structured language approach to defining responsibilities. Although the only outlined the approach, it shows how responsibility modelling can be useful in identifying conflicts between different actor-roles in an organisation.

Strens and Dobson [30] first proposed the use of responsibility modelling as a means of better understanding the appropriate configuration of security policies in an organisation. Later, Feltus and Petit [12] proposed a formalisation of responsibility in an organisational context as a means of modelling and reasoning about organisational policies. Feltus et al. [11] extended this work by developing a methodology for modelling organisational policies using responsibilities as a formalism.

In early work in the DIRC[1] project, Dobson and Sommerville [9] showed the use of responsibility models as a means of capturing the different roles undertaken in a socio-technical system. Sommerville et al. [29] applied the responsibility modelling techniques developed in the DIRC project to contingency planning for civil emergencies. The analysis was used to capture the responsibility vulnerabilities that caused some of the disruption during the response to a major civil incident. The paper demonstrated that responsibility modelling could be applied to an inter-organisational view of a socio-technical system.

Lock and Sommerville [21] also applied responsibility modelling to understanding the evolution of larger scale systems and systems. The work showed that responsibility modelling could be applied to the modelling, analysis and understanding of risks of collections of systems that are loosely coordinated for some larger purpose, but remain under autonomous control of independent organisations.

As noted by Baxter and Sommerville [2], less consideration has been given to the methods and notations which support the engineering of socio-technical systems by providing information of use to a systems engineer.

Sommerville et al. [28] began to explore this challenge by using responsibility models as a means of deriving early stage information systems requirements. The technique derived requirements based on the likely information needs of an actor discharging a responsibility. These requirements can then be used to

---

[1] Dependability Interdisciplinary Research Collaboration.

support the configuration of information systems based on enterprise resource planning frameworks, rather than the complete development of new systems. This approach was illustrated by developing information requirements for an inter-organisational emergency management system.

In general, previous work on responsibility modelling did not deliver the unified approach that was hoped for. The graphical representation and underlying primitives varied between different works; some papers used a large set of entities, while others paired this down to a common core. Tool support was limited, and as a result analysis often had to be performed by hand.

# 3   Formalism

## 3.1   Notation

Responsibility modelling uses a simple notation, consisting of responsibilities, actors and resources as well as the relationships between them. These elements can either be represented graphically or textually, and tools to convert from one to the other are under development. Figure 1 provides a simple example of the graphical notation.

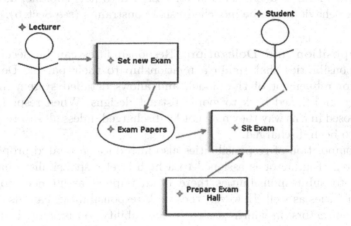

**Fig. 1.** Sample responsibility model for a university exam. The exam papers are produced and consumed; the Sit Exam responsibility is dependent on both the actor Student and the responsibility Prepare Exam Hall.

**Responsibilities.** Responsibilities are duties that must be discharged by the system. They are the core of responsibility modelling, with all other artefacts either discharging these responsibilities; or resources that are produced by or provide support that enables the responsibility to be discharged. Responsibilities can be specified at any level of detail from high level abstractions to specific implementation approaches.

**Actors.** Actors are entities within the system that act to discharge responsibilities. Actors can either be human, technical or organisational. Human actors are roles within the system (rather than individuals) and technical actors are automated processes such as software daemons or machinery. The different types of actors are treated homogeneously in the notation: all actor types can be assigned to responsibilities, which indicates they have a responsibility to discharge them.

**Resources.** Resources represent objects that are required in order for a responsibility to be discharged, such as documents required to complete a managerial task or physical equipment required to complete a practical task. Responsibilities cannot be discharged unless the appropriate resources are available, and resources can either be produced by other responsibilities or can be initialised as already existing.

## 3.2  Properties and Relations

**Assignment.** Actors are assigned to responsibilities, indicating that the actor holds a duty to discharge that particular responsibility. In the standard case the responsibility can be successfully discharged (assuming all other requirements are met) as long as at least one actor assigned to it is capable, although more complex behaviour can be modelled using constraints (see Sect. 5).

**Decomposition and Delegation.** Responsibilities can be decomposed into sub-responsibilities that retain a relationship to their parent. Decomposition allows for refinement of the model, and allows detailed system models to be produced and linked back to more abstract designs. When responsibilities are decomposed in this way they may not be discharged unless all sub-responsibilities have also been discharged.

Decomposition of responsibilities also introduces a related property, that of delegation. If an actor is assigned to a high-level responsibility that is decomposed into sub-responsibilities there is an implied assignment to those sub-responsibilities as well. However, these sub-responsibilities can also be assigned to different actors, in which case the responsibility to discharge is delegated.

**Supervision.** When responsibilities are delegated the original actor no longer plays an active role in discharging those responsibilities. However, they are still responsible for the high-level responsibility, which cannot be discharged without also discharging the delegated responsibilities. This creates an implicit relationship of supervision between the actor assigned to the high level goal and the actors that responsibilities have been delegated to. This enables responsibility modelling to generate a model of the organisation hierarchy within the model, despite this not being explicitly specified. In particular, this approach can highlight when the in-practice hierarchy implied in the system design is different from the formal managerial structure.

**Scope.** Generally in responsibility modelling the scope of the system is implicit, relying on those interpreting the model to understand how the system sits in the wider context. However this approach is subjective, and can easily lead to ambiguity, especially when refining from a high level model down to an implementation design. Therefore objects on the edge of the system scope can be explicitly indicated. These objects should not be further refined, and can be considered to operate as black boxes. They are particularly useful when indicating the boundary between the system currently modelled and another, interacting social-technical system.

### 3.3 Applications

Responsibility modelling can be applied at two main levels - requirements analysis and system analysis. When used at the requirements level, responsibility modelling can produce sets of responsibilities, resources and relevant actors based on business requirements, regulation and legal requirements and technical proposals. At the requirements level the model may consist of unrelated fragments that are not directly linked - for example, there may be a legal requirement for a pilot to sign-off on a cargo manifest, and a business requirement for cargo containers to be scanned as they loaded onto the aircraft. These two requirements are completely separate, but are both in the scope of an aircraft cargo management system.

At the system analysis level the responsibility model should aim for completeness. By this stage of development all elements of the system should have been decided upon, and hence any ambiguity or omissions in the Responsibility model represent ambiguities and omissions in the system structure itself. Separated or unattached sections indicate a lack of integration within the system, or that certain elements are not related to the core tasks of the system.

## 4   Modelling

This section illustrates the use of responsibility models in formally analysing the structure of socio-technical systems. For motivating examples, two software development team models are considered: the surgical team described by Brooks [5] and the Scrum agile team structure described by Schwaber and Beedle [26].

### 4.1   The Surgical Team

The surgical team is a model for small-scale software development. Figure 2 illustrates the surgical team using the responsibility modelling notation described above.

The model proposes a team structure consisting of ten roles, two of which are core developers (the surgeon/chief developer and the co-pilot/junior development) with the rest comprising a support staff. The surgical team is a not a software lifecycle model and we do not attempt to model it as such; its focus

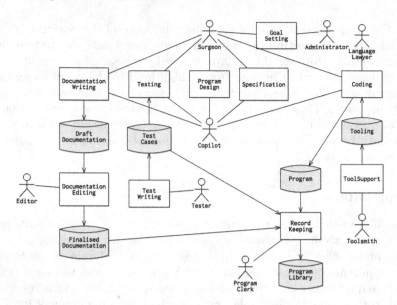

**Fig. 2.** Responsibility Model of the surgical team proposed by Brooks [5]

is on allocating members of a development team to responsibilities to maximise productivity and minimise organisational overhead.

Inspecting our model reveals a number of issues with the surgical team concept. The relationship between surgeon and the copilot is not well defined, as they share responsibility for almost all functions they perform, excepting administration. The surgical team proposal does not define the process by which the surgeon and copilot divide and allocate tasks, which suggests that this is an additional process that should be implemented when the surgical team is used.

The role of the language lawyer is also shown to be ambiguous. The only concrete responsibility they are involved in is coding, by optimising routines and improving the quality of code where possible. While several other roles (such as acting as an advisor) are suggested they are not formally included.

The record keeping activities of the Program Clerk are shown to be peripheral to the overall team activities. They are not required to perform the main responsibilities of the team and their absence does not prevent any of the core responsibilities from being discharged. We have shown the Program Clerk's responsibility to depend on the production of test cases, documentation and program code, since we *assume* this responsibility includes curation of these artefacts. However, this is not made explicit in the description by Brooks [5].

Responsibility modelling has highlighted the non-explicit and non-core elements of the system. An absence of assignments or linked responsibilities where expected highlights the parts of the system that are implicit, revealing sections that may not operate in practice as the designers of the system intended. It is also possible to identify non-core actors that are not directly involved with the key responsibilities, and likewise it is clear which actors are involved with the core system functions. Additionally, we can identify how the team will function

if lacking certain staff by removing those actors and attempting to meet all the
responsibilities. Undischarged responsibilities will be identified, as well as actors
that will have increased workload.

## 4.2   Scrum

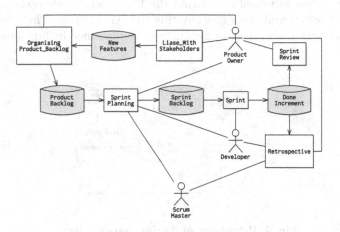

**Fig. 3.** Responsibility model of Scrum.

The Scrum process is an agile development framework for software development. Scrum is an iterative approach, where the product is developed in a series
of sprints, and requirements are expressed by a product owner. Additionally,
the Scrum team lacks a hierarchy and does not contain managers or assigned
roles and groupings. Instead all team members take part in all Scrum activities,
which are overseen by a Scrum Master who acts as a facilitator. Our model of
the responsibilities in the Scrum process are illustrated in Fig. 3.

The figure shows that work is organised around responsibilities for planning,
undertaking and reviewing a sprint. In contrast to the surgical team, the iterative
structure of the responsibilities (and thus the overall process) is evident in the
model.

In addition, the model suggests that Scrum is a more collaborative process
than the Surgical team. Although there are distinct roles for Product Owner
and Scrum Master, these do not hold responsibilities that are analogous to the
Administrator or Surgeon in the Surgical team. Rather, all roles collaborate in
many different responsibilities in different ways. For example, Developers are
responsible in collaboration with the Scrum Master and Product Owner for
Scrum Planning, in which the set of objectives for the next Sprint is decided.
Similarly, all actors collaborate in the conduct of the Retrospective and Sprint
Review, but with distinct sub-responsibilities.

Note that this example demonstrates that actors are roles, not individuals;
in Scrum, it is common for the Scrum Master to also be a Developer. As a result,
extra care (ideally aided by tool support) is necessary when considering the risk

of overload, as one actual individual or organisation may be acting in a number of different roles.

A responsibility can be decomposed in order to understand how agents collaborate to discharge the overall responsibility. Figure 4 illustrates how the Sprint responsibility is decomposed to show the assignment of sub responsibilities. The Developers retain responsibility for undertaking development of new features or remedy of features, as prioritised during the Daily Scrum. However, the Scrum Master shares responsibility for coordinating the Daily Scrum. The exact division of responsibilities within the Daily Scrum may be identified by further refinement if desired.

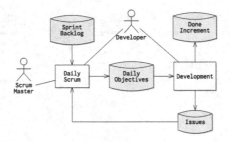

**Fig. 4.** Refinement of 'Sprint' responsibility.

The figure also illustrates the modelling of heterogeneous human, organisational and technical components consistently as agents with responsibilities. The development team is an organisational agent consisting of several (unidentified) developers. Responsibility for integration testing is delegated to a Continuous Integration Environment, a software application that is configured to monitor for changes to the target system's code base. Problems with the new feature are reported as Issues that must be resolved before integration is permitted.

The decomposed model is consistent with the overall model presented in Fig. 3. Resources that are inputs and outputs to the Sprint responsibility (Sprint Backlog and Done Increment respectively) are similarly represented as boundary elements for the decomposed diagram. Similarly, the agents that hold the overall responsibility for the Sprint (Developer and Scrum Master) are present in the decomposed diagram. The Continuous Integration environment does not hold responsibility for conducting the overall Sprint, so only appears in the sub-diagram in association with its specific responsibilities. Depending on the modeller's preference and the target audience, these refinements can either be presented separately, or used to expand the core responsibility model.

### 4.3  Observations

Many process and structure models (in all types of domains) contain unformalised behaviour that is nonetheless implied or referred to by the formal element of the model. This may be an explicit decision to keep parts of the system out of scope (such as the intra-team behaviour in Scrum) or may reflect uncertainty over the use of that part in practice (such as the language lawyer of the surgical team). In some models these unformalised elements are clearly signposted; however, many models do not distinguish them clearly. This opens up the possibility of inconsistent application of the model and important elements left undone due to their non-formalised nature. Responsibility modelling can clearly identify non-formalised or ambiguous formalised elements, allowing clear discussion of potential issues. Equally, where these variations are not pertinent to a discussion responsibility modelling provides for convenient abstraction.

Responsibility modelling is especially effective when comparing deployments or implementations against the theoretical standard. The complexity and variation of social-technical systems means that many real systems vary significantly from their conceptual model, but these differences are not regularly formalised. As a result, analysis is often performed on abstract models of the system that do not represent real-world usage, leading to analysis that does not capture actual behaviour and provides a false sense of security.

Responsibility modelling can alleviate this by allowing both high-level and implementation-level models of the system to be produced using the same scheme. The well-defined semantics of responsibility modelling will allow sections of the implementation-level model to be mapped automatically to the relevant responsibilities in the high-level model, so that the completeness of implementations can be checked directly against the original specification.

## 5 Prototype Tool Support

A prototype tool for responsibility modelling has been implemented using Eclipse Sirius, as displayed in Fig. 5. The tool currently allows the graphical creation and editing of responsibility models, with all types of objects and relations supported. Models are created by dragging components from the toolbar, and once placed in the model they can be rearranged and modified at will. Relations can be added by selecting the appropriate type and selecting the two objects to be related. Model elements can also be enabled and disabled, allowing analysts to examine the effects of individual failures on the wider system. The underlying representation of models is built using the Eclipse Modelling Framework, which provides an additional cross-platform XML representation.

**Automatic Analysis.** The existence of a formal structure for responsibility modelling enables wide ranging analysis to be performed automatically on models produced with this toolkit, with several analysis techniques implemented and more planned.

Basic analysis can be performed by triggering a model validation, which performs around half a dozen local checks. Entities are checked for their completeness, locating unproduced resources and actors without assignments. In many cases incomplete elements will indicate that further modelling detail is required, but they may also indicate fundamental shortcomings in the system being modelled.

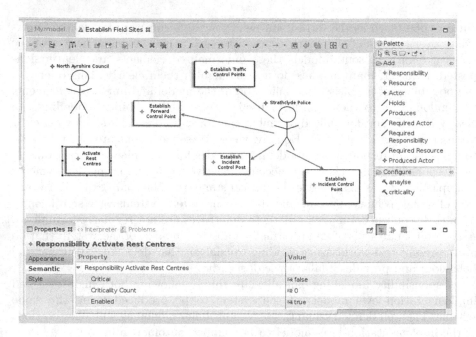

**Fig. 5.** Eclipse-based responsibility modelling tool

Thresholds can be set to determine potentially overloaded actors that hold an excessive amount of responsibilities, potentially leading to degraded operation. Actors holding large amounts of responsibilities might become overloaded and perform poorly if attempting to simultaneously manage different tasks. Likewise, resources that are consumed by multiple responsibilities highlight potential issues over resource allocation or exhaustion (Fig. 6).

Additionally, for each actor a set of other actors that it relies on is generated - as actors may hold certain responsibilities, but rely on other actors to ensure that they are discharged.

Two specialist forms of analysis are also possible, which operate across the entire model. Criticality analysis detects the most critical entities - the resources, responsibilities and actors that contribute the most to the system and would cause the highest number of responsibility failures if they failed to operate.

The second form of model-wide analysis is responsibility discharge detection, which is augmented with a powerful constraint language. By default, responsibilities are considered to be successfully discharged if all required elements (the entities to which they are linked by relations) are active. However, sometimes the discharge criteria for a responsibility are more complicated. A responsibility may for example be dischargeable by either one of two separate actors, or may rely on the availability of a subset of different resources. In these cases, the more complex behaviour can be expressed using constraints.

When discharge analysis is performed, initial checks are made on entities without complex constraints to determine if they can be discharged. After this,

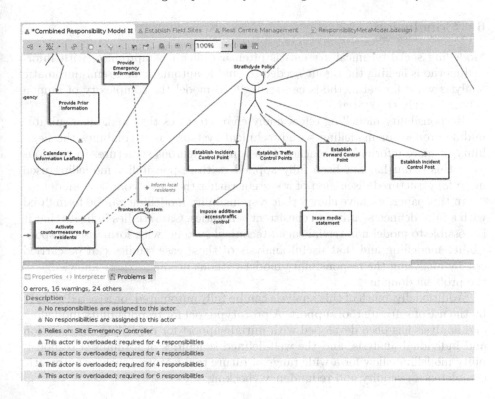

**Fig. 6.** Analysis in progress, showing reliance, overload and selectively disabled responsibilities

the constraints defined on complex entities are evaluated by a constraint parser, and responsibilities that fail to discharge are indicated. If combined with the selective disabling of model elements this technique allows for an effective analysis of system failure modes. This allows for the examination of fault tolerance and redundancy within the system, and further automation allows the most serious points of failure to be determined by checking the number of undischarged responsibilities caused when each object in the system is disabled.

In responsibility modelling actors are intended to be roles or positions, rather than actual individuals. However, in any actual implemented systems these roles will clearly be filled by specific actors or organisations. This could lead to vulnerabilities not captured by conventional modelling if an actual individual or organisation takes on the responsibilities of multiple actors. This could lead to overloading and hence a performance risk, or the same individual may hold actor roles that conflict or require them to perform multiple tasks simultaneously. While not currently implemented, we plan to develop tooling that can enable this to be taken into consideration by providing a model view that allows real-world entities to be mapped to actors, enabling automatic detection of overloaded entities and a visualisation of potential conflicts of interest.

# 6    Conclusion

Modelling social-technical systems is often a difficult compromise, with informal methods lacking the rigour needed to enable automatic and semi-automatic analysis while formal methods can struggle to model the complexity of human activity within the system.

Responsibility modelling offers many characteristics that make it a suitable middle ground for modelling social-technical systems, as it combines the flexibility of more informal approaches with a more rigorous structure. In previous work this rigour has not been fully applied, with responsibility modelling used more for structured discussion of a system rather than as a complete model.

In this paper, we have shown that responsibility modelling can be formalised with a fully-defined syntax and consistent semantics. Case studies indicate that it is possible to model non-trivial social-technical systems with formalised responsibility modelling and that useful analysis of these case studies can be carried out by analysing the responsibility model without needing expert knowledge of the problem domain.

Additionally, much of this analysis can be fully automated, or assisted greatly by the use of software tool support. A prototype tool for responsibility modelling and analysis has been developed with initial support for modelling construction and individual analysis, and the well-defined semantics of formalised responsibility modelling allow for a wide range of future tool features, such as automatic completeness, validity and redundancy checking.

# References

1. Basnyat, S., Chozos, N., Johnson, C.: Incident and accident investigation techniques to inform model-based design of safety-critical interactive systems. In: Gilroy, S.W., Harrison, M.D. (eds.) DSV-IS 2005. LNCS, vol. 3941, pp. 51–66. Springer, Heidelberg (2006)
2. Baxter, G., Sommerville, I.: Learning lessons from the failures of socio-technical systems design, April 2008. (for submission to Interacting with Computers)
3. Besnard, D., Baxter, G.: Human compensations for undependable systems. Tech. Rep. CS-TR-819, School of Computing Science, Newcastle University, Newcastle upon Tyne, UK, November 2003
4. Blyth, A.J., Chudge, J., Dobson, J.E., Strens, M.R.: ORDIT: A new methodology to assist in the process of eliciting and modelling organisational requirements. In: Kaplan, S. (ed.) Proceedings on the Conference on Organisational Computing Systems, pp. 216–227. ACM Press, Milpitas 1993)
5. Brooks Jr., F.P.: The Mythical Man-Month, 9th edn. Addison Wesley, Reading (1995)
6. Cholvy, L., Cuppens, F., Saurel, C.: Towars a logical formalization of responsibility. In: Proceedings of the 6th International Conference on Artificial intelligence and Law, pp. 233–242. ACM Press, Melbourne, June–July 1997
7. Darimont, R., Delor, E., Massonet, P., van Lamsweerde, A.: GRAIL/KAOS: an environment for goal-driven requirements engineering. In: Adrion, W.R. (ed.) ICSE 1997: Pulling Together, Proceedings of the 19th International Conference on Software Engineering, pp. 612–613. ACM Press, Boston, Massachusetts, May 1997

8.  Dewsbury, G., Dobson, J. (eds.): Responsibility and Dependable Systems. Springer-Verlag London Ltd, London (2007)
9.  Dobson, J.E., Sommerville, I.: Roles are responsibility relationships really, dIRC Project Technical Report, October 2005
10. Feiler, P., Gabriel, R.P., Goodenough, J., Linger, R., Longstaff, T., Kazman, R., Klein, M., Northrop, L., Schmidt, D., Sullivan, K., Wallnau, K.: Ultra-Large-Scale Systems, The Software Challenge of the Future. Software Engineering Institute, Carnegie Mellon University, 4500 Fifth Avenue, Pittsburgh, June 2006
11. Feltus, C., Incoul, C., Aubert, J., Gateau, B., Adelsbach, A., Camy, M.: Methodology to align business and IT policies: use case from an IT policy. In: 2009 International Conference on Availability, Reliability and Security. IEEE Computer Society, Fukuoka, March 2009
12. Feltus, C., Petit, M.: Building a responsibility model including accountability, capability and committment. In: 2009 International Conference on Availability, Reliability and Security. IEEE Computer Society, Fukuoka, March 2009
13. Garion, C., van der Torre, L.W.N.: Design by contract deontic design language for multiagent systems. In: Boissier, O., Padget, J., Dignum, V., Lindemann, G., Matson, E., Ossowski, S., Sichman, J.S., Vázquez-Salceda, J. (eds.) ANIREM 2005 and OOOP 2005. LNCS (LNAI), vol. 3913, pp. 170–182. Springer, Heidelberg (2006)
14. Gerber, A., Kotzé, P., van der Merwe, A.: Towards the formalisation of the togaf content metamodel using ontologies. In: Filipe, J., Cordeiro, J. (eds.) ICEIS 2010 - Proceedings of the 12th International Conference on Enterprise Information Systems, vol. 2, pp. 54–64. SciTechPress, Funchal (2010)
15. Harper, R., Newman, W.: Designing for user acceptance using analysis techniques based on responsibility modelling. In: Tauber, M.J. (ed.) CHI 1996 Conference Companion on Human Factors in Computing Systems, pp. 217–218. ACM Press, Vancouver (1996)
16. Hause, M.: The sysml modelling language. In: 5th European Systems Engineering Conference, INCOSE, Edinburgh, Scotland, UK, September 2006
17. Kobryn, C., Sibbald, C.: Modeling dodaf compliant architectures the telelogic approach for complying with the dod architectural framework. White paper, Telelogic, October 2004
18. Lapouchnian, A.: Goal-oriented requirements engineering: an overview of the current research. Depth report, Department of Computer Science, University of Toronto, June 2005
19. Leveson, N.G.: A systems-theoretic approach to safety in software-intensive systems. IEEE Trans. Dependable Secure Comput. 1(1), 66–86 (2004)
20. Leveson, N.G., Dulac, N.: Safety and risk-driven design in complex systems-of-systems. In: Proceedings of the 1st NASA/AIAA Space Exploration Conference: Continuing the Voyage of Discovery. American Institute of Aeronautics and Astronautics, Orlando, Florida, USA, January-February 2005
21. Lock, R., Sommerville, I.: Modelling and analysis of socio-technical system of systems. In: 10th International Conference on Engineering Complex Computer Systems, pp. 224–232. IEEE Computer Society, Oxford, March 2010
22. Lock, R., Storer, T., Sommerville, I.: Responsibility modelling for risk analysis. In: Proceedings of European SREL (ESREL) 2009, Prague, Czech Republic, pp. 1103–1109, September 2009
23. Meyer, J.J.C., Weiringa, R.J.: Applications of deontic logic in computer science: A concise overview. In: Meyer, J.J.C., Weiringa, R.J. (eds.) Deontic Logic in Computer Science: Normative System Specification, pp. 17–45. Wiley, Chicester (1993)

24. Mumford, E.: The story of socio-technical design: reflections on its successe, failures and potential. Inf. Syst. J. **16**, 317–342 (2006)
25. Padmanabhan, V., Governatori, G., Sadiq, S., Colomb, R., Rotolo, A.: Process modelling: the deontic way. In: Stumptner, M., Hartmann, S., Kiyoki, Y. (eds.) Proceedings of the 3rd Asia-Pacific Conference on Conceptual Modelling. Conferences in Research and Practice in Information Technology Series, vol. 53, pp. 75–84. ACM Press, Hobart (2006)
26. Schwaber, K., Beedle, M.: Agile Software Development with SCRUM. Prentice Hall, Englewood Cliffs (2001)
27. Sommerville, I., Lock, R., Storer, T.: Information requirements for enterprise systems. In: Calinescu, R., Garlan, D. (eds.) Monterey Workshop 2012. LNCS, vol. 7539, pp. 266–282. Springer, Heidelberg (2012)
28. Sommerville, I., Lock, R., Storer, T., Dobson, J.: Deriving information requirements from responsibility models. In: van Eck, P., Gordijn, J., Wieringa, R. (eds.) CAiSE 2009. LNCS, vol. 5565, pp. 515–529. Springer, Heidelberg (2009)
29. Sommerville, I., Storer, T., Lock, R.: Responsibility modelling for civil emergency planning. Risk Manag. **11**(3–4), 179–207 (2009b)
30. Strens, R., Dobson, J.: How responsibility modelling leads to security requirements. In: NSPW 1992–1993: Proceedings on the 1992–1993 Workshop on New Security Paradigms. pp. 143–149. ACM Press, New York (1993)
31. Trist, E.: The evolution of socio-technical systems. a conceptual framework and an action research program. Occasional paper 2, Ontario Quality of Working Life Centre, June 1981
32. Yu, E.S.: Towards modelling and reasoning support for early-phase requirements engineering. In: 3rd IEEE International Symposium on Requirements Engineering (RE 1997), pp. 226–235. IEEE Computer Society (1997)

# Multidimensional Modelling from Open Data for Precision Agriculture

Jan Tyrychtr[1]([⊠]), Jiří Brožek[2], and Václav Vostrovský[2]

[1] Department of Information Technologies,
Faculty of Economicsand Management, Czech University of Life Sciences
Prague, Kamýcká 129, 165 21 Prague 6 Suchdol, Czech Republic
tyrychtr@pef.czu.cz
[2] Department of Information Engineering,
Faculty of Economics and Management, Czech University of Life Sciences
Prague, Kamýcká 129, 165 21 Prague 6 Suchdol, Czech Republic

**Abstract.** The multidimensional data models are most often used for decision support in Business Intelligence field. This paper presents innovative approach for support of knowledge analysis in precision agriculture, where such analytical approach offers great potential for the future. Corner stone of our approach is the creation of knowledge rules based on open data and information available from inside a particular agricultural company. In the next step such explicit knowledge is transformed into multidimensional database and an analytical model for decision support of the farm's managers is designed. Our approach is demonstrated on example concerning knowledge analysis of one of the agricultural problems – infestation of farm plants by aphids.

**Keywords:** Multidimensional modelling · Knowledge rules · Open data · Multidimensional database · Precision agriculture

## 1 Introduction

One of the possible approaches to simplification of decision processes in companies is the support of analytical tasks using *Business Intelligence* means [1–3]. Business Intelligence (BI) is a set of methods, concepts and technologies for manager decision support using multidimensional views of data. The purpose of BI is to transform the working data of information systems into analytical form and provide important information about key indicators of a company in the form of contingency tables, graphs and reports. This paper presents innovative approach based on usage of knowledge engineering and open data. *Knowledge engineering* [4, 5] concerns methods for gathering, formalization, coding and testing of knowledge gained from human sources or inductively gained from other information sources (databases, scientific and technical text, etc.). The combination of explicit knowledge from inside the company, data from company information systems and e-government open data offers a great potential in the field of precision analytical systems design.

© Springer International Publishing Switzerland 2015
J. Barjis et al. (Eds.): EOMAS 2015, LNBIP 231, pp. 141–152, 2015.
DOI: 10.1007/978-3-319-24626-0_11

## 1.1    Open Data of Agricultural E-Government

The issue of the open data [2–4] has recently been subject of intense research and discussions. This topic is relevant especially in relationship with the public sector, in which it is implemented following the principles of:

- publishing: "What is not secret can be published",
- openness: make available as much information about your own activities, decisions, rules, and financial flows as possible,
- availability: publish the information in available and understandable form,
- client-side control: transfer the relevance control of open data from publisher to recipient,
- free access: keep the open data available free of charge,
- open standards: comply with open standards and data quality standards.

An Obvious need of value-added information dedicated to decision making in small and medium agricultural companies was identified during the previous research [2]. A lack of this information can be easily eliminated by open data acquired through the open agricultural e-government. It is in the interest of the Ministry of Agriculture to make the data available to all parties with as low legal and licensing restrictions as possible and also in the highest possible technical quality. The prosperity of the economic subjects and the whole sector can be enhanced by activities that will bring new values (i.e. data with added value) that the agricultural companies will be willing to pay for.

In the Czech Republic, there is a good quality of e-government in the agriculture facilitated by the Czech Ministry of Agriculture [2]. The core component of the agricultural e-government in the Czech Republic is eAGRI portal maintained by the Ministry of Agriculture.

## 1.2    Theoretical Principles of Multidimensional Databases

Currently, the knowledge base of explicit knowledge is often implemented as relational databases [2–5]. This paper presents an innovative approach to storing the explicit knowledge using multidimensional databases.

Multidimensional databases are implemented for this reason. *Multidimensional databases* are suitable for storage of large amount of (multidimensional) data that are mostly analysed and summarized for the purpose of decision-making. The term *multidimensional data* represents data of aggregated indicators that were created with various groups of relational data aimed for online analytical processing (OLAP). OLAP is an approach to decision support that serves for data warehouse, data mart retrieval [6]. The solely way of data organization in multidimensional database is implemented as data cube.

*Data cube* is a data structure for storage and analysis of huge amount of multidimensional data [7]. In general, it is interpreted as a basic logical structure that describes multidimensional databases in the same manner as a relation describes relational databases. Data cube represents an abstract structure that, in contrary with classical relational structure, has not the unique definition. There are plenty of formal definitions of data cube operators, a compact overview is e.g. in [8]. At large, the data cube consists of dimensions and measures. *Dimension* is a hierarchically organized set of dimensional values that provide category information characterizing certain aspects of data [9]. *Measures* (observed indicators) of cube are mainly quantitative figures that could be analysed. However, some interesting approaches using textual measures are starting to emerge at the present time [10].

Several technologies can be used for physical storage of multidimensional data (and the implementation of OLAP applications). The two main ways to store data include so-called *multidimensional OLAP* (MOLAP) and *relational OLAP* (ROLAP) [11]. MOLAP physically stores the data in an array like structures that are similar to data cube. In the ROLAP approach, data is stored in a relational database using a special scheme instead of the traditional relational schema. There are also other approaches, so-called *hybrid OLAP* (HOLAP) combining the properties of ROLAP and MOLAP [12] and so-called *desktop OLAP* (DOLAP). DOLAP is capable to connect to a central data store and download the required subset of the cube to a local computer [13].

For the design of multidimensional databases we use the means of the multidimensional modelling. *Multidimensional modelling* nowadays is mostly based on the relational model, or on the multidimensional data cube. *Multidimensional models* categorize the data either as facts with associated numerical measure, or as dimensions that characterize the facts and are mostly in text form. Facts are objects that represent the subject of the required analysis that has to be analysed for better understanding of its behavior [14].

The multidimensional data model based on the relational model distinguishes two basic types of sessions that are called dimension tables and tables of the facts. They can create a star structure (*star schema*) [15–19], various forms of snowflakes (snowflake schema) [16,17,19] and constellations (constellation schema) [20]. The issue of choosing an appropriate structure is solved in the paper Levene et al., [21].

Business Intelligence tools provide new and aggregated views of the current data and also views of the key indicators calculated from such data. They also allow to conduct mathematical and statistical analysis of the data helping the decision making processes of the farm management. Effects and benefits of using BI have been discussed in [30–32]. In this paper we present our innovative approach for decision support in agriculture using BI means. Unlike other expert systems for decision support our approach allows to analyze the knowledge by various dimensions (time, agents, cultivar, etc.).

## 2   Methods

For the design of our innovative solution to capture the knowledge of agricultural activities through multidimensional databases, we use the databases of the Farmer's Portal and databases ÚKZÚZ (Central Institute for Supervising and Testing in Agriculture) run by the Czech Ministry of Agriculture. These databases are basically implemented using standard relational tables containing cultivar registry (open data), crop protective agents registry (open data), aphid flight activity and infestation risks data (open data), sums of effective temperatures (open data), amount of aphid infestation, costs of protective agents and the total effectivity of the agent (explicit internal knowledge) (see example Table 1).

**Table 1.** Relational table containing a set of registered cultivars and applied agents

| Cultivar name | Crop | Agent | Area of application | 1 ha dosage (volume of agent /volume of water) |
|---|---|---|---|---|
| Finka | Potato | Actara 25 WG | 8103/1 | 0,08 kg/200-500 |
| A 2 | Apple | Calypso 480 SC | 8202 | 1,5-2 ml 2-6 |
| 4799 | Hop | Warrant 700 WG | 9301/1 | 0,008 % 2000 |
| Alice | Potato | Agri Pirimicarb 50 WG | 8103/2 | 0,5 kg/ha 300-400 |
| Baltika | Potato | Biscaya 240 OD | 8103/3 | 0,3 l/ha 300-600 |

This paper is based on authors' previous research and is a follow-up to their previously published work [30]. The contribution of this paper is the combination of knowledge coming not only from the company internal data but also from external data concerning farming activities (open data). The conceptual schema is designed as a Multidimensional Entity Relation model (MER model) [21] with the star scheme [18]. The prototype of the multidimensional knowledge is created using the ROLAP technology and PowerPivot software. The reason for this choice is the flexibility of the solution in creating of ad-hoc queries and the ability to work with relational databases instead of creating a data warehouse. For these purposes the design method by [22] is used. The basic assumption of the designed prototype is that the requirements analysis represents only and just demand for analytical application of the knowledge-based rules in agriculture.

Knowledge retrieval in the farm is a very complex and time consuming development stage of the development of an usable knowledge system. If the agricultural business entity stores its explicit knowledge in existing database applications, such knowledge can be effectively used for support of managerial decisions of this business entity. These databases can be processed using specialized tools to create the knowledge base (in the form of rules) for applied knowledge system. Creating a knowledge base, however, is a nontrivial problem, because when storing explicit knowledge in database it reverses transformation of knowledge to data. Such an approach to storing the knowledge tends to be incomplete, inconsistent and almost invalid.

Suppose for example the following explicit knowledge rule of an agricultural company:

IF *aphid flight activity (quantity 3000)* AND *crop (apple)* AND *cultivar (A 2)*
    AND *effective temperature sum (3.4)* AND *quarter (Q3)* THEN *aphid infestation (35%)*                                        (1)

The above knowledge rule can then be interpreted as follows: If the farm grows apple trees (cultivar A 2) and in the third quarter of the year the flight activity of aphids is 3000 specimens, then the amount of infestation of apple trees by aphids reaches

35 %. Such explicit knowledge is without any doubt invaluable for farmers. However if such knowledge is combined with knowledge gained from available open data, it may lead to more effective decision making of farmers. For example the following rule (2) was defined using open data and information from ÚKZÚZ portal.

IF *aphid flight activity (quantity 3000)* AND *crop (apple)* AND *cultivar (A 2)*
AND *sums of effective temperatures (3.4)* AND *quarter (Q3)* THEN *agent*
*(Calypso 480 SC)* AND *dose (1.5-2 ml 2-6)*    (2)

The above mentioned knowledge rule can then be interpreted as follows: If the infested crop is apple tree (cultivar A 2), it is the third quarter of the year and the flight activity of aphids is 3000 specimen, then the recommended agent is Calypso 480 SC with dosage of 1.5-2.0 ml per 2-6 liters of water.

Such rule is useful for selecting the right agents and its dosage. However, a rule formulated like this and stored inside a knowledge database does not directly imply whether the rule is still valid, especially if such rule is based on internal knowledge. Also there is no efficient tool for analysis of such explicit knowledge at the moment.

The multidimensional approach for storing explicit knowledge allows analysing the knowledge in this context by various dimensions such as the time, the place, the weather changes, etc. These dimensions in terms of the agricultural sector are very useful since it is possible to determine not only the recommended agents (quantity and efficiency), but also to find out how their efficiency has changed in time and in space (i.e. location) compared to other monitored agents. In this context it should be noted that the knowledge gained in the past may not be applicable in full at present (e.g. due to changes of technology, growing styles, etc.). And this analytical approach allows to edit / create new explicit knowledge to increase (economic, technical) efficiency of the agricultural enterprise.

Finally, the general scheme for the design of multidimensional databases is specified in order to improve the quality of the databases used for storing explicit knowledge that leads to the elimination of these problems.

## 3    Results

### 3.1    Transforming Knowledge Rules

Using open data and farmer's explicit knowledge we can derive examples of knowledge-based rules similar to rules (1 and 2). Such rules are beneficial as the farm can effectively decide on the use of suitable equipment. However, as mentioned above we lack an effective tool for analysis of such knowledge (stored in a relational database). Suppose there is a set of knowledge rules defined as IF **E** THEN **H** where **E** and **H** are predicates in implication (according to [3]) then for multidimensional approach it is needed to limit **H** predicates to those related to observed indicators. Knowledge rule that complies with this condition can look like this:

IF *aphid flight activity (quantity 4800)* AND *crop (potato)* AND *cultivar
(Finka)* AND *effective temperature sum (6.8)* AND *quarter (Q3 2015)* AND
*agent (Actara 25 WG)* AND *dosage (0.08 kg 200-500)* THEN *aphid
infestation (5%)* AND *costs (8,500 CZK)* AND *efficiency (85%)*          (3)

Rule (3) may be interpreted as follows: If during the 3d quarter of 2015 we use
Actara 25 WG protective agent dosed at 0.08 kg per 200-500 litres of water to prevent
aphid infestation of potatoes (Finka cultivar), then we can reach 85 % protection
efficiency at total costs of 8,500 CZK.

This type of explicit knowledge will allow farm managers to decide what product to
choose in comparison with other criteria such as efficiency and cost. Sometimes it may
be advantageous for agricultural enterprise to use cheaper alternatives with lower
efficiency, and sometimes vice versa. This given type of explicit knowledge can be
transformed into a multidimensional schema for the purpose of knowledge-based
analysis. Further, default conceptual and logical schema for the design a multidimensional database will be created.

In the first phase of conceptual design of the multidimensional database, a fact table
in an empty conceptual schema must be created. Based on the knowledge rule (2) it can
be stated that **E** predicates will represent dimensional tables while **H** predicates are
particular measures (indicators) in the fact table. Because there is a predicate concerning time (Quarter) in the knowledge rule (3), the scheme will also contain time
dimension. Fact table will be associated using roll-up relationship (N:1) with all necessary dimensions. During the transfer to the logical schema, each dimension will be
assigned a numerical primary key and will be associated with the foreign key in the fact
table (Fig. 1).

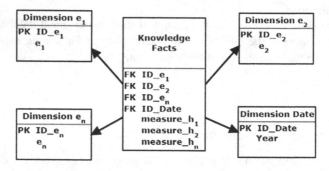

**Fig. 1.** Logical scheme of the transformation of the knowledge rules (own work).

At this stage we achieved the analogy of the knowledge rules with the multidimensional paradigm, and it was possible to transform these rules into the conceptual
and logical multidimensional data model. The authors of this paper believe that the
multidimensional database created using such approach allows to design OLAP
applications for the knowledge-based decision support of the responsible managers of
agricultural businesses.

## 3.2   Creation of the Prototype

To get an accurate preview of the future OLAP solution, the prototype of a multidimensional database is created using the transformation of knowledge rules. Creating a prototype allows us to find the advantages and limitations of the proposed process of knowledge transformation into a multidimensional database. For creating the prototype we use the following knowledge rule:

*IF* aphid flight activity ∧ crop ∧ cultivar ∧ effective temperature sum ∧ quarter
∧ agent *THEN* aphid infestation % ∧ efficiency % ∧ costs CZK.          (4)

**Conceptual Design Prototype.** Transformation of the knowledge rule (4) leads to identification of measures and dimensions of the conceptual schema. The whole diagram contains only one fact table (due to the fact that the approach uses the star scheme). Identified measures then represent attributes of the fact table.

The result of the transformation of verdicts of knowledge of the rules at the dimensions and measures (Table 2) allows the creation of conceptual schema.

**Table 2.**  Description of the results of the transformation of knowledge-based rules (4).

| Measure | Dimension | Dimension Date |
|---|---|---|
| Aphid infestation | Flight activity | Date |
| Efficiency (%) | Crop | |
| Costs (CZK) | Cultivar | |
| | Temperature sum | |
| | Agent | |
| | Dosage | |

**Logical Design Prototype.** In the logical design we associate the identified dimensions with fact tables. The basic logical scheme is extended by the additional dimension attributes.

For the Crop dimension we create attributes Name and Crop Group. For the Cultivar dimension we create attributes Name, Cultivar No. and Status (protected cultivar, registered cultivar, etc.). The Agent dimension is described with attributes Name, Registry No., Infestant, Area of Use, Active Component. The Flight Activity dimension contains attributes Place and Risk of Spreading. In the Temperature Sum dimension we create attributes Average Daily Temperature, Lower Development Threshold, Effective Daily Temperature and Effective Temperature Sum. These attributes are not measurements but already calculated values acquired from agricultural e-government open data. For the Dosage dimension we create attributes Volume and Unit. The Date dimension contains attributes that will allow analysis both in the short term (Period of Application, Month, Week and Day) and in the long term (Year). For the knowledge analysis it is important to implement the analytical processing in both the short and the long term, since not all knowledge expressions remain unchanged in the short term. In this stage of design of the logic scheme prototype the snapshot granularity of data is selected. Data (relating to individual knowledge statements) then will be input into the database at the same time intervals (e.g. quarterly). The time dimension takes into account the year and the application period. Only in these intervals it is possible to identify changes in each dimension (statements). The diagram of the resulting logical prototype is shown in Fig. 2.

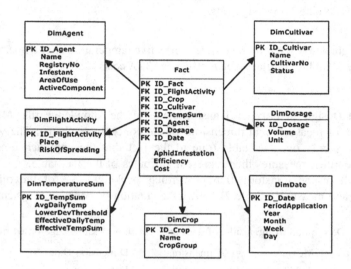

**Fig. 2.** Logical schema of the prototype (self-authored).

**Physical Design Prototype.** Our methodological approach utilizes Microsoft Excel 2013 and PowerPivot software for the design of the prototype.

First, the relational data and open data (in XML or XLS format) are imported into fact tables and particular dimensions in PowerPivot, then the relations are created based on the proposed logical scheme (Fig. 2). Integrated data does not represent specific data of a large agricultural business. Data are only theoretical (from Table 1), represent a small farm. Integrated tables contain attributes designed in the logical schema. Other attributes, especially those that were added as sub-attributes to individual dimensions are not included in the prototype.

Physical design of the prototype enables not only to verify that the logical model of our designed approach is viable, but also verifies whether the solved transformation of knowledge rules into multidimensional databases for OLAP has practical meaning.

For example, to answer the following analytical questions:

– What is the average effectivity of Actara 25 WG agent applied during Autumn in years 2012-2015?
– What was the total cost (in CZK) of protection against aphids?
– How did the aphid infestation of potatoes level changed in comparison to previous years?

To answer these analytical questions and to test prototypes of multidimensional databases in practice the corresponding pivot tables are created in PowerPivot. This type of output is mostly supported by all client applications for OLAP. In the physical design, the rate is selected so that it will be displayed inside the pivot table and dimensions are placed in rows and columns where their values are calculated within (Fig 3).

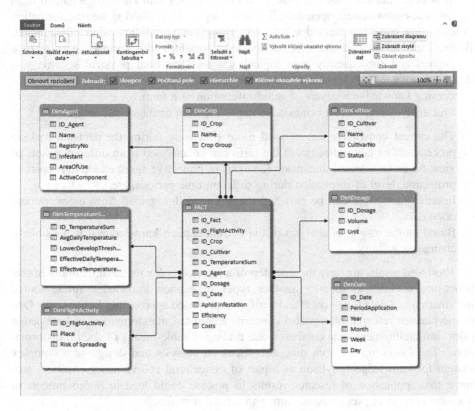

**Fig. 3.** Multidimensional model in PowerPivot 2013 (self-authored).

By using the contingency tables and graphs the farm management can increase effectivity of their decision making using already available internal explicit knowledge and knowledge acquired from agricultural e-government open data. Data presented in contingency tables allow farm managers to analyze the knowledge in more detail and also update it if needed. This can result in beneficial analysis of probability of pest infestation, effectivity of protective agents and other analyses important for decision making in precision agriculture.

Our approach to analytic model design using the PowerPivot tool is useful for agricultural businesses that do not want to or cannot invest into robust Business Intelligence solutions. The main reason is that MS Excel with PowerPivot add-on is easily available and also most of the farmers already use MS Excel for their agendas.

# 4   Conclusion

The paper presented innovative approach to analytical processing of explicit knowledge in precision agriculture. Our approach utilizes explicit internal knowledge stored in knowledge database. Such knowledge is then enriched with knowledge gained from agricultural e-government open data. The next step of the method is the transformation of such knowledge (represented as knowledge rules) into multidimensional data model. Before creating such model it is necessary to transform the knowledge rules to a conceptual and subsequently to a logical schema. The final physical schema was designed using MS PowerPivot. This approach was demonstrated on the example concerning knowledge analysis of aphid infestation of a farm.

Our analytical approach brings advantages for farm managers, such as:

- The current knowledge can be used more effectively during the decision making processes. The key indicators of the farm can be analysed from different points of view based on selected dimension (analysis of protective agent effectivity, costs of protection, level of infestation during different time periods, etc.).
- Internal knowledge can be enriched using knowledge gained from e-government open data.
- Based on the results of analysis of the current explicit knowledge it is possible to change its validity.

Presented results are only the first step of a more complex research. Authors of this paper are working to identify another types of explicit knowledge rules, source information and data (open data) and verify the proposed approach in larger scale. One of the planned research phases also concerns automated transformation of knowledge rules into multidimensional databases and finding suitable means of such transformations. The follow up research may also focus on analysis and design of a complex system for knowledge provision as a part of agricultural eGovernance. Authors presume that application of research results in practise could lead to improvements in decision support in precise agriculture and related domains.

**Acknowledgments.**  The results and knowledge included herein have been obtained owing to support from the IGA of the Faculty of Economics and Management, Czech University of Life Sciences in Prague, grant No. 20141040, "New methods for support of managers in agriculture".

# References

1. Sauter, V.L.: Decision Support Systems for business intelligence. Wiley, New York (2014)
2. Fisher, D., Drucker, S., Czerwinski, M.: Business intelligence analytics. Comput. Graph. Appl. **34**(5), 22–24 (2014)
3. Tyrychtr, J., Ulman, M., Vostrovský, V.: Evaluation of the state of the business intelligence among small czech farms. Agric. Econ. **61**(2), 63–71 (2015)
4. Feigenbaum, E.A.: The art of artificial intelligence. 1. Themes and case studies of knowledge engineering, Stanford Univ CA Dept of Computer Science (1977)

5. Feigenbaum, E., Mccorduck, P.: The Fifth Generation: Artificial Intelligence and Japan's Challenge to the World (1983)
6. Charvat, K., Esbri, M.A., Mayer, W., Campos, A., Palma, R., Krivanek, Z.: FOODIE— Open data for agriculture, In: IST-Africa Conference Proceedings (2014)
7. Lausch, A., Schmidt, A., Tischndorf, L.: Data mining and linked open data – New perspectives for data analysis in environmental research. Ecol. Model. **295**, 5–17 (2015)
8. Piedra, N., Tovar, E., Colomo-Palacios, R., Lopez-Vargas, J., Chicaiza, J.A.: Consuming and producing linked open data: the case of OpenCourseWare. Program: Electron. Libr. Inf. Syst. **48**(1), 16–40 (2014)
9. Rysová, H., Kubata, K., Tyrychtr, J., Ulman, M., Šmejkalová, M., Vostrovský, V.: Evaluation of electronic public services in agriculture in the Czech Republic. Acta Univ. Agriculturae et Silviculturae Mendelianae Brunensis **61**(2), 437–479 (2013)
10. Fonkam, M.: On a Composite Formal-ism and Approach to Presenting the Knowledge Content of a Relational Database. In: Advances in Artificial Intelligence, pp. 274–284 (1995)
11. Hawryszkiewycz, I.: Knowledge Management: Organizing Knowledge Based Enter-prises, Palgrave Macmillan P (2009)
12. Vaníček, J., Vostrovský, V.: Knowledge acquisition from agricultural data-bases. Sci. Agriculturae Bohemica **39**, 82–85 (2008)
13. Pankowski, T.: Using Da-ta-to-Knowledge exchange for transforming relational databases to knowledge bases. Rules on the Web Res. Appl. **7438**, 256–263 (2012)
14. Abelló A., Romero, O.: On-Line Analytical Processing. In: Liu, L., Özsu, M.T. (eds.), pp. 1949–1954. Springer (2009)
15. Pedersen, T.: Cube. In: Liu, L., Özsu, M.T. (eds.) Dictionary of Gems and Gemology, pp. 538–539. Springer, US (2009)
16. Vassiliadis, P., Sellis, T.: A survey of logical models for OLAP databases. ACM SIGMOD Rec. **28**, 64–69 (1999)
17. Pedersen, T., Dimension, L.L., Özsu, M.T. (eds.) p. 836. Springer US (2009)
18. Mendoza, M., Alegría, E., Maca, M., Cobos, C., León, E.: Multidimensional analysis model for a document warehouse that includes textual measures. Decis. Support Syst. **72**, 44–59 (2015)
19. Datta, A., Thomas, H.: The cube data model: a conceptual model and algebra for on-line analytical processing in data warehouses. Decis. Support Syst. **27**(3), 298–301 (1999)
20. Khan, A.: SAP and BW Data Warehousing: How to Plan and Implement, Khan Consulting and Publishing, LLC (2005)
21. Tyrychtr, J.: Provozní a analytické databáze, Praha: ČSVIZ (2015). http://www.csviz.cz/kniha-provozni-a-analyticke-databaze/
22. Pedersen, T.: Multidimensional Modeling. In: Liu, L., Özsu, M.T. (eds.) pp. 1777–1784. Springer US (2009)
23. Wu, M., Buchmann, A.: Research Issues in Data Warehousing, Ulm, Germany (1997)
24. Chaudhuri, S., Dayal, U.: An Overview of Data Warehousing and OLAP Technology, vol. 26, pp. 65–74 (1997)
25. Ballard, C., Herreman, D., Schauer, D., Bell, R., Kim, E., Valencic, A.: Data Modeling Techniques for Data Warehousing, 1, IBM International Technical Support Organization (1998)
26. McGuff, F.: Designing the Perfect Data Warehouse (1998). http://members.aol.com/fmcguff/dwmodel/index.htm
27. Boehnlein, M., Ende, A.: Deriving initial data warehouse structures from the conceptual data models of the underlying operational information systems, Kansas City, USA (1999)

28. Abdelhédi, F., Zurfluh, G.: User Support System for Designing Decisional Database, Nice, France: IARIA (2013)
29. Levene, M., Loizou, G.: Why is the snowflake schema a good data warehouse design? Inf. Systems **28**, 225–240 (2003)
30. Edwards, M.: Best practices in data warehousing award winners, Bus. Intell. J. **6**(4) (2001)
31. Elbashir, M.Z., Collier, P.A., Davern, M.J.: Measuring the effects of business intelligence systems: the relationship between business process and organizational performance. Int. J. Account. Inf. Syst. **9**(3), 135–153 (2008)
32. Popovič, A., Hackney, R., Coelho, P.S., Jaklič, J.: Towards business intelligence systems success: Effects of maturity and culture on. Decis. Support Syst. **54**, 729–739 (2012)
33. Vostrovský, V., Tyrychtr, J., Ulman, M.: Knowledge support of information and communication technology in agricultural enterprises in the Czech Republic. Acta Univ. Agric. Silvic. Mendel. Brun. **63**(1), 327–336 (2015)

# Enterprise Optimisation

# Lessons Learned from Experimental Prototype Development for KPI Acquisition and Modeling from Legacy ERP Systems

Gundars Alksnis[✉], Erika Asnina, Anita Finke, and Marite Kirikova

Institute of Applied Computer Systems, Riga Technical University, Meza iela 1 k-4,
Riga 1048, Latvia
{gundars.alksnis,erika.asnina,anita.finke,
marite.kirikova}@rtu.lv

**Abstract.** In this paper we consider a business case of an Enterprise Resource Planning (ERP) system vendor who needs to introduce qualitative features without making great investments in the legacy source code. We propose to extend legacy ERP system's functionality by applying the Leading System paradigm so that business process management can be introduced. This enables business process awareness and provides opportunity for qualitative feature set introduction in a legacy ERP system. As a result, Key Performance Indicator (KPI) acquisition, modeling and analysis from the process aware legacy ERP system becomes possible. The main focus in this paper is on lessons learned about a suitable prototype architecture for KPI acquisition, modeling and analysis, and about best practices for KPI analysis from log data of business process execution.

**Keywords:** Legacy ERP systems · Process awareness · Key performance indicators modeling

## 1 Introduction

In this paper we consider the research problem that was brought by the Enterprise Resource Planning (ERP) system vendor who wanted to introduce qualitatively new features in the ERP system without making great investments in the legacy source code. This is a rather common situation – over time ERP systems become more and more complex and at some point the vendor has to decide whether the system is to be substantially re-architected or external components are to be introduced to enable more flexible and extensible solutions. The lack of flexibility and extensibility may hinder competitiveness of client enterprises and they may have to decide whether to stay with the current ERP system vendor or to make, usually substantial, financial investments in evaluating offers of other vendors and migrating to a new system. Gradual evolution or continuous improvement have been advocated as more business friendly strategies to compare with re-engineering approaches [1]. Therefore, the motivation for this research is to provide options how to extend the capabilities of legacy ERP system with advanced features.

© Springer International Publishing Switzerland 2015
J. Barjis et al. (Eds.): EOMAS 2015, LNBIP 231, pp. 155–170, 2015.
DOI: 10.1007/978-3-319-24626-0_12

In particular, we focus on how to introduce Key Performance Indicator (KPI) acquisition, modeling and analysis in the context of legacy ERP systems.

Let us illustrate the general features of a business case which we use to illustrate the problem. An ERP system vendor has many customers, mostly, small and medium size enterprises. Each customer uses the ERP solution for its specific needs, integrates it with its own and/or third party information systems (IS) and other ERP systems. It is quite common for a business process (BP) to span among several participants from different enterprises, which therefore must collaborate to obtain business value by using multiple ISs. The particular ERP vendor, however, has limited possibility to change or enhance the functionality of the third party ISs. Also in the context of legacy ERP systems, workflows supported by process engines might not be directly applicable. Thus, when the knowledge about business processes is only in the heads of end users or at the best in some decoupled descriptions, understanding and managing how process instances are being executed in reality becomes the hardly achievable task. Therefore, we assume that if it would be possible to detect changes in the ERP system's business objects externally, they could be used to provide user guidance and also to perform monitoring of KPIs from the log data of executing business processes.

The research objective is to provide an approach for extending the capability of legacy ERP systems with KPI acquisition, modeling and analysis functionality. The constraint to be taken into consideration is that in legacy ERP systems there is no clear mechanism how to obtain KPIs from business process execution log data; and although experienced users might know their tasks and execution order, they still are not able to analyze current and past business process execution characteristics.

As a research method we use prototyping and lessons learned format of presentation by grouping research questions into categories and for each research question stating an issue, analyzing a problem, and providing summarizing recommendations. From the research objective we have identified eight research questions and for each give a literature review, applied approach, motivation and achieved results.

The rest of the paper is organized as follows. Section 2 outlines general architecture of the prototype with which we have modeled KPI data. Section 3 provides detailed discussion about the role of KPIs. Section 4 discusses KPI acquisition methods from business process simulation tools. Section 5 discusses KPI analysis and visualization tools and demonstrates example obtained from the implemented prototype. Finally, Sect. 6 concludes the paper with the summarization of main results and outlines future work.

## 2    General Architecture of the Prototype

In this section we provide assumptions and detailed description regarding the general architecture of the prototype that was used during the modeling and experimental development for obtaining KPIs.

**Research Question 1: Is it possible to validate specific components of the prototype against the general architecture in relation to KPI acquisition, modeling and analysis?**

*Procedure.* We assume that the proposed prototype must be based on an architecture as described in  [2]. The authors of [2] have evaluated different business modeling

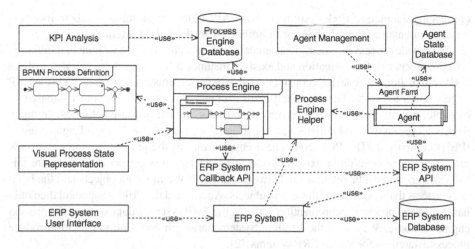

**Fig. 1.** General architecture of the prototype for KPI acquisition and modeling.

paradigms and concluded that for the non-disruptive introduction of process awareness (which is essential for KPI acquisition, modeling and analysis) the Leading System paradigm is the most optimal conceptual tool, though it comes with limitations on the business process definitions. The general architecture of the prototype is depicted in Fig. 1.

The following are the main components of the architecture:

- Process Engine – the main task of which in our context is to react on signal messages sent by external agents, call Service Tasks and maintain process definitions and their states. We use Camunda[1] process engine.
- (Legacy) ERP System – ensures business data processing via user interface and external Application Programming Interface (API) for agents and the process engine in order to obtain and modify the database of ERP system.
- Agent Farm – by accessing the API of ERP System, agents monitor the business data for specific states and notify process engine when predefined conditions are met.

Initially, the process engine was embedded in the web application that ran in the context of JavaEE application server. This simplified prototype implementation and testing. For example, by default the embedded process engine used H2 in-memory database. Therefore it was possible to start with new process engine structure each time it was launched. In order to test in a production-like environment, however, the process engine was implemented as a separate application that uses persistent storage and provides callback API to the ERP system. The goal of the callback API is to provide Business Process Model and Notation (BPMN) Service Tasks with the ability to call ERP system API. During the process execution the process engine

---

[1] http://camunda.org. The particular selection is not in the scope of this paper, however it should be noted that there was done evaluation among multiple process engines.

creates an instance of ERP system callback API component, makes calls to its operations and ensures that changes are committed in the ERP system database.

To provide process instance advancements and state changes, we assume that initiators for new process instance creation and existing instance advancement are end users of the ERP system. For example, let's consider a case when user registers new invoice via the ERP system's user interface. This ultimately leads to changes in the ERP system's database (for example, new records in the tables are created). As a result of these activities, an agent detects these changes and initiates sending a signal message to the Process Engine Helper (PEH) component. The PEH component ensures that in the process engine either new process instance creation or existing instance advancement is performed. To ensure this behavior, there must be relationship between the ERP system's data objects and the business process that correlates to these data objects. Agents and the PEH component then only have to ensure proper synchronization between the ERP system's database and the process engine database. We call it the Leading System paradigm and it allows us to introduce process awareness for legacy ERP systems [2].

From the process engine viewpoint, the behavior of the process instance must map to the data model in such a way that, upon receiving signal messages from the ERP system, the advancement of the process instance is made (it is ensured by external agents and the PEH). This behavior can be modeled with such elements of BMPN 2.0 standard as User Task, Receive Task, Timer and Catch Events. For example, when the process instance state reaches a particular User Task element, the process engine creates a new task instance which must be completed for the process instance to advance further. Such task can be related to a particular user or role in the ERP system. Receiving a signal message indicates that a particular task is completed, the process instance is advanced accordingly (i.e., in the ERP system database the state has changed and therefore detected by an agent rule). It is possible not only to receive the signal message about the fact that a particular task has been completed, but also to attach related data to it. For example, this data can be mapped to the process instance variable. Therefore it is possible to make branching decisions during a process instance execution (modeled as BPMN XOR Gateway elements).

To simplify synchronization between the ERP system and the process engine, we enforce the constraint that each process definition must be related to only one business entity (object). With a business entity we denote anything that has a unique business key (identifier) and during its lifecycle can be in different states. As a result, there can be multiple business process instances, but each is related to the unique business entity. For example, business entity "Invoice" can be related to and used in the "Invoice management process."

Another important aspect is that the PEH is able to return the state of successfully applied signals and also to show, which signals were not applied. This information is used by agents in order to not resend the same state signal messages multiple times.

Let's review how these principles can be applied for modeling a simple coordination business process as shown in Fig. 2. The testing of this model can be performed for the following execution scenario:

1. The PEH receives a signal message (containing a business entity name and an identifier) that corresponds to the start event rule of the process definition. As a result,

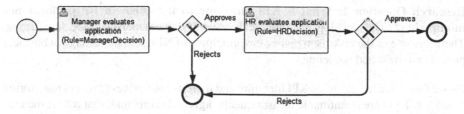

**Fig. 2.** An example of a simple coordination business process

the new process instance is created and automatically advanced to the first user task – "Manager evaluates application."

2. Next, the PEH receives a signal message from an agent that the rule "ManagerDecision" has been completed. This message contains also data about the decision (approved or rejected).
3. Assuming that the approval decision was made, the process instance advances and stops at the second user task "HR evaluates application."
4. Next, the PEH receives another signal message from an agent that the rule "HRDecision" has been completed. This message contains also data about the decision.
5. Assuming that also the second approval decision was made, the process instance advances to the end state.

To provide support for BPMN Service Tasks we assume that process definitions can contain references to Java classes, which during process execution are instantiated, and via the callback API perform automated activities in the ERP system.

However, the important aspect of the process engine behavior is that it saves details about each process instance execution history in its database. This information then can be used as a base for KPI acquisition, modeling and analysis. This aspect is the main subject of discussion in further sections.

*Summary.* By applying the Leading System paradigm, the prototype application was developed and placed between the ERP system and the process engine. We created various BPMN process definitions and by applying process testing classes, we performed unit and integration tests. Unit and integration tests mostly simulated agents that send signal messages to the process engine thus creating/advancing/ending process instances and providing the feedback to the ERP system.

To monitor process engine states we used Camunda Cockpit web application. It allows visualization of information about executing process instances and their states. This information is important not only for evaluation of the current status of the process engine from different perspectives, but also KPI and Business Intelligence (BI) analysis can be performed on the base of this information.

# 3   Key Performance Indicators

In this section we give general definitions of Key Performance Indicators (KPI) and their usage in business process analysis and modeling.

**Research Question 2: What is KPI and how to use them in BP performance monitoring?** The developed prototype foresees business performance monitoring. Therefore one of the tasks is to review the principles of KPIs and their usage in business process analysis and modeling.

*Procedure.* We have studied KPI literature and their use in business process monitoring solutions. KPIs are quantifiable measurements, agreed beforehand, that reflect the critical success factors of an organization [3]. In other words, they are a set of quantifiable measures that a company or industry uses to gauge or compare performance in terms of meeting their strategic and operational goals [4]. KPIs are used in areas like revenue improvement, cost reduction etc. In this case, the goal is to collect business process performance KPI metrics for further business process performance modeling and analysis.

There are many of KPIs available to help to measure BP performance. Examples of such KPIs are [5]:

- Percentage of processes where completion falls
- Average process overdue time
- Percentage of overdue processes
- Average process age
- Percentage of processes where the actual number of assigned resources is smaller than planned number of assigned resources
- Sum of costs of stopped active processes
- Average time to complete a task
- Sum of deviation of time (for example, in days) against the planned schedule of all active projects

Different opinions exist about the types and quantity KPIs needed for successful BP performance measurement [6]. For example, Hope and Fraser [7] recommend to use no more than ten KPIs. Others, like Kaplan and Norton [8] recommend using no more than twenty KPIs. We see that in practice, the amount and specific features of KPIs depend on the specific features of the organization and goals. Another way is to use the rule "10/80/10" [9]. It means that an organization should have about ten Key Result Indicators (KRIs), up to eighty Performance Indicators (PIs) and Result Indicators (RIs), and ten KPIs. Parmenter [10] recommends to use one or two daily or in real-time (24/7) updated KPIs and five important KPIs that are updated once a week. In those seven KPIs, a number of KRIs are required.

KPI measures have at least four aspects: budget, scope, time and quality. Parmenter [10] indicates that a correct performance KPI must be related to one or more organizational success factors and quality models. Less important KPIs can be related only to success factors of an organization.

KPIs are used for different purposes, for example, for organization's strategic, tactical and operational measurement management [6, 11]. It is more difficult to create KPIs for strategic levels, for example, to measure organizations strategic objectives. It is because usually strategic objectives are related to more than one business process and it means that processes differ each from other. One more difficulty is that in practice the validation usually can be performed only when KPIs are already integrated into systems and used organizations. Only then it is possible to see whether these KPIs really give needed information. There are situations when KPIs are to be modified or changed, for example, when the organization changes its objectives or existing KPIs fail to bring relevant information for decision makers [10].

Modeling of KPIs can be carried out by at least two methods – a protocol modeling method and an alternative "attributes" method. The protocol modeling method is based on quality requirements of the organization combined with business strategic, tactical and operational goals. And the "attributes" method is based on concept of meta-type attributes like measurements. An example of such attributes might be the "average number of employees" of an organization.

*Summary.* In each situation it is recommended to use a collection of ten KPIs that show the most important measurements. Of course, there can be more than ten indicators that will help to define the most important KPIs. KPIs development can be made mathematically, but the real validation can be performed only during KPIs usage on a daily basis.

Measurements can have at least four aspects: budget, scope, time and quality. The prototype, discussed in this paper, does not cover the financial aspect, so only three other aspects will further be discussed.

In addition, KPIs have an operational and tactical perspective. In the prototype the main focus is on internal processes, specifically – on business process management and performance quality control. The prototype does not restrict the types of KPIs, for example, whether they are related to strategic, tactical or operational goals. This helps to create a solution for wide range of business processes. The prototype permits that KPI measurements can be taken on a past, present and future process executions, and it can be done regularly with different time intervals or upon request.

In the next section the tools that support KPIs creation and necessary data import are described.

## 4   Acquiring KPIs from Business Process Simulation Tools

**Research Question 3: What best practices exist for performance metrics of BPs?**
The prototype concept foresees such business performance metrics that touch the scope, time and quality in operational and partially tactical perspectives. One of the tasks is to discover what best practices exist for business performance metrics, since they are the foundation for KPIs.

*Procedure.* We have checked specifications of four business process modeling tools, which have well-developed mechanisms for measuring business processes either during simulation or in runtime mode. These tools are Grade-BM v4.1, IBM WebSphere Business Modeler Advanced v7.0, MicroStrategy Analytics Enterprise v9.3 and v9.5, and ARIS Process Performance Manager.

Specifications of MicroStrategy [12] and ARIS [13] lack the description of available performance metrics and KPIs in details. However, ARIS suggests functionality for analysis of process instances using simulation, KPIs evaluation in online mode, as well as data mining. KPIs touch process time, costs, resources, quality and performers. MicroStrategy defines the metric as one or more aggregate functions applied to table columns (or expressions/functions of them) at a particular level of metric [14]. Micro-Strategy does not contain a predefined list of KPIs, but has two pre-packed applications that include two business-specific modules, namely, "Customer Analysis" and "Financial Analysis." Both of them were not appropriate due to lack of required data in the prototype. Nevertheless, MicroStrategy suggests more than 300 embedded mathematical, OLAP, financial and statistical functions to help in creating KPIs at any level of complexity.

Grade-BP [15] is intended for business process modeling and simulation in order to discover bottlenecks in the processes during the design. Additionally, it is possible to ground user-specified business metrics on defined metrics in the tool and to simulate their achievement at defined resources and time periods. The accumulated statistics then can be used for analysis of tasks, events and performers. From the Grade-BM statistics view, a transaction is also a task. If applicable, Grade-BP provides aggregated measurements for one simulation session (complete or partial) in the form of total, maximal, minimal and average values in the time period.

IBM WebSphere Business Modeler Advanced v7.0 [16] foresees monitoring global processes without any code generation or deployment, at any level of detail and with or without event distribution. Processes are analyzed dynamically at runtime and during event origin. It is possible to analyze time, costs, resource allocation, "free float" activity time, the most critical and the shortest paths of processes, as well as a process case.

*Summary.* The analysis gave us the general view on the process business performance metrics provided by the MicroStrategy, Grade-BM and IBM WebSphere Business Modeler Advanced. The levels of measuring can be the following: a task, an activity instance, a set of activity instances (or an activity), a process instance, a set of process instances (or a process), a process case instance, a set of process case instances (or a process case), an event queue, a resource, and a performer. Fifty one candidate for process performance metrics have been elicited and then analyzed in more detail.

**Research Question 4: What raw data are required to collect the appropriate process performance metrics from the elicited ones?** As previously mentioned, the prototype has limitations on costs (related to financial KPIs at the enterprise units level), resources and performers characteristics. Therefore, not all of the elicited metrics may be appropriate from the available raw data. However, some of the required data potentially may be added to the process definition scheme as an extension part.

*Procedure.* During the research, raw data that may be required for each of fifty one elicited metric evaluation are identified. Those metrics, which require data that potentially are hard to be obtained from the prototype at the present, were set as inappropriate and excluded from the list.

*Summary.* The refined performance metrics include measurements at the action (a task, an activity, a transaction, a process, etc.), queue and performer levels. They include all possible execution and delay durations, successful completeness and failure rates, deviations from the planned indicators, performers load, etc.

Based on the results of the assessment of the required raw data, we conclude that for performance metrics the prototype should be able to collect the following data:

- For activity instances and process instances: start time, end time, failed end label (an indicator that an instance finished its execution unsuccessfully), planned execution duration, and work start time
- For queues: since the prototype events also are related only to the process instances and activity instances, these metrics use instances data
- For performers: instance performer and previously mentioned data of instances.

**Research Question 5: What best practices exist for KPI templates?** The task is aimed to analyze those performance metrics which could be considered as KPIs.

*Procedure.* We have analyzed best practices in offers of KPI libraries. Since KPIs are very business function/area specific, we have searched KPIs libraries in scientific literature [17–19]; stakeholders' communities KPI Institute [20], KPI Library [21], and APQCs Process Classification Framework [22]; and BI tools [16, 23]. A number of KPIs is huge. Therefore, we have focused only on those, which may touch quality of business process execution.

KPI Institute and KPI Library have many suggestions for KPI identification, however most of them are particular business specific. We have elicited 2 KPIs from KPI Institute and 20 KPIs from KPI Library (mostly related to project/program management).

APQCs Process Classification Framework (PCF) used in IBM WebSphere Business Modeler Advanced v7.0, is applied from enterprise levels 2.0 "Develop and Manage Product/Services" up to 8.0 "Manage Financial Resources." Most of the presented KPIs had a close relationship with financial indicators, managerial decisions, sales/services specifics, staff costs, management of quality assurance activities, and narrow business specifics. However, as for the prototype general performance indicators were needed, we have elicited only twelve KPI candidates from more than 200 indicators. In turn, Klipfolio tool provides KPI examples for different functional areas: sales, marketing, supply chain, call centers, help desk, assurance, small enterprise, health care, social media and SEO KPIs. Unfortunately, all the provided KPIs are particular business specific. Therefore, they were not included in the KPI candidate list.

*Summary.* We have elicited 2 general KPIs from enterprise knowledge management metrics [19], 28 KPIs related to client orientation and internal processes of Balanced Scorecard areas [17], and 12 KPIs from the recommended ones in [18] at the process and sub-process levels used to measure execution bottlenecks. The result is the list of 76 KPIs candidates.

**Research Question 6: What raw data are required to collect the appropriate KPIs from the elicited ones?** The same as in case of performance metrics we required additional analysis of raw data necessary to measure KPIs.

**Table 1.** Summary of available raw data for KPI calculation from the prototype

| No. | KPI | Data availability |
|---|---|---|
| 1 | Daily log | Full |
| 2 | Completeness status (%) | Not enough, because of missing source data and computation of process execution scenarios |
| 3 | Work schedule achievement in the planned period | Partly, because can be applied only to finished processes |
| 4 | Incomplete process task rate | Full |
| 5 | Yield (%) | Full |
| 6 | Total turnaround time (for a business process) | Full for finished processes |
| 7 | Total lead time | Full for finished processes |
| 8 | Deviation from planned work hours (%) | Full for finished processes |
| 9 | Deviation from the schedule (hours) | Full for finished processes |
| 10 | Delayed process activities (%) | Partly, because can be applied only to finished processes |
| 11 | Milestones missed in the time period (%, #) | Not enough, because of missing source data |
| 12 | Average delay duration of process activities | Not enough, because of missing source data |
| 13 | Average close duration of process activities | Full for finished processes |
| 14 | Close duration rate of process activities | Full for finished processes |
| 15 | Queue rate of process activities | Full |
| 16 | Planned hours for activities (#) | Full |
| 17 | Forecast accuracy one period before the production | Full for finished processes |
| 18 | Incomplete work messages as well as their statuses and sizes | Full, if process owner is the same as executor |
| 19 | Work success and failure rate | Full |
| 20 | A number of new process instances (#) | Partly, because can be applied to started processes, but can't be applied to planned start date/time |
| 21 | On time completed process (%) | Full, if planned end date can be calculated dynamically |
| 22 | Date when ancillary work must be completed (for main processes only) | Full for delegated activities |
| 23 | Processes completed on time and on budget | No enough, because of missing data about expenses and budget |
| 24 | Main work that subcontractors perform | Partly |
| 25 | Execution/performance time for top ten projects/processes | Full for finished processes and if process executor is also process owner |

*Procedure.* The 76 KPIs candidates selected in the previous step have been refined with their assessment formulas and required raw data. Those candidates that required additional data on finance, costs and staff work time periods have been excluded from the final KPI candidate list. The final list contains 25 KPIs and availability of the necessary data for which are summarized in Table 1.

The required raw data the prototype should be able to collect are the following:

- For activity instances: end time, work start time, performer, category, name, number, planned end time, planned execution duration, planned start time, start time;

- For process instance: path, alternate path, end time, budget, owner, costs, performer, planned end time, planned execution time, planned start time, start time;
- For milestone instances: occur time, planned occur time.

Unfortunately not all required data could be obtained from the process engine database used in the prototype. Such data as "planned duration" of the activity and the process, and the "process owner" have to be obtained from the process definitions themselves. But data about startup time of a task, planned startup time of an activity, planned occur time for a milestone, alternative path for a process, process budget, process execution path, and process expenses are not retrievable at all.

*Summary.* We have elicited an initial list of process performance metrics and KPIs that are general enough. Both metrics and KPIs require a small set of raw data related to activities, processes, milestones, and performers/owners. All raw data can be exported by the prototype either from the runtime/historical raw data, or from the process declaration schemas. Not all KPIs are measurable within the prototype however – 17 KPIs can be measured completely, 4 only partially and for 4 KPIs the process engine does not provide enough data.

# 5  Data Import into KPI Analysis and Visualization Tools

**Research Question 7: What possibilities give tools which support KPIs analysis and visualization?** Today in the market many KPIs analysis and visualization tools that allow to operate with data from external data sources (for example other information systems) are available.

*Procedure.* We have checked specification of KPIs tools, which have support for data analysis and visualization. These tools are represented in Table 2.

Not all of these tools support OLAP, Extract, Transforms and Load (ETL), Data Mining and KPIs at the same time [24]. For example, only the following open source tools support above-mentioned possibilities – SpagoBI, Pentaho and Vanilla. Such open source tools like OpenI, JasperSoft and Palo do not support KPIs.

According to [25], the ten most recommended tools for BI are Pentaho, Sisence, Bayound Intelligence, Birst, TARGIT Decision Suite, iDashBoards, TIBCO Spotfire, IBM Cognos Business Intelligence, Quadbase Systems and Tableau.

The most widely used BI tools research [26] mentions tools like Adaptive Insights, Birst, GoodData, Jedox, Logi Analytics, Pentaho, Tableau, TIBCO, Actuate, Information Builder, Qlik, Dimensional Insight, Dundas, Jinfonet, Klipfolio, Phocas, Targit and the tools from IBM, Microsoft and SAP. The authors of this research mention that small and medium organizations mostly use dashboards and service solutions.

Performance measurements are based on data or facts stored in databases. Even in small and medium organizations there is more than one data source, so there could be need for data extraction. Therefore it is recommended to use various ETL technologies for necessary data extraction and transformation for further use in OLAP cubes and analysis.

*Summary.* The most widely supported data sources are relational databases (creating a direct connection to one or more databases), connections with web service or systems data thought API (including ERP systems databases). Second most popular data imports are from MS Excel spreadsheets and flat files. Less popular is data import from XML files and connection to non-relational databases, for example, multi-dimensional databases and document databases.

Many of BI tools support ETL technology, but not always this means that they also support OLAP cubes.

**Research Question 8: Is it possible to export raw data from the prototype and to import them for KPI creation?** The task was to import data in one of the most supported format, CSV, and to create a KPI in some popular tool.

*Procedure.* Among a number of tools that support building and tracking the KPIs, MS Excel is one of the most popular tool. It allows to import data from different data sources, supports data charts, PivotTables, many statistical and mathematical functions as well as connections from one MS Excel file to other [27]. MS Excel has also risks and disadvantages related to unpredictable processing of large amount of data, versioning issues, unstable dashboards due to changes in charts, graphics or data structures, as well as uncontrolled editing that can lead to data integrity loss. However, its numerous functions, data analytics, calculations and visualization possibilities make this tool suitable for our experiments.

The procedure of using MS Excel as a KPI monitoring includes such actions as [28]: select necessary data, for example, import from the database; identify data pools for measurements; select and create graphs and charts needed to show on a dashboard; and create a spreadsheet where to place all the graphs and charts and put some filters on them, for example, pivot table charts, colored schemes/indicators, etc.

During our experiments, we selected raw data of the process shown in Fig. 2 as a plain denormalized table, then imported this data to MS Excel; selected the data we need to monitor and create PivotTable; and created filters and a chart for process activities durations.

*Summary.* Multiple experiments have been successfully completed. All 17 KPI's with the complete data set and 4 KPI's with the partially available data set have been modeled successfully. To get an insight into obtained results, an example pivot table for coordination business process KPI "Average close duration of process activities" is shown in Fig. 3.

**Table 2.** Summary of Business Intelligence tool comparison

| BI tools | Technologies | | | | | | | | |
|---|---|---|---|---|---|---|---|---|---|
| | Connection with RDBMS | Connection with DBMS dimension | Excel spreadsheets | Flat file (text, CSV) | Web Services and API | XML | JSON | ETL | Internal OLAP |
| Actuate BIRT | v | v | v | v | v | v | | | |
| Adaptive Insights | v | | v | | v | | | v | |
| Beyound Intelligence | v | | v | | v | v | | v | v |
| Birst | v | v | | v | v | v | v | | v |
| iDashBoards | v | | v | | v | v | v | | v |
| Dimensional Insight The Driver | v | | v | v | v | v | | v | |
| Dundas | v | v | v | | v | v | | v | v |
| GoodData | v | v | | v | v | v | v | | |
| IBM Cognos Business Intelligence | v | v | v | | v | v | | v | v |
| Information Builder | v | v | | v | v | v | v | v | |
| Jedox | v | | v | v | v | v | | v | v |
| Klipfolio | v | | v | v | v | v | v | | |
| MicroStrategy | v | | v | v | v | | | v | v |
| Pentaho | v | v | v | | | v | | v | v |
| Phocas | v | | v | v | v | | | v | |
| QlikView | v | | v | v | v | v | | | |
| Quadbase Systems | v | | | | v | v | | | |
| Sisence | v | | v | v | v | v | | | v |
| SpagoBI | v | v | | | v | | | v | v |
| Tableau | v | v | v | v | v | | | v | v |
| TARGIT | v | v | v | v | v | | | v | v |
| TIBCO | v | v | v | v | v | | | v | |
| Vanilla | v | v | | | v | | | v | v |

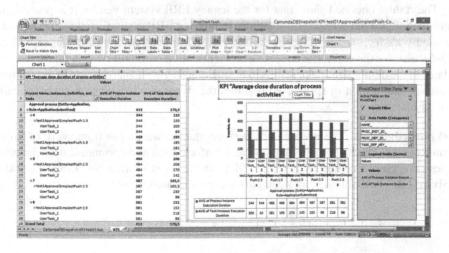

**Fig. 3.** The resulting pivot table for KPI "Average close duration of process activities"

# 6 Conclusions

In this paper we described our experiences and lessons learned from the experimental prototype development for KPI acquisition, modeling and analysis in the context of legacy ERP systems for which the process awareness has to be introduced.

It was shown that by implementing the Leading System paradigm, it is possible to introduce BP execution support for such legacy ERP systems that originally do not have explicit process awareness thus providing new qualitative features without making huge investments in the legacy source code. The implemented prototype allowed us to acquire additional data about business process executions and use them for KPI modeling and analysis.

One of the research tasks was to discover what kind of KPI metrics exist and what are the best practices for BP performance modeling. There are many opinions regarding types and quantity of KPIs that are needed for successful BP performance measurement and how to correctly apply them. However, usually it is recommended to use a selection of no more than ten KPIs that provide the most important measurements.

We have elicited original list of 76 KPIs from related works. This list then have been refined with their assessment formulas and required/available raw data. KPI candidates that required additional data on finance, costs and staff work time periods were excluded. Thus the final list for modeling and analysis consisted of 25 KPIs. Unfortunately not all required data could be obtained from the process engine database to calculate these KPIs: 17 KPIs can be measured completely, 4 only partially and for 4 KPIs the process engine does not provide enough data. The 21 KPI with the complete and partial data sets has been modeled successfully.

Among the tools that support building and tracking the KPIs we have selected MS Excel that was the simplest tool fitting our requirements for data input and representation. During the experiments, we selected raw simulation data of the multiple BP executions, imported these data to the Excel spreadsheet and created calculations, filters and pivot charts from process activities.

The results obtained show that for the legacy ERP system vendor it is possible to introduce additional services substantially improving ERP system's feature set that can be used both for existing and new customers. We hope that our conclusions will be helpful also for the enterprise modeling and simulation community. The future work is related to the demonstration of results to business and system analysts and based on their feedback elaboration of specific KPIs into more dynamic visualization environments, like dashboards.

**Acknowledgments.** The research has been conducted within the framework of European Regional Development Fund's project "Information and communication technologies competence center" Nr. KC/2.1.2.1.1/10/01/001 (Contract No. L-KC-11-0003) activity 1.2. "Technologies for managing services in workflows."

# References

1. Sneed, H.M.: An incremental approach to system replacement and integration. In: Proceedings of 15th European Conference on Software Maintenance and Reengineering, pp. 196–206 (2005). doi:10.1109/CSMR.2005.9
2. Alksnis, G., Asņina, Ē., Kirikova, M., Meiers, E.: Enabling Support of Collaborative Cross-enterprise Business Processes for Legacy ERP Systems. In: Journal of Complex Systems Informatics and Modeling Quarterly (CSIMQ). RTU Press online, pp. 1–18 (2015). doi: 10.7250/csimq.2015-2.01
3. Key Performance indicators (KPI): How an organization defines and measures progress toward its goals (by F. John Reh). http://management.about.com/cs/generalmanagement/a/keyperfindic.htm
4. Key Performance Indicators – KPI. http://www.investopedia.com/terms/k/kpi.asp
5. KPI Examples. http://www.pnmsoft.com/resources/bpm-tutorial/key-performance-indicators
6. Livieri, B., Di Cagno, P., Bochicchio, M.: A bibliometric analysis and review on performance modeling literature. In: Journal of Complex Systems Informatics and Modeling Quarterly (CSIMQ). RTU Press online, pp. 56–71 (2015). doi:10.7250/csimq.2015-2.05
7. Hope, J., Fraser, R.: Beyond Budgeting: How Managers Can Break Free from the Annual Performance Trap. Harvard Business School Press, Boston (2003)
8. Kaplan, R.S., Norton, D.P.: The Balanced Scorecard: translating strategy into action. Harvard Business School Press, Boston (1996)
9. The New Thinking on KPIs – part 3 of 4. http://www.strategydriven.com/2010/06/04/the-new-thinking-on-kpis-part-3-of-4
10. Parmenter, D.: Key Performance Indicators: Developing, implementing, and Using Winning KPIs. Wiley, Hoboken (2007)
11. Roubtsova, E., Michell, V.: A method for modeling of KPIs enabling validation of their properties. In: Proceedings of the 5th ACM SIGCHI Annual International Workshop on Behaviour Modelling - Foundations and Applications (BMFA 2013), Article 3, 10 pp. ACM, New York (2013)
12. MicroStrategy. http://www.microstrategy.com/
13. ARIS Process Performance Manager. http://www.softwareag.com/
14. Moraschi, D.: Business Intelligence with MicroStrategy Cookbook. Packt Publishing, Birmingham (2013)
15. Grade-BP. http://www.gradetools.com/
16. IBM WebSphere Business Modeler Advanced. http://www-03.ibm.com/software/products/en/modeler-advanced
17. Parmenter, D.: Key Performance Indicators: Developing, Implementing, and Using Winning KPIs, 2nd edn. Wiley, Hoboken (2010)
18. Keyes, J.: Knowledge Management, Business Intelligence, and Content Management: The IT Practitioner's Guide. Auerbach Publications, Boca Raton (2006)
19. Jeston, J., Nelis, J.: Business Process Management: Practical Guidelines to Successful Implementations. Elsevier, Oxford (2006)
20. KPI Institute Homepage. http://kpiinstitute.org/
21. KPI Library Homepage. http://kpilibrary.com/
22. APQCs Process Classification Framework. http://www.apqc.org/pcf
23. Klipfolio KPI Examples. http://www.klipfolio.com/resources/kpi-examples
24. Tereso, M., Bernardino, J.: Open source business intelligence tools for SMEs. In: 6th Iberian Conference on Information Systems and Technologies (CISTI), pp. 1–4. IEEE (2011)

25. Compare Business Intelligence (BI) Software Tools. http://www.softwareadvice.com/bi/
26. Dresner Advisory Services: Small and Mid-sized Enterprise Business Intelligence Market Study (Licenced for Klipfolio (2014). http://www.klipfolio.com/downloads/dresner-sme-2014
27. Connect data in another workbook to your workbook. https://support.office.com/en-au/article/Connect-data-in-another-workbook-to-your-workbook-3a557ddb-70f3-400b-b48c-0c86ce62b4f5
28. KPI Dashboard Creation in Excel (by Brigitta Schwulst) (2014). https://blog.udemy.com/kpi-dashboard/

# Model Checking Web Services Choreography

Arbia Ben Azaiez and Zohra Sbaï[✉]

Universit de Tunis El Manar, École Nationale d'Ingnieurs de Tunis,
BP. 37 Le Belvédère, 1002 Tunis, Tunisia
arbia.azaiez@yahoo.fr, zohra.sbai@enit.rnu.tn

**Abstract.** By exploiting the open standards of Web and by assuring a weak coupling of components, Web service technology provides a flexible and universal approach to the inter-operability of heterogeneous systems. This service composition is one of the major challenges of the emerging paradigm of Service Oriented Computing (SOC). Existing works suggest resolving this problem by the orchestration of services. However, this approach is centralized around a composition engine and there is a static service composition which follows a predefined pattern. To overcome this, a composition approach based on decentralized cooperation between a collection of services has been proposed, known as a choreography. The formal verification of such a composition is a very interested subject in the research area. Our contribution in this area is to provide a formal framework ensuring the verification of a choreography described in WS-CDL. For this, we propose first to model this choreography by a composition of open workflow nets: a special class of Petri nets. Then, we detail how to check behavioral properties specified in temporal logic using the model checker NuSMV.

**Keywords:** Web services choreography · WS-CDL · Formal analysis · Petri nets · Temporal logic · Model checking

## 1 Introduction

The emergence of Web services paradigm was a significant development in the history of Internet, which was destined to play the role of a data exchange vector. With Web services, Internet becomes a platform of software components, self-descriptive, easily integrated and loosely coupled. Web services were born to cover the problems that companies faced in terms of inter-operability, by implementing a Service Oriented Architecture (SOA) based on a standards set.

Web services are limited to relatively simple features that are modeled by a collection of operations. However, it is necessary to build new applications by composing services to meet more complex requirements with added value. Different canvas called methods have been proposed and implemented to manage and write the coordination of service based applications operations. We distinguish two categories of coordination processes: processes which implement the choreography of services and processes implementing their orchestration.

© Springer International Publishing Switzerland 2015
J. Barjis et al. (Eds.): EOMAS 2015, LNBIP 231, pp. 171–186, 2015.
DOI: 10.1007/978-3-319-24626-0_13

In a choreography, each participant involved in the overall process describes its role in the interaction. This is ensured through the description of Web services calls between pairs. Various languages have been proposed for the choreography of Web services among which we use Web Services-Chorography Description Language (WS-CDL). This language is the best known and the most used in the description of Web services choreography.

As they interact together, conflicts can be generated in the choreography of Web services. It is therefore necessary to check whether the composition of these services has errors or undesirable behavior. Indeed, this checking cannot be performed directly on a WS-CDL description. For this, several studies have tried to take advantage of formal methods to conduct a reliable verification based on the transformation of composition process towards a formal specification.

In this context, we propose in this paper an approach to analyse, model and formally verify the choreography of Web services and implement it in our platform D&A4WSC [13]. This approach allows to take a given WS-CDL specification as input and to generate a model based on open workflow nets that will be directly verified by our platform. For this formal verification, we invoke the NuSMV model checker [8] in order to check properties specified in CTL temporal logic [5]. Properties of interest which can be verified by the platform are soundness, deadlock freeness and compatibility properties.

The rest of this paper is composed of the following: Sect. 2 introduces the WS-CDL language as well as the open workflows nets (oWF-nets), which are used to prepare to WS-CDL analysis. After providing in Sect. 3 how WS-CDL can be translated into oWF-nets, Sect. 4 shows the steps for a formal verification of Web services choreography. Section 5 presents some experimental results and Sect. 6 discusses the related work. In Sect. 7, we summarize our work and give some future work.

## 2   Preliminaries

In this section, we expose an overview of WS-CDL specification and open workflow nets modeling.

### 2.1   WS-CDL Language

The WS-CDL description is a specification based on an XML document which aims to describe the collaborative observable behavior of multiple services which interact to achieve a common goal. A WS-CDL specification is composed of two parts [16] as described in Fig. 1:

(i) **Static part**: which specifies the entities which cooperate in WS-CDL description such as:
   - RoleType: Specifies the implementation process given by a participant with a specific role.
   - ParticipantType: An entity having a particular set of roles in the choreography.

– RelationshipType: Defines the relation between the roles and declares that two role Types have a need to interact to achieve some set of Web services.
– ChannelType: the medium used to communicate between participantType with specifying the where and how information is exchanged.

(ii) **Dynamic part**: describes interactions between the participants and their temporal interdependencies. It includes a definition of the set of variables used to realize the data dependent behavior of the choreography.

The choreography activity construct presents the basic building block of WS-CDL. It describes the behavior of the choreography, while an exception block defines the handling of exceptional events during the execution of the choreography activity, and a finalize block describes the actions to be taken upon termination of the choreography. There are three classes of activities:
– Basic Activities: Interaction is the principal basic activity. It describes the communication between two roles with exchanging information.
– Structural Activities: Refers to activities which present the scheduling rules in a choreography.
– Work-unit Activities: It is a conditional and looping construct combined in an enclosing activity.

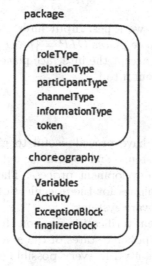

**Fig. 1.** WS-CDL document

## 2.2  Petri Nets

Petri nets are a major formalism for modeling business processes. The strength of such formalism is that it provides a strong mathematical basis with a graphical representation [6].

A Petri net is a tuple N = (P, T, F, W) in which P and T are two finite sets of places and transitions respectively. $F \subseteq (P \times T) \cup (T \times P)$ define the flow relation and $W: (P \times T) \cup (T \times P) \longrightarrow \mathbb{N}$ define the weight function of N which satisfy $W(x,y) = 1$ $if(x,y) \in F, else$ $W(x,y) = 0$.

If $W(u)=1$ $\forall$ u$\in$F then N is said to be an ordinary net and it is denoted by $N = (P,T,F)$.

We define a marking of a Petri net N by a function $M : P \longrightarrow \mathbb{N}$. $M_0$ is used to denote the initial marking of N.

A transition $t \in T$ is enabled in a marking M (denoted by $M[t\rangle$) if and only if $\forall$ p $\in$ $^{\bullet}t : M(p) \geq W(p,t)$. $^{\bullet}x$ represents the input nodes of $x$.

Petri nets are drawn as follows: the places are represented by circles and the transitions by rectangles. For the flow relation, an arc is drawn between x and y for each (x,y) in the relation. The weight function labels the arcs in case their weights are greater than 1. For the marking M of a Petri net, we draw $M(p)$ tokens into the circle representing the place p [20].

We propose to model the choreography with a composition of open workflow nets (oWF-nets) [17,19] which are a special class of Petri nets. They generalize classical workflow nets [2] by introducing interfaces for asynchronous messages passing. Intuitively, an oWF-net is an ordinary Petri net $N = (P, T, F)$ where:

- N has an input place i (i.e. $^{\bullet}i = \phi$),
- N has an output place f (i.e. $f^{\bullet} = \phi$), where $x^{\bullet}$ represents the output nodes of $x$,
- N has interface places of two types: Input interface places $IIP = \{p \in P/ \, ^{\bullet}p = \phi\}$ and Output interface places $OIP = \{p \in P/ \, p^{\bullet} = \phi\}$,
- for each node n $\in$ (P$\cup$T) except the interface places, there exists an itinerary from i to n and a path from n to f.

## 2.3   Model Checking

Formal methods and tools have proved useful to give high level and precise descriptions of computer systems, and to analyze exhaustively these systems at early phases of the system development process. They are a particular kind of mathematically-based techniques for the specification, development and verification of software and hardware systems.

Model checking is a formal verification method that is based on its ability to explore exhaustively all the possible states of the model and then to verify if the desired requirement is guaranteed in every possible execution. In addition, this formal method permits to produce a counter example if the checked property is violated and hence it facilitates the process of error characterization as well as its correction. For this reason, we choose to use the model checking method.

Tools automating the model checking method are as well available. Among many model checkers, we choose to use one of the main model checkers: NuSMV which is based on SMV (Symbolic Model Verifier) [15]. NuSMV is an extension and re-implementation of SMV symbolic model checker, the first model checking tool which is based on Binary Decision Diagrams (BDDs) [4]. The tool has been designed to be an open architecture for model checking. It has been developed in a joint project between ITC-IRST, the University of Genoa, the University of

Trento and Carnegie Mellon University. It offers many features including essentially the navigation of a counter example. In fact, all the model checkers can generate a counter example, the particularity of NuSMV is that it offers the possibility to the user to move from one state to another and even to assess the temporal logic expression of the counter example status [1].

NuSMV verifies temporal logic properties over finite state systems. It uses a symbolic representation of the specification in order to check if a model satisfies a property. NuSMV is able to verify properties specified in LTL (Linear Temporal Logic) as well as in CTL (Computation Tree Logic) [12]. We chose to use in this work CTL since it permits to use universal as well as existential quantifiers which allow us to reason on states and many future states possible for it.

CTL formulas are inductively defined as follows:

$$\varphi ::= \top | \bot | p | \neg \varphi | \varphi \wedge \varphi | \varphi \vee \varphi | \varphi \to \varphi | AX\varphi | EX\varphi | AF\varphi | EF\varphi | AG\varphi | EG\varphi | A[\varphi \sqcup \varphi] | E[\varphi \sqcup \varphi]$$

Where A models all possible paths from the current time, E models at least one path from the current moment. A and E are usually followed by one of the following prefixes: X, U, G and F.

A CTL formula f is built from atomic propositions corresponding to variables, boolean operators such as : $\neg, \vee, \wedge, \longrightarrow$ and temporal operators. Each temporal operator consists of two parts. A path quantifier (A or G) followed by a temporal modality (F, G, X, U). The temporal operators are interpreted relative to a current state s. The path quantifier indicates if the temporal operator expresses a property that should hold on all paths starting at s (denoted by the universal path quantifier A), or at least on one of these paths (denoted by the existential path quantifier E). The temporal modalities are interpreted as follows:

- Xp (neXt time p) is true if the formula p is true in the state reached immediately after the current state in the
- Fp (Future p) is true if there exists a state in the path where the formula p is true.
- Gp (Globally p) is true if p is true at every state in the path.
- pUq (p Until q) is true if there is a state in the path where q is true and p is true in all preceding states (if any). This definition is the so called strong until. Weak until would also be true when q holds forever. path.

# 3    Mapping WS-CDL Elements to oWF-net Constructs

This research consists of developing an approach to analyze WS-CDL document using model checking techniques. So, we propose, first, to establish a mapping between WS-CDL elements and oWF-nets constructs. We briefly represent oWF-nets modeling for WS-CDL elements.

– **Interaction Element**

Interaction element is the basic block in a choreography. It reflects the information exchange between roleTypes [9] which are represented by places and referred to as the *fromRoleType* (the sender of message) and the *toRoleType* (the receiver of message).

There is two types of exchange messages between roleTypes: request or response. Request is made always from the *fromRoleType* to *toRoleType* and response is made in the opposite direction. These messages are represented with tokens. An example of interaction is represented in Fig. 2.

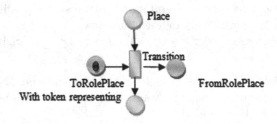

**Fig. 2.** oWF-net Model for request-response exchange messages

– **Activity Element**

Activity element defines the ordering rules of records performed into a choreography element [9]. There are three types of structural activities namely Sequence, Parallel and Choice.

– *Sequence Activity* represents one or more activities performed in the same order as their definition (Fig. 3.a).
– *Parallel Activity* represents one or more activities performed at the same time (Fig. 3.b).
– *Choice Activity* represents the performing of one activity chosen among a set of activities (Fig. 3.c).

# 4    Formal Verification Approach

Due to the difficulty of verifying directly the choreography with the model checking method and the expressive power as well as the graphical nature of Petri nets on the other hand, we propose to model first the choreography of Web services in open Workflow nets and then to translate the obtained model into SMV. Afterwards, we propose to specify in CTL the compatibility property to be verified. Finally, we invoke NuSMV to verify if the model meets the requirements.

This approach, described in Fig. 4, consists therefore of three steps:

1. Analyse the WS-CDL document (a syntactic verification),
2. Generate a model based on oWF-nets,
3. Verify this model with NuSMV model checker.

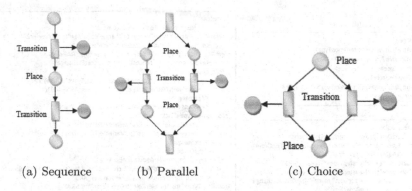

(a) Sequence      (b) Parallel             (c) Choice

**Fig. 3.** Sequence, Parallel and Choice activities

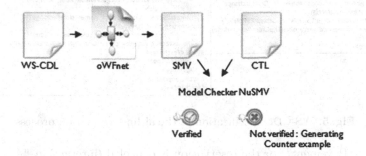

**Fig. 4.** Approach of formal verification of choreography

In order to better clarify our approach, we aim to treat a simple example of airline ticket reservation process to enhance the three operations. This process is composed of two services: Traveler and Airline Reservation System (ARS).

The reservation system works as follows: the traveler send a trip request to the ARS which replies with a list of available flights in a specific date. Then, if there is available flights, he may order a reservation for the best flight and finally will pay a ticket. Else, the request may be canceled.

## 4.1 Analysis of the WS-CDL Document

The first operation consists of considering a WS-CDL document, which represent an XML-based document, as input for analysis. Here, we just check the syntax of the WS-CDL document.

The WS-CDL description of airline ticket process is drawn in Fig. 5.

From this description, we define our services: the Traveler and the ARS, and the various interactions between them described by the choreography tag that presents the heart of the Web services choreography.

As shown in the figure, it is a first single interaction entitled "TripOrder" that presents the reservation request by the traveler. Then a choice of two inter-actions: Either the booking is made so the traveler pays the ticket (interaction

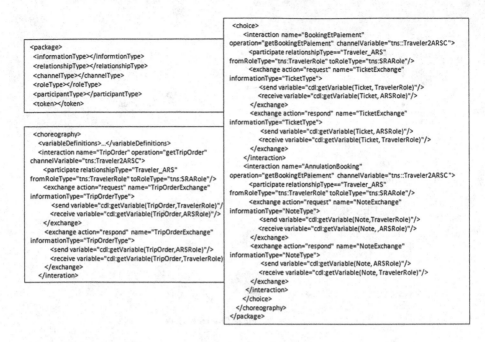

**Fig. 5.** WS-CDL specification of the airline reservation process

"BookingEtPayement") or the reservation is canceled (interaction "Annulation-Booking").

### 4.2   Generation of the oWF-nets Based Model

After analyzing the WS-CDL specification, the formal representation of the specific choreography is generated based on the applying of the mapping discussed in Sect. 3. As mentioned in the preliminary section, we especially used open workflow nets to model Web services which communicate with other services.

Open workflow nets (oWF-nets) result from the extension of workflow nets (WF-nets) by adding external places for the communication of the external environment of the considered Web services [3]. A WF-net is a Petri net with two special places: input place i containing initially x tokens (x is the number of instances ready for execution) and a final place f. In a WF-net, each node is in a path from i to f. For the choreography of Web services, each Web service is modeled by an oWF-net describing the control flow between the tasks ensured by this service and containing interface places used to communicate with other Web services. The overall obtained model is a Petri net with a set of input places, a set of output places and a set of interface places.

For our example, the model based on oWF-nets is shown in Fig. 6.

This model describes the interactions between Web services, mentioned previously, through the exchanged messages TripOrderExchange, TicketExchange and NoteExchange.

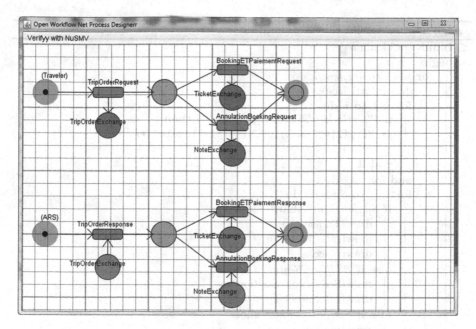

**Fig. 6.** oWF-net model of Airline reservation process

This generation is done according to algorithm 1, knowing that $PT$ represents an array of services and $S$ represents the array of interactions for each service.
In this algorithm, we assume the following definitions:

- $Int$ : a transition will be drawn with its input interface if the service is the receiver or output if the service is the sender.
- $SeqInt$ : a series of transitions will be displayed with corresponding interfaces according to the role of the service. A sequence has at least two interactions.
- $ChInt$ : if the service is involved in two different interactions with two different services and has to choose between them, so two arrows will be drawn each one is followed by a transition and its appropriate interface.
- $ChSeqInt$ : the same principle of "ChInt" except that it is a sequence of transitions to draw.
- $ParaInt$ : if the service is involved in two interactions that take place at the same time. So two arrows will be drawn each one is followed by a place and a transition with appropriate interface.
- $ParaSeqInt$ : the same principle of "ParaInt" except that it is a sequence of transitions to draw.

### 4.3   Formal Verification of the Model

Once we have a model based on oWF-nets of a WS-CDL specification, we propose to proceed to a formal verification of this model. For this, we choose to adopt an approach based on model checking [5], and then, we proceed to specify in CTL [4]

---

**Algorithme 1 .** oWF-nets generation

---

**Input** : pt,i,k,n:integer
**begin**
    **for** $pt=1$ **to** $PT.length$ **do**
        draw(StartPlace);
        **for** $i=1$ **to** $n$ **do**
            **if** $PT[pt]=M[i][2]$ or $PT[pt]=M[i][3]$ **then**
            /* M[i][2]="FromRole",M[i][3]="ToRole" */
                fill(S);
            **end if**
        **end for**
        **for** $k=1$ **to** $S.lenght$ **do**
            **if** $S[k][0]="Int"$ **then**
                draw(Transition);
                draw(InterfaceO/I);
                draw(place);
            **else if** $S[k][0]="SeqInt"$ **then**
                draw(SequenceTransition);
                draw(InterfaceO/I);
            **else if** $S[k][0]="ChInt"$ **then**
                draw(place);
                draw(ChoiceTransition);
                draw(InterfaceO/I);
            **else if** $S[k][0]="ChSeqInt"$ **then**
                draw(ChoiceSequenceTransition);
                draw(InterfaceO/I);
            **else if** $S[k][0]="ParaInt"$ **then**
                draw(ParallelTransition);
                draw(InterfaceO/I);
            **else if** $S[k][0]="ParaSeqInt"$ **then**
                draw(ParallelSequenceTransition);
                draw(InterfaceO/I);
            **else**                /* "FinalizerBlock/ExceptinoBlock" */
                draw(Transition);
                draw(InterfaceO/I);
                draw(EndPlace);
            **end if**
        **end for**
    **end for**
**end**

---

properties of interest and automatically check them by NuSMV model checker. Before this CTL model checking, we translate the oWF-nets based model to SMV language (the input language for NuSMV model checker) [14].

We implemented the automatic verification of any CTL property and especially we implemented the analysis of compatibility property. We studied different classes of compatibility such as those proposed in [20]: weak compatibility, compatibility and strong compatibility.

For example for the weak compatibility, a composite system N which does not suffer from deadlock problem is said weakly compatible.

$$\text{weak compatibility} \Leftrightarrow \text{deadlock-freeness}$$

It is necessary to ensure that each final place is reached to deduce that there is no deadlock encountered. In CTL, this stand for checking the following formula:

$$A(not\ deadlock\ U\ P)$$

Where $P$ is a proposition on marking asserting the following:

$$\underset{s=1}{\overset{n}{\&}}\,(M(f_s) > 0)$$

And *deadlock* is a variable (boolean) which is defined in the $TRANS$ section of the SMV specification. It is $True$ only if all places and transitions remain unchangeable.

This announces that for all the possible executions, we will attend, from every state, a state where all the final places of the services involved are marked.

Note also that n is the number of involved services and $f_s$ is the final place of a service s.

We automated the mapping to SMV and the invocation of NuSMV to verify CTL properties on the SMV model in our platform D&A4WSC [13].

The Fig. 7 presents the result returned by NuSMV model checker when checking for weak compatibility of the airline reservation process.

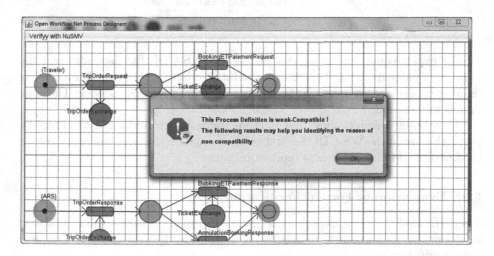

**Fig. 7.** Result of choreography verification

# 5    Approach Evaluation

In this section, we expose experiments made on different choreographies by extending the size of the WS-CDL file by increasing the number of participating services and the number of interactions per service. These experiments are made with an Intel Core Duo microprocessor 3, 2.10 GHZ and 4 GHZ memory.

## 5.1    Complexity of Modeling Algorithm

We now study the complexity of our modeling algorithm (Algorithm 1) which consists of two loops "for". The first loop concern the number of services and the second presents the number of interactions for each service. If we suppose that $i$ (resp $j$) is the number of operations made by the first loop (resp. the second loop), then the complexity is in the order of $O(i*j)$.

In order to confirm this study, we did experiments on some choreographies presented in Table 1.

**Table 1.** Time spent to generate oWF-nets model

| Nb of services | Nb of interactions | | | | |
|---|---|---|---|---|---|
| | 2 | 5 | 10 | 20 | 40 |
| 2 | 10 | 30 | 55 | 70 | 110 |
| 5 | 30 | 40 | 65 | 80 | 130 |
| 10 | 40 | 80 | 135 | 190 | 215 |
| 20 | 60 | 130 | 190 | 240 | 332 |
| 40 | 120 | 203 | 330 | 409 | 580 |
| 50 | 280 | 350 | 410 | 452 | 590 |

For experiments, we varied the size of the WS-CDL file depending on the number of participants and the number of interactions per service. For a specific number of services, we increase the number of interactions per service. The time unit is millisecond.

The obtained results show that the time increases proportionally and rapidly rising the size of the WS-CDL file and we can conclude that our translator allows to generate complex oWF-nets representations.

## 5.2    Evaluation of Formal Verification

We performed the same experiments previously made to assess the time issued for formal verification and the results are summarized in the Table 2. The time unit is millisecond.

The time changes proportionally with the number of participating services and the number of interactions per service and take more than an hour to see the result. This delayed response of the model checker is explained by the large

**Table 2.** Time spent to formal verification

|  | Nb Interactions | | | | |
| --- | --- | --- | --- | --- | --- |
| Nb Service | 2 | 5 | 10 | 20 | 40 |
| 2 | 3623 | 4140 | 6376 | 32905 | +2h |
| 5 | 4118 | 6943 | 260228 | 2216708 | +3h |
| 10 | 11725 | 446525 | 4061865 | 10121332 | +3h |
| 20 | 112280 | +5h | +5h | +5h | +5h |

number of participating services and the large number of interactions per service. These experiments show therefore that even the choreography becomes more complex, the verification is well assured.

# 6   Related Work

Formal approaches are used in analyzing and verifying properties of Web services choreography. Xiangpeng et al. [21] proposed a language called CDL, which covers the functionality of WS-CDL regarding the roles of participants and collaboration between those roles. Subsequently, they applied the model-checking technique to verify the accuracy of a given CDL specification, translating it into Promela, the input language of Spin model checker. However, to use this approach, developers would need to know a new language to understand the collaboration of Web services within a choreography. In addition, the properties to be checked are expressed by temporal logic LTL which does not quantify all execution paths.

Pu et al. [18] defined an approach that uses Java as a modeling language for WS-CDL specification. Then, they applied the Java Path Finder model checker (JPF) by adding a keyword Assert as an activity to check whether the specification complies with the requirements and assertion checking as well as the deadlock property expressed in LTL. However, the defined Java model can not provide a clear representation of the interactions in a choreography. In addition, it requires user effort by adding the keyword Assert to facilitate the verification process, which presents a barrier for its use.

Foster et al. [11] presented an approach to verify safety properties, deadlock and liveness of a composite Web service. Indeed, this approach is based on modeling a WS-CDL choreography as a message sequence chart (MSC) which will be transformed into a finite state process (FSP). From this description FSP, the authors generate the LTS model that will be taken as input by the LTSA model checker to verify the desired properties. However, the message sequence charts (MSC) provide a static view for a specific scenario therefore can not be effective to represent the sets of scenarios contained in WS-CDL. In addition, LTSA does not provide a counter example in order to locate the source of eventual error.

E. Caliz et al. [7] presented an approach based on the transformation of a specification in a colored Petri net (CP-nets) as an intermediate model. Then, it will be analyzed using formal verification and simulation environment provided by CPN Tools. However, this approach requires that developers should interpret the result report of properties and must have knowledge of the modeling language.

Finally, Diaz et al. [10] defined an approach that translates a given WS-CDL specification to a timed automata as an intermediate model to verify the accuracy of Web services generated with the model checker UPPAAL. However, timed automata can not handle errors and exceptions of a composite Web service and the objective of the authors was to generate WS-BPEL documents and not necessarily to analyze and verify WS-CDL specifications.

# 7    Conclusion

We presented in this paper a formal approach of Web services choreography analysis. This choreography is described in Web Services-Choreography Description Language (WS-CDL). Due to the expressive power of Petri nets, we proposed to translate a WS-CDL specification into a composition of open workflow nets which stand for a sub class of Petri nets dedicated to model processes communicating with partners and to ensure the communication between services via interface places. Then, we apply a model checking on this composition to check for behavioral properties such as compatibility of Web services. These properties are described in Computation Tree Logic (CTL) and verified by NuSMV model checker. In case of failure, NuSMV generates a counter example that we analyse and present to the user in order to help him to find the error and then to correct the process. We benefited from model checking as a powerful technique to verify and to detect the eventual errors at an early stage.

This research contributes to the Web services domain, by extending application of open Workflow nets modeling technique to analyze Web service choreography specifications. We have shown that our platform can translate and verify complex WS-CDL specifications.

Towards the semantics and verification of full WS-CDL, oWFnets focus on just a few key issues related to Web service choreography. The goal in the design of oWFnets is to make the proof of their properties as concise as possible, while still capturing the core features of WS-CDL. The features of WS-CDL that oWFnet models include information Type, participant Type,token, variables, activities (control-flow and interaction), choreography, exception and finalize blocks. oWFnets omits some advanced features such as activities(workunit, skip, assignment). Other features missing from oWFnets include basic types (channel Type and relationship type), token locator, expressions and some basic activities such as silent and perform.

Extending oWFnets to include more features of WS-CDL will be one direction of our further work. ALso, we investigate to integrate time constraints in modeling and verifying of choreography and we propose to study other qualitative as well as quantitative properties of Web services choreography and orchestration.

# References

1. Cimatti, A., Clarke, E., Giunchiglia, E., Giunchiglia, F., Pistore, M., Roveri, M., Sebastiani, R., Tacchella, A.: NuSMV 2: an opensource tool for symbolic model checking. In: Brinksma, E., Larsen, K.G. (eds.) CAV 2002. LNCS, vol. 2404, pp. 359–364. Springer, Heidelberg (2002)
2. van der Aalst, W.M.P.: Verification of workflow nets. In: Azéma, P., Balbo, G. (eds.) ICATPN 1997. LNCS, vol. 1248, pp. 407–426. Springer, Heidelberg (1997)
3. van der Aalst, W.: The application of petri nets to workflow management. J. Circuits Syst. Comput. **8**, 21–66 (1998)
4. Antonik, A., Huth, M.: Efficient patterns for model checking partial state spaces in CTL intersection LTL. Electr. Notes Theor. Comput. Sci. **158**, 41–57 (2006)
5. Baier, C., Katoen, J.P.: Principles of Model Checking (Representation and Mind Series). The MIT Press, Cambridge (2008)
6. Barkaoui, K., Ben Ayed, R., Sbaï, Z.: Workflow soundness verification based on structure theory of petri nets. Int. J. Comput. Inf. Sci. (IJCIS) **5**(1), 51–61 (2007)
7. Caliz, E., Umapathy, K., Sánchez-Ruíz, A.J., Elfayoumy, S.A.: Analyzing web service choreography specifications using colored petri nets. In: Jain, H., Sinha, A.P., Vitharana, P. (eds.) DESRIST 2011. LNCS, vol. 6629, pp. 412–426. Springer, Heidelberg (2011)
8. Cimatti, A., Clarke, E.M., Giunchiglia, F., Roveri, M.: NuSMV: a new symbolic model checker. Int. J. Softw. Tools Technol. Transfer **2**(4), 410–425 (2000)
9. Decker, G., Overdick, H., Zaha, J.M.: On the suitability of WS-CDL for choreography modeling. In: Proceedings of Methoden, Konzepte Und Technologien Fur Die Entwicklung Von Dienstebasierten Informationssystemen (EMISA 2006) (2006)
10. Diaz, G., Cambronero, M.E., Pardo, J.J., Valero, V., Cuartero, O.: Model checking techniques applied to the design of web services (2007)
11. Foster, H., Uchitel, S., Magee, J., Kramer, J.: Model-based analysis of obligations in web service choreography. In: International Conference on Internet and Web Applications and Services (AICT-ICIW 2006), IEEE Computer Society (2006)
12. Frappier, M., Fraikin, B., Chossart, R., Chane-Yack-Fa, R., Ouenzar, M.: Comparison of model checking tools for information systems. In: Dong, J.S., Zhu, H. (eds.) ICFEM 2010. LNCS, vol. 6447, pp. 581–596. Springer, Heidelberg (2010)
13. Guerfel, R., Sbaï, Z.: D&A4WSC as a design and analysis framework of web services composition. In: Proceedings of the International Workshop on Petri Nets and Software Engineering (PNSE 2014), in conjunction with Petri nets and ACSD, pp. 337–338 (2014)
14. Guerfel, R., Sbaï, Z., Barkaoui, K.: Modeling and formal verification framework of web services composition. Int. Conf. Control Eng. Inf. Technol. (CEIT 2013) **2**, 140–145 (2013)
15. Henzinger, T., Nicollin, X., Sifakis, J., Yovine, S.: Symbolic model checking for real-time systems. Inf. Comput. **111**(2), 193–244 (1994)
16. Hongli, Y., Xiangpeng, Z., Zongyan, Q., Geguang, P., Shuling, W.: A formal model of web service choreography description language(WS-CDL. Technical report) (2006)
17. Massuthe, P., Reisig, W., Schmidt, K.: An operating guideline approach to the SOA. Ann. Math. Comput. Teleinformatics **1**, 35–43 (2005)
18. Pu, G., Shi, J., Wang, Z., Jin, L., Liu, J., He, J.: The validation and verification of WSCDL. In: Asia-Pacific Software Engineering Conference. IEEE, Los Alamitos. pp. 81–88 (2007)

19. Sbaï, Z., Barkaoui, K.: Vérification formelle des processus workflow - extension aux workflows inter-organisationnels. Revue Ingnierie des Systmes d'Information (ISI) **18**(5), 33–57 (2013)
20. Sbaï, Z., Barkaoui, K.: On compatibility analysis of inter organizational business processes. In: Barjis, J., Pergl, R. (eds.) EOMAS 2014. LNBIP, vol. 191, pp. 171–186. Springer, Heidelberg (2014)
21. Xiangpeng, Z., Hongli, Y., Chao, C., Xiwu, D., Zongyan, Q.: Verification of WS-CDL choreography. In: Asian Working Conference on Verified Software. UNU-IIST, Macao SAR, China (2006)

# ICNETS: Towards Designing Inter-Cloud Workflow Management Systems by Petri Nets

Sofiane Bendoukha[1], Hayat Bendoukha[2], and Daniel Moldt[1]([✉])

[1] Theoretical Foundations of Computer Science, Department of Informatics,
University of Hamburg, Hamburg, Germany
{sbendoukha,moldt}@informatik.uni-hamburg.de
[2] Department of Computer Science, Faculty of Mathematics and Computer Science,
University of Science and Technology USTOMB, Oran, Algeria
bendoukhayat@univ-usto.dz

**Abstract.** The design of a Cloud ecosystem is usually tackled in technical way and it is vendor-dependent. There is a lack of conceptual foundation to specify the processes (workflows) running in the Cloud and their life-cycle. Furthermore, enabling workflows in such an environment still encounter many obstacles regarding workflow definition, deployment and execution. In fact, each Cloud provider has its own specification and APIs, which affects negatively their accessibility for both Cloud developers and Cloud consumers. The objective of this paper is to address these issues differently by introducing the Inter-Cloud Nets (ICNETS), which are a set of Petri net-based modeling and implementation techniques to specify Cloud-based workflows and their management. Our work aims at reducing the complexity of designing and implementing components that target Inter-Cloud environments. Moreover, we provide practical examples clarifying the concepts discussed through the paper. The examples are related to the remote sensing domain and implemented over a private Cloud based on the OpenStack framework. Another feature of this work is to avoid interoperability issues when developing Inter-Cloud based applications. For this purpose, we provide a supplementary layer to retrieve services from different Cloud providers.

**Keywords:** Inter-Cloud · Workflows · Petri nets · Modeling · Multi-agent systems · Grid computing

## 1 Introduction

The Cloud technology is a recent computing paradigm, which has been defined by NIST [12]: *"a model for enabling convenient, on-demand network access to a shared pool of configurable computing resources (e.g., networks, servers, storage, applications, and services) that can be rapidly provisioned and released with minimal management effort or service provider interaction"*. Nevertheless, complex applications require several services that a single Cloud is not able to satisfy. Unavailability of a Cloud service may lead to unsatisfied contracts established

© Springer International Publishing Switzerland 2015
J. Barjis et al. (Eds.): EOMAS 2015, LNBIP 231, pp. 187–198, 2015.
DOI: 10.1007/978-3-319-24626-0_14

between Cloud providers and Cloud consumers. Therefore, Inter-Cloud computing is considered as the next natural evolution of Cloud computing [15]. There
are two terms to design the Inter-Cloud: *Federations* and *Multi-Clouds* [15].
The term *Federations* deals more with interoperability and *Multi-Clouds* with
the portability of the applications between the Clouds. The research on the
Inter-Cloud is still at an early stage of development. A semi-automated process
to guide consumers to work with different Clouds based on monitoring tools for
the quality of services, is unfortunately not yet technically possible. The main
challenges for the emerging Inter-Cloud Computing identified up to now are
application and data interoperability and portability, governance and management, service metering and monitoring, as well as security.

Hence, the construction of such complex systems remains a problem as soon
as there are several independent partners involved in the design and the execution of these systems. What is missing is the support of processes in this
environments. For complex systems with independent partner expressive and
powerful software systems have to be provided.

Workflow concepts are strong candidates to address the previous issues. Their
advantage is the automation of processes and efficient coordination and collaboration between various entities composing the system. However, Workflow
Management Systems (WfMS) usually do not address the special aspects of
Cloud-based systems. New concepts and constructs to overcome this problem
are necessary. Therefore, this work provides a conceptual and technical solution for the modeling and design of complex systems in Cloud-like environments
with a special emphasis on processes. Our contribution consists of the introduction of the Inter-Cloud NETS (ICNETS). The ICNETS are predefined Petri net
structures that allow modeling of Cloud-based workflows and the management
system. By ICNETS, we introduce a new form of Petri net *places/transitions*.
The latter have specific functionalities, which consist of invoking Coud services
directly from the net. The complexity of the (Inter-) Cloud environment is hidden
by a gateway layer. Furthermore, Cloud developers and Cloud consumers will
not be confronted to issues like model transformation (instantiating the system
and the processes) or interoperability. In this paper we emphasize on workflow
modeling, service discovery and Cloud service brokerage then deployment, monitoring and migration of applications. In order to illustrate their usability, *data*
management operations have been implemented by ICNETS. The operations
include allocating and accessing containers and objects in the Cloud.

The remainder of the paper is organized as follows. In Sect. 2 we present some
related work and compare it to our approach. In Sect. 3 we discuss a motivating
scenario that will be used through the paper. Section 4 provides an overview
about Grid-based WfMSs. ICNETS are presented in Sect. 5, the architecture we
propose for Cloud-based workflow management is introduced in Sect. 6. Finally,
Sect. 7 concludes the paper and discusses future work.

## 2    Related Work

In term of specification of Cloud-based applications and systems, the Cloud Modeling Language (Cloud) is a tool-supported domain-specific language (DSL) [8].

It relies on model-driven techniques and methods and allows developers to model the provisioning and deployment of a multi-Cloud application at two levels of abstraction: (i) the Cloud Provider-Independent Model (CPIM), which specifies the provisioning and deployment of a multi-Cloud application in a Cloud provider-agnostic way; (ii) the Cloud Provider-Specific Model (CPSM), which refines the CPIM and specifies the provisioning and deployment of a multi-Cloud application in a Cloud provider-specific way [8]. The strength of CloudML is that the description of the deployment is causally connected to the real running system: any change on the description can be enacted on demand on the system, and, conversely, any change occurring in the system is automatically reflected in the model.

The Cloud Application Modeling Language (CAML) [4] enables representing Cloud-based deployment topologies directly in the Unified Modeling Language (UML) and refining them with Cloud offerings captured by dedicated UML profiles. In general, the purpose of CAML is (i) to enable the representation of models from the reverse engineering perspective and the forward engineering perspective and (ii) to provide guidance in terms of optimization patterns for turning Cloud independent models into Cloud specific models from which Cloud optimized application code can be generated as a prerequisite for the deployment on the selected Cloud environment.

The EU-funded mOSAIC[1] project [11] proposes a complementary solution based on software agents and semantic data processing. It allows transparent and simple access to heterogeneous Cloud resources and to avoid vendor lock-in. It fulfills this goal by its Cloud ontology that describes services and their interfaces. Moreover, a unified cross platform API that is platform and language independent is provided by mOSAIC. The mOSAIC platform is targeted mainly at Cloud application developers. The mOSAIC approach is based on a *Cloud Agency* gathering client and provider agents in a brokerage process working with service level agreements [3]. It is used as a Multi-Cloud resource management middle-ware, it plays the role of run-time environment in the model-driven engineering project named MODAClouds [2]. MODAClouds, a MOdel-Driven Approach for the design and execution of applications on multiple Clouds that aims at supporting system developers and operators in exploiting multiple Clouds and in migrating their applications from Cloud to Cloud as needed. To do so, MODA-Clouds proposes an advanced quality-driven design, development and operation method based on the Model-Driven Development (MDD) paradigm.

## 3   Motivating Example

In order to introduce the features that ICNETS can deliver to both Cloud consumers and developers, we consider an example related to the remote sensing domain. Consider a scenario where we have to implement an image processing workflow (see Fig. 1) such as image classification[2]. Due to unavailability

---

[1] http://www.mosaic-fp7.eu/ (Last accessed 15.02.2015).

[2] Image classification refers to the task of extracting information classes from a multi-spectral raster image. The resulting raster from image classification can be used to create thematic maps.

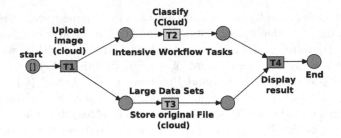

**Fig. 1.** Cloud-based image processing workflow

of required softwares or performance issues at local site, the workflow holders decided to adopt a Cloud-based solution. The workflow holders are provided with a graphical user interface (GUI)[3] for uploading/submission of the workflow and the required data. Consequently, the entity that performs the classification as well as the required data are hosted in the Cloud. The objective of this section is not to explain the classification process itself but only to show the features of the ICNETS for modeling/running such kind of workflows.

The life-cycle of this workflow can be summarized as follows:

- (T1) Cloud consumers upload all required images to the *selected Cloud*
- (T2) on the *selected Cloud*, specific softwares or Web services perform the classification and generate another image as a result
- (T3) in parallel with (T2), the original image is for security stored in a Cloud-based database
- (T4) the resulted (classified) image is communicated to the Cloud consumers

Although the above workflow looks straightforward in term of complexity. Executing workflow tasks in a Cloud environment or invoking Cloud services requires special skills. Adopting a Cloud solution has also many challenges. Which Cloud provider to select for the execution of the workflow tasks? How one can use services from different Cloud providers? These are questions that should be answered prior the implementation. These issues apply for both Cloud developers and Cloud consumers. Concerning the example scenario, transitions T1, T2 and T3 require Cloud services. To retrieve these services, an appropriate selection mechanism needs to be available in order to select the best Cloud provider that fits their requirements. Furthermore, Cloud consumers should be able to express their requirements properly (at design time). Another important issue is Cloud interoperability. With the growth of the Cloud computing technology there are currently a plenty of Cloud providers. Each of these providers has its own data models, interfaces, authentication and authorization mechanisms. Thus programming against the Cloud is arduous. There should be a strategy to communicate with different Cloud providers. A run-time API (vendor independent) is the appropriate solution for this issue. Our approach strives to overcome the issues mentioned above and to provide a user-friendly environment for the development of Cloud-based applications. This is discussed in the following section.

---

[3] Web or desktop, both are possible.

# 4    Grid-Based Workflow Management Systems

As the origin of Cloud computing is Grid computing, there are several similarities between both computing paradigms. Workflow management is no exception. Thus, current Cloud-based WfMS are extensions of Grid workflow systems. Yu et al. give a detailed taxonomy of workflow management systems [17] based on workflow design, workflow scheduling, fault management and data movement. The study includes also a characterization and classification of different approaches for building and executing workflows on Grids. Korupa et al. [10] give a model of grid-based workflow management systems. The latter register their services in the grid information service to perform role resolution. The WfMSs belong to different organizations and they are responsible of scheduling and monitoring of their own tasks. It is the same for the grid nodes which perform local scheduling on the basis of the work lists they get from the WfMSs. In this model, one resource can hold several work lists. Hence, further scheduling parameters need to be included such as priority and deadlines. They also outline existing Grid worklfow systems with key features and differences. The development of distributed and scientific workflow systems with grid paradigm has significantly grown during the last decade. A workflow enactment service can be built on top of the low level grid middleware (eg. Globus Toolkit[4], Condor [14] and UNICORE[5], through which the workflow management system invokes services provided by grid resources [17]. At both the build-time and run-time phases, the state of the resources and applications can be retrieved from grid information services. There are actually many grid workflow management systems in use; in the following a few examples of such systems: Pegasus[6], Taverna[7], Kepler[8], GridFlow[9] and Triana[10]. The new features introduced in this paper concern mainly the build-time level. Here we have proven that reference nets and RENEW can be also utilized for modeling scientific workflows. Moreover, unlike Grid systems which are originally free of charge, we provide a mechanism that allows Client customers to specify their workflows and most important their requirements in term of budget. At run time, our approach provide a user-friendly platform to execute workflows in different Clouds.

# 5    Inter-Cloud NETS

In this section we introduce the ICNETS and their role in the architecture that we propose in Sect. 6. As their name indicates, ICNETS are based on Petri nets. Petri nets are a simple, graphical modeling formalism with a strong mathematical

---

[4] http://www.globus.org/toolkit/ (Last access 20.03.2015).
[5] http://www.unicore.eu/.
[6] http://pegasus.isi.edu/.
[7] http://www.taverna.org.uk/.
[8] https://kepler-project.org (Last access 20.04.2015).
[9] http://gridflow.ca/ (Last access 15.09.2014).
[10] http://www.trianacode.org/ (Last access 10.12.2014).

basis. Their efficiency for workflow modeling does not need to be proven [1]. Nevertheless, traditional Petri nets only allow modeling control flow[11]. Furthermore, the resulted workflow model usually needs a translation to an intermediary (executable) model in order to be instantiated and executed by a workflow engine. Therefore, we use a special kind of Petri nets called reference nets [9], which combine the *nets-in-nets* paradigm [16] and *synchronous channels* from [6]. Reference nets play an important role in this work. Firing a transition can also create a new instance of a subnet in such a way that a reference to the new net will be put as a token into a place. This allows for a specific, hierarchical nesting of networks, which is helpful for building complex systems in these formalisms. We exploit this feature for the implementation of the architecture presented in Sect. 6. The components are in form of Petri nets models communicating with each other through synchronous channels.

With respect to traditional *Petri nets* or even reference nets, we introduce new kinds of *place/transition*. The new *places/transitions* can be distinguished by their color. Their principle role is to separate between ordinary activities and those requiring Cloud services for their execution. For the latter, a whole mechanism has been implemented to allow the interaction with different Cloud providers. In general, there are two category of places/transitions: *storage places/transitions* and *compute places/transitions*. Moreover, there are also special arcs to rely these new elements. These arcs allow an appropriate connection between the places and the transitions. For example a *storage place* can only be connected with a *storage transition*. There is also the notion of *Type* for the information passed to the transitions. *Storage places* contain mostly data to be stored in the Cloud and the *compute places* hold script file to be executed in the Cloud. The first category concerns all workflow tasks making use of Cloud-based storage services and the second category involves all tasks related to computing activities. These new *places/transitions* are clearly identified in Fig. 2. In that example, only *storage places/transitions* are highlighted with yellow color and blue color respectively.

In order to illustrate the features of ICNETS, we have implemented some workflows dealing with storage in the Cloud. These workflows consist on performing some data transfer and management on an OpenStack Cloud. With respect to the motivating example from Sect. 3 the data handled within the operations are satellite images. These operations (models) can be *reused* on-demand and be part of another workflow. Moreover, they can communicate with each other, instantiate new nets through *synchronous channels*[12]. We also implemented a *CloudGateway* to avoid interoperability issues and to invoke Cloud services from

---

[11] A workflow schema is a combination of three essential dimensions: control flow, data flow, and resource flow.

[12] Synchronous channel inscriptions consist of two types of inscriptions, *up-links* and *down-links*. Up-links are used in object nets while down-links in system nets. They consist of at least two transitions where one of the transitions is seen as the initiator of the communication having a down-link inscription.

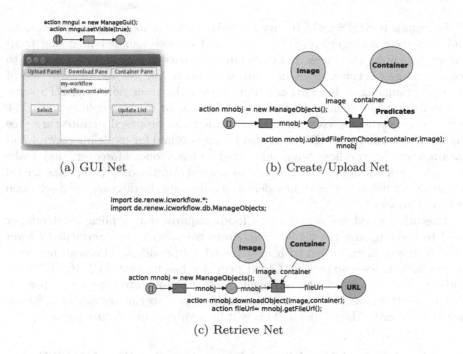

Fig. 2. Cloud operations with ICNETS (Color figure online)

different Cloud providers. For that purpose we integrated the *jclouds*[13] library, which simplifies the support to migration and multiple deployment of applications on different Cloud providers and provides a unified programming interface to access Cloud resources. The library is divided into two categories, one for *compute* and the other for *blob* storage like Amazon S3. During the modeling phase, developers just need to specify the Cloud provider that they require. The rest is performed by the *CloudGateway*. Each operation has a number of parameters. In the context of image processing, the important inputs are: the image and the container where the image is stored. Figure 2 shows some of the operations modeled by the ICNETS. In our approach, all the behavior is captured by reference nets. The latter should be executed/simulated to perform the Cloud operations. For example, executing the first net (Fig. 2a) triggers the display of the GUI, thus Cloud consumers can select the image to upload/retrieve and also in which container is considered. After the specification of these two parameters, their values are passed to the correspondent net. In this figure, the values are required for the upload and the retrieve nets (Fig. 2c and b respectively).

For now, the operations specified by ICNETS concerned only the Cloud consumers. They allow them to model the workflow and to specify the parameters. Nevertheless, The ICNETS have another functionality, which is the design and the implementation of the Cloud-based system, that manages the workflows. This will be illustrated in the following section.

---

[13] https://jclouds.apache.org/ (last access date: 05.02.2015).

In resume ICNETS make it easy to design complex Inter-Cloud applications and also their management. They are based on well-founded modeling techniques, which are Petri nets and especially reference nets. The latter permit to reduce the gap between modeling and implementation, by allowing the use of Java programming as inscription language over the transitions. ICNETS serve to specify/implement internal and external behavior of the whole system. The behavior concerns the components composing the proposed architecture (see Fig. 3). Furthermore, ICNETS can also be appropriate for modeling control and data flow of the workflow being submitted to the Cloud. Moreover, they make it easier for modelers and developers to orchestrate (invoke) composite Cloud services from different Cloud providers and automate the discovery and selection of Cloud providers.

Executing workflows in different Clouds requires that application developer need to code against the Cloud. Therefore, we provide an intermediary layer to allow the communication with multiple Cloud providers. This feature avoids vendor lock-in issue since each Cloud provider has its own API. ICNETS are both the conceptual and the technical basis of the architecture we propose in Sect. 6. Furthermore, we are actively working on the elaboration of a formal model to describe the ICNETS. This will be a subject of a future paper.

# 6    Cloud-Based Workflow Management with ICNETS

In this section we present the second feature of ICNETS, which is the design and the implementation of the system that manages the workflows mentioned above. It describes the entities responsible of workflow submission, deployment and execution in an Inter-Cloud environment.

## 6.1    Architecture

The architecture that we propose is depicted in Fig. 3. The components of the architecture are: *CloudBroker*, *CloudPersister*, *CloudRegister*, *WorkflowGUI* and the *CloudGateway*. The components and their roles will be explained gradually as we describe the architecture. As mentioned in the introduction we focus more on process management, (Cloud) service discovery and matching than security or monitoring issues. Before going further, an important information about our approach needs to be taken in account. Most of the components of the architecture and their internal behavior (control flow) are modeled by reference nets. These nets execute tasks only after being instantiated (simulated). The components can communicate with each other, instantiate other components and transmit variables using *synchronous channels*.

Workflow holders start by modeling their workflows using RENEW[14]. Modeling a workflow consists of specifying clearly the control and data flow of the

---

[14] RENEW (www.renew.de) is an editor and simulation tool for different kind of Petri nets especially reference nets.

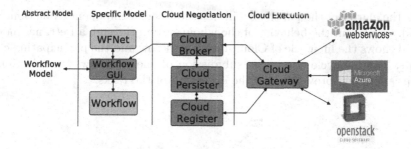

**Fig. 3.** Cloud-based workflow management architecture

tasks. Considering the example presented in Sect. 3, the image path as well as the service needed by the task (storage or compute) need to be communicated. These concrete information can be specified either directly in the *places* as *Strings* or through the *WorkflowGUI*, which provides forms (see Fig. 2a). Such forms can also be provided and handled by the *Workflow* and the *WFNet* plug-ins. These plug-ins are highlighted with different color only to indicate they are not critical for the specification of the workflow but can provide more facility.

The next step is to invoke the *CloudBroker* with the given parameters. A request consists of the required Cloud service and optionally the name of the Cloud provider. The role of the *CloudBroker* is to check for available Cloud providers, (and their actual status) that fit the QoS of the Cloud consumers. For this purpose, it invokes the *CloudPersister* and gets the list of available Cloud providers. This list is communicated to the workflow holder in order to approve the offer or to reject it. This mechanism is exclusively provided by the *WFNet* plug-in.

The *CloudPersister* consists of a central (or distributed) data base (we use mongodb[15] for persistence) that contains useful information about the Cloud providers such as: Id, Name as well as instance and availability status. These informations are obtained by the *CloudRegister*. In opposite to other approaches [5], this is the responsibility of the *CloudRegister* to communicate with the Cloud providers and request information about their status.

The *CloudGateway* is an essential component in the architecture. All the communication with the Cloud providers is performed through this component. Its role is to provide an unified layer to communicate with different Cloud providers regardless of their specifications and APIs. Therefore, we took advantage from current technologies and techniques to hide complexity of an Inter-Cloud ecosystem and provide an interface to most known Cloud providers (Amazon AWS, Openstack, Windows Azure). The *CloudGateway* serves as a gateway for both *CloudRegister* and the *CloudBroker*. It allows the *CloudBroker* to check the availability of a specific Cloud provider and permits to the *CloudBroker* to perform operations on different Clouds. To illustrate this, we performed some Cloud-based operations on a private Cloud managed by *OpenStack* framework.

---

[15] http://www.mongodb.org/ (Last access date 10.01.2015).

For the clarity of the paper we will not show each component's functionality. Instead, we present the behavior of the whole system through a Petri net model. Figure 4 shows the life-cycle of Cloud-based workflow and the participating components. The life-cycle covers the submission of the workflow, the selection of appropriate Cloud providers and the execution of the tasks.

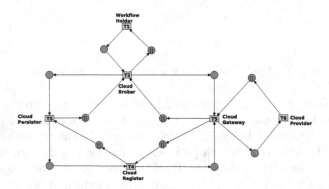

**Fig. 4.** Workflow life-cycle through petri nets

As already mentioned several tasks can be performed by ICNETS. For instance task T4 is responsible of contacting the Cloud provider and get the status of the Cloud instance. Like in the example presented in Sect. 5 the process is coded in Java methods that can be instantiated from the transitions. We have to notice here that this model does not reflect the behavior of each component. Although tasks which are performed by the components are represented by one single transition, the concrete behavior is captured by another net model that should triggered from this transition. This is allowed by using synchronous channels, which permit the instantiation of net models (see Sect. 5).

## 7    Conclusion

In this paper, we proposed a new approach to manage workflows and design Inter-Cloud systems. Our significant contributions are both at conceptual and technical level. We have proven that ICNETS (see Sect. 5), which are based on the reference nets formalism can be a powerful modeling and implementation technique for building complex systems such as Clouds. We proposed an architecture that covers on the one hand Inter-Cloud management issues such as: interoperability and vendor lock-in. On the other hand, workflow concepts have been adopted in order to specify, deploy and execute tasks that make use of Cloud services. Our approach has been tested successfully in a concrete Cloud environment managed by the *OpenStack* framework. The tests consisted of the specification and the execution of storage operations in the Cloud.

The natural next step is to go beyond *Data* management and cover another important aspect, which is process management in the Cloud. Our main objective is to handle processes (workflows) in an Inter-Cloud environment. Thus new functionalities need to be implemented in order to support such *cloudification* of traditional workflows. The entity responsible of managing those process we call it DROP-ENGINE (see Sect. 1). Furthermore, we are investigating the extension of the list of QoS parameters (budget[16] and deadline[17]). Another planed future work consists of providing a formal definition for ICNET. This includes the specification of each element such as the storage and compute places/transitions. Further research directions include the consider the components of the architecture proposed in Sect. 6 as *Agents*. This is possible by using the MULAN/CAPA framework [7, 13]. This framework allows building agent-based applications following the PAOSE approach[18].

# References

1. van der Aalst, W.M.P.: The application of petri nets to workflow management. J. Circ. Syst. Comput. 8(1), 21–66 (1998)
2. Ardagna, D., Di Nitto, E., Mohagheghi, P., Mosser, S., Ballagny, C., D'Andria, F., Casale, G., Matthews, P., Nechifor, C.-S., Petcu, D., Gericke, A., Sheridan, C.: Modaclouds: a model-driven approach for the design and execution of applications on multiple clouds. In: 2012 ICSE Workshop on Modeling in Software Engineering (MISE), pp. 50–56 (2012)
3. Aversa, R., Di Martino, B., Rak, M., Venticinque, S.: Cloud agency: a mobile agent based cloud system. In: Barolli, L., Xhafa, F., Vitabile, S., Hsu, H.-H. (eds.) CISIS 2010, Krakow, Poland, 15–18 February 2010, pp. 132–137. IEEE Computer Society (2010)
4. Bergmayr, A., Troya, J., Neubauer, P., Wimmer, M., Kappel, G.: UML-based cloud application modeling with libraries, profiles, and templates. In: Paige, R.F., Cabot, J., Brambilla, M., Rose, L.M., Hill, J.H. (eds.) Proceedings of the 2nd International Workshop on Model-Driven Engineering on and for the Cloud Co-located with the 17th International Conference on Model Driven Engineering Languages and Systms, CloudMDE@MoDELS 2014, Valencia, Spain, 30 September 2014, CEUR Workshop Proceedings, vol. 1242, pp. 56–65 (2014). CEUR-WS.org
5. Buyya, R., Ranjan, R., Calheiros, R.N.: InterCloud: utility-oriented federation of cloud computing environments for scaling of application services. In: Hsu, C.-H., Yang, L.T., Park, J.H., Yeo, S.-S. (eds.) ICA3PP 2010, Part I. LNCS, vol. 6081, pp. 13–31. Springer, Heidelberg (2010)
6. Christensen, S., Hansen, N.D.: Coloured petri nets extended with channels for synchronous communication. In: Valette, R. (ed.) ICATPN 1994. LNCS, vol. 815, pp. 159–178. Springer, Heidelberg (1994)
7. Duvigneau, M., Moldt, D., Rölke, H.: Concurrent architecture for a multi-agent platform. In: Giunchiglia, F., Odell, J.J., Weiss, G. (eds.) AOSE 2002. LNCS, vol. 2585, pp. 59–72. Springer, Heidelberg (2003)

---

[16] Cost payable for using the Cloud services.
[17] Time taken for application execution.
[18] www.paose.net.

8. Ferry, N., Rossini, A., Chauvel, F., Morin, B., Solberg, A.: Towards model-driven provisioning, deployment, monitoring, and adaptation of multi-cloud systems. In: 2013 IEEE Sixth International Conference on Cloud Computing (CLOUD), pp. 887–894, June 2013

9. Kummer, O.: Referenznetze. Logos Verlag, Berlin (2002)

10. Kuropka, D., Vossen, G., Weske, M.: Workflows in computation grids. In: GCC Workshops, pp. 296–301. IEEE Computer Society (2006)

11. Di Martino, B., Petcu, D., Cossu, R., Goncalves, P., Máhr, T., Loichate, M.: Building a mosaic of clouds. In: Guarracino, M.R., Vivien, F., Träff, J.L., Cannatoro, M., Danelutto, M., Hast, A., Perla, F., Knüpfer, A., Di Martino, B., Alexander, M. (eds.) Euro-Par-Workshop 2010. LNCS, vol. 6586, pp. 571–578. Springer, Heidelberg (2011)

12. Grance, T., Mell, P.: The nist definition of cloud computing. Technical report, National Institute of Standards and Technology, Information Technology Laboratory (2011). http://csrc.nist.gov/publications/nistpubs/800-145/SP800-145.pdf

13. Rölke, H.: Modellierung von Agenten und Multiagentensystemen - Grundlagen und Anwendungen. Agent Technology - Theory and Applications, vol. 2. Logos Verlag, Berlin (2004)

14. Thain, D., Tannenbaum, T., Livny, M.: Distributed computing in practice: the condor experience. Concurrency - Pract. Experience 17(2–4), 323–356 (2005)

15. Toosi, A.N., Calheiros, R.N., Buyya, R.: Interconnected cloud computing environments: challenges, taxonomy, and survey. ACM Comput. Surv. 47(1), 7 (2014)

16. Valk, R.: Petri nets as token objects - an introduction to elementary object nets. In: Desel, J., Silva, M. (eds.) ICATPN 1998. LNCS, vol. 1420. Springer, Berlin Heidelberg (1998)

17. Jia, Y., Buyya, R.: A taxonomy of workflow management systems for grid computing. J. Grid Comput. 3(3–4), 171–200 (2005)

# Interactive Transformation Path Generation Using Business Support Maps

Philipp Diefenthaler[1,2](✉), Melanie Langermeier[2], and Bernhard Bauer[2]

[1] Softplant GmbH, Munich, Germany
philipp.diefenthaler@softplant.de
[2] Software Methodologies for Distributed Systems, University of Augsburg,
Augsburg, Germany
{melanie.langermeier,bernhard.bauer}@informatik.uni-augsburg.de

**Abstract.** Enterprise architecture (EA) management supports transformation path planning to facilitate the change from the current to the target architecture. We create parts of these transformation paths automatically using the information from current and target business support maps. Restrictions on the business support maps, i.e. areas which shall remain stable and which shall be transformed, are modeled by an enterprise architect to allow for a goal oriented transformation path generation. The transformation paths serve as project proposals for the project portfolio management. Necessary changes to the EA are prioritized and estimated. Our solution uses a graph transformation based approach to allow for an interactive creation of possible transformation paths. The transformation paths are the state transitions of a graph transition system, which we create from an EA model. We weigh the effort of each transformation according cost, time and risk.

**Keywords:** Enterprise architecture planning · Graph transformations · Decision support

## 1 Introduction

Diverse challenges drive the need of an enterprise to adapt itself in order to stay competitive. These challenges range from implementing business models, to introducing new technologies, to (re-)engineering business processes to comply with new laws and regulations. Enterprise architecture management (EAM) helps to foster this adaptation by creating transparency on the current enterprise architecture (EA) and collecting demands for change. Based on this transparency EAM creates a target EA and possible transformation paths to reach the target [1]. EA models describe the enterprise and its information technology, including the interdependencies of different artifacts, on an aggregated level [21]. They are used to support the creation of transparency for analyzing and planning changes. Furthermore, they aid in the communication with other decision making domains within the enterprise, like the project portfolio management. By creating alternative transformation paths it is possible to provide decision support and derive

© Springer International Publishing Switzerland 2015
J. Barjis et al. (Eds.): EOMAS 2015, LNBIP 231, pp. 199–213, 2015.
DOI: 10.1007/978-3-319-24626-0_15

changes from the EA models, which serve as project proposals. However, the creation and evaluation of different transformation paths based on the current and target EA model is primarily a manual task. Additionally, several restrictions can be posed on the target EA model which have to be considered during transformation path generation. Furthermore, it is important to allow for the distinction between good and better transformation paths.

Current approaches support only parts of this process, we combine several methods in order to provide a sound decision support for enterprise architects. Therefore, we take a current business support map and restrictions imposed within a target business support map, as a starting point to create different transformation paths by applying graph transformations on them. We consider the model underlying a business support map as part of the EA model. A priori constraints are modeled before the creation of the transformation paths within the target business support map and are considered during the creation. We provide a description of the initial and goal state of the graph transition system. Furthermore, we present the transformation actions which enable the interactive transformation path generation. Weighting factors allow us to differentiate the effort of each transformation action.

## 2    Related Work

EAM can support project portfolio planning with the identification of change projects, that contribute most to the goals of the enterprise and furthermore, the project initialization by EA models that help in scoping projects and avoiding redundant work [3]. Existing work regarding a method and its implementation in order to support portfolio planning based on EA models is scarce. In the following subsections we introduce approaches for information technology (IT) consolidation decision support (1), formalization of actions (2), and tool support (3). Combinations of those research results will be used to build our method.

### 2.1    IT Consolidation in the Context of Enterprise Architecture

Franke et·al. [9] present a binary integer programming approach to optimize the consolidation of applications and their functionality for supporting business processes. Their solution creates an optimal decision on applications which should retain and be removed. Furthermore, the solution considers costs for adding functionality to applications to allow them to support further business processes. Iacob et al. [12] describe how to support IT portfolio valuation based on ArchiMate models. From the current architecture the application costs and possible consolidation costs are derived. The goal is to cut the overall costs to a minimum. Furthermore, the ArchiMate models use constraints which the optimization and the resulting target architecture has to adhere to.

### 2.2    Actions as Possible Transformations

Lautenbacher et al. [13] provide an approach for transformation path generation using an action repository which allows for the creation of sequences of actions.

The sequence is defined by a logical ordering of the actions. A goal state for planning is modeled as an explicit state. Weighing the actions is not considered. Sousa et al. [17] use Action-Threat-Opportunities (ATO) Trees to assess risk and opportunities in a project plan for changing the EA. A goal, e.g. profit, is supported by several architecture principles which in turn are realized by actions. The actions may have risk or opportunities attached to them. The different types of nodes in the tree are the hierarchical levels of a so called planning tree. Nodes at the same hierarchical level are either exclusively disjunctive or conjunctive alternatives that constitute to the upper hierarchy element. Considering risks and opportunities, as the elements at the lowest hierarchy level, allows considering the benefits of actions and therefore to determine the most valuable set of actions.

## 2.3   Tool Supported Planning

Dam et al. [6] present a tool supported approach for change propagation to allow for an evolution of the enterprise architecture. They provide formal repair operations based on first order logic Alloy models to restore the consistency in the models after a user has deleted elements or connections. The inconsistencies can be reasoned in the Alloy models. Their approach is an extension to the Systemic Enterprise Architecture Methodology [20]. Gringel and Postina [10] present a tool supported approach for performing a gap analysis on a current and ideal application landscape. It is coupled to the tool independent Quasar Enterprise approach, which can be used to develop service-oriented application landscapes. To be able to perform their gap analysis it is necessary to model the current application landscape consisting of current application components, current application services, current operations of the application services and business objects. The ideal landscape is modeled with ideal components, ideal services, ideal operations and domains. Based on these two models the tool generates a list of actions. The suggested procedure is to allow an architect to select actions that result in a target architecture. How the different actions interfere with each other is not considered and actions require the ideal landscape with all details modeled to be derivable.

## 3   Preliminaries

In the following we present the preliminaries, required to perform the interactive transformation path generation (Sect. 4). We introduce the EA concepts we rely on as well as the relationships between them. Enterprise architecture modeling is done using business support maps. Section 3.2 provides the meta model used for the representation. Finally we present the derivation and definition of transformation actions.

### 3.1   Enterprise Architecture Model

A *process activity* is part of a business process and it is performed by an employee acting in the responsible *role*. A *role* is responsible for certain tasks within an enterprise and the same employee may act in different roles within different business processes. An *application service* is an implemented functionality that allows to automate tasks or parts thereof. An actual implementation that performs the functionality is called *application*. We use *information services* as an implementation independent concept of an *application service* to express its functionality. Furthermore, we consider *information objects* as part of the EA model. *Information objects* are detailed enough to specify their content, but implementation independent. We consider an *information object* and *information service* as virtual artifacts. Virtual artifacts are neither part of the business nor the IT architecture and are used for decoupling both architectures [2]. It is possible to relate *application services* to present and future process activities and roles, whereas *information services* are only related to future process activities and roles. *Information services* are a means for an enterprise architect to model a demand for business support within a process activity raised by a stakeholder.

## 3.2    Meta Model for Business Support Maps

A landscape map is a visualization based on a model that spans a matrix. Elements of the same type are used for each axis and elements of a certain type populate the cells of the landscape map [19]. In models, which allow only binary relations between elements, the ternary relations underlying the landscape maps are modeled by introducing a cell element for linking axis positions and cell content (c.f. [4]). A special type of landscape maps are business support maps. We call the cell element of the business support maps a business support element. These serve as the starting point for planning purposes. The desired future business support is modeled in the target business support map. They can be used for planning purposes by creating business support maps for different points in time. Enterprise architects use current business support maps for creating transparency on application services and applications currently used in business processes. By doing so an enterprise architect is able to identify redundancies of application services and lacking business support. Within the target business support map enterprise architects express the desired future, which should be realized. They explicitly specify application services to be used or information services for which application services are to be built. Both business support maps can be compared to identify necessary changes using a gap analysis [7]. We focus within this paper on the business support maps considering *process activities* (x-axis) and *roles* (y-Axis) localizing *application services* and *information services*. Figure 1 provides the meta model used to represent an enterprise architecture with a business support map. The current and target business support elements are used to localize *application services*. A process activity localizes a current and target business support element. Target business support elements additionally allow to localize information services.

## 3.3    Definition of Transformation Actions

A transformation action is a formal specification of a change, relevant in transformation path generation. Furthermore, they are models of possible changes and

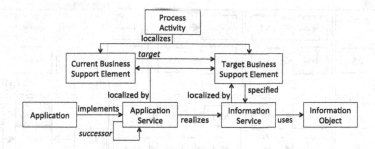

**Fig. 1.** Type graph for the business support maps.

apply changes to the model of an enterprise architecture allowing to explore different transformation paths. For the formalization of transformation actions we use typed graph productions. Typical changes are the removal of redundancies, the population of empty business support elements or explicit replacement. These changes correspond to changes in IT transformations [16] on a different level of detail, as we consider services and not the applications in the first place. A transformation pattern is an abstraction from a modeled situation. The abstraction allows to leverage from individuals to types. Each transformation pattern represents a statement of change or planned stability. From each transformation pattern it is possible to derive necessary changes. An applicable transformation action is an option for a given situation in a current and target business support map that can be deployed. The selected transformation actions that transform the current into the target business support map constitute the transformation path. All possible transformation paths are defined by all sequences of applicable transformation actions. Figure 2 shows seven different transformation patterns that can be present in a business support map using application and information services as localized elements.

An explicit usage of an application service is modeled by an enterprise architect with the transformation patterns (a), (b) and (c) shown in Fig. 2. Transformation pattern (a) states that a certain application service is to be used in the future for a certain business process by a certain role. In contrast (b) specifies that an application service currently in use is not to be used in the future and instead another application service is to be used. (c) states that the business support remains stable. If transformation pattern (d) is present, currently no business support through applications takes place. However, in the future such business support should take place without specifying which certain application service, respectively application is responsible for the support. Transformation pattern (e) states that there is currently no business support and that no change should take place. In contrast transformation pattern (f) states that a business support is to be removed without replacement. With (g) the modeler states that an application service currently supporting the business is to be replaced. However, (g) does not restrict the replacement to a certain application service or application in contrast to transformation pattern (b).

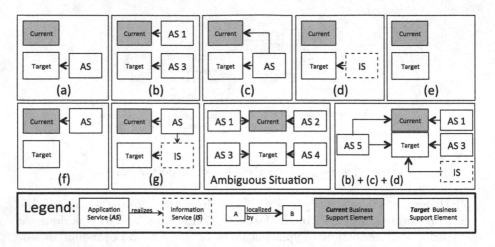

**Fig. 2.** Transformation patterns in business support maps for current and target business support elements with the same localization, including a combined pattern and an ambiguous situation.

These seven transformation patterns are the atomic transformation patterns we assign a meaning to as described above. Through combinations of them, every meaningful change between current and target business support maps is describable. The combination of the transformation patterns (b), (c) and (d), as shown in Fig. 2, has still a meaning that is reconstructable. In contrast Fig. 2 shows an ambiguous situation that could be a combination of several different transformation patterns, for example a combination of patterns (b) and (b) or patterns (a), (a), (f) and (f). For ambiguous situations the intended meaning is not reconstructable and may lead to different interpretations of the model given different stakeholders. In order to ensure that no ambiguous situations are present in an EA model, model consistencies checks at design time can be done using appropriate techniques, for example reasoning [5]. In order to derive a complete set of transformation actions, we analyzed the seven transformation patterns. Every transformation pattern can be specified as graph pattern which in turn serves as the foundation for the specification of transformation actions. In the following we introduce the transformation actions, that are derivable from the transformation patterns shown in Fig. 2. For the transformation patterns (c) and (e) no transformation actions are specified as no changes are to be performed between current and target. The transformation action *replace an application service with an application service* is applicable for transformation pattern (b). Transformation pattern (d) and (g) allow for further transformation actions to be executed. The transformation actions provided here are *functional enhancement of an existing application service, develop new application service for existing application, develop new application service and new application*, and *reuse existing application service*.

All these four transformation actions are alternatives for the transformation patterns (d) and (g). Reusing an existing application service is possible, if an application service in the EA model exists that implements the information service localized by a target business support element. The functional enhancement of an application service corresponds to a realization of an information service with an existing application service. Another alternative is the realization of a new application service via an existing application. Furthermore, it is possible to realize a new application service via a new application to implement the modeled demand for business support, specified through the information service of the target business support map. Through the definition of transformation actions via transformation patterns, we ensure to capture all possible instantiations.

## 4   Interactive Transformation Path Generation

In the following section we introduce the formalisms for the representation of EA models as graphs and transformation actions as graph transitions of a graph transition system. Furthermore, we show how the transformation actions are ranked to differentiate from their efforts and finally explain how the path generation is performed.

### 4.1   EA Models as Graph States

We consider the model of the EA, including models of current and target business support maps, as a directed labeled graph $G = (N, E, source, target, label)$ with a finite set of nodes $(N)$ and edges $(E)$. The source and target function map each edge to its outgoing and incoming node. As a consequence in G the edges are connecting exactly two nodes. The function label allows us to use named edges. Parallel edges with the same label are forbidden, i.e. an edge with a label and the same source and target cannot exist twice in $G$.

### 4.2   Transformation Actions as Graph Transitions

After defining our EA model and meta-model as a graph we now define the graph transition system $GTS = (G_0, TA)$ which allows us to create the transformation paths. Figure 3 shows an abstract $GTS$. Each transformation action $TA = (LHS, RHS, NAC)$ consists of a left-hand side $(LHS)$, a right-hand side $(RHS)$, and a negative application condition $(NAC)$. Each transformation action's $LHS$, $RHS$, and $NAC$ is defined on the type graph through graph patterns, which are matched on each graph G later on. A graph pattern is a triple of the form $(Vt, Et, Vt)$. The triple (*Application Service, realizes, Information Service*) is an example of one graph pattern. The $LHS$ contains all the patterns, which have to be present in $G_*$; whereas the $NAC$ specifies which patterns are not allowed in $G_*$ for $TA$ to be applicable. In contrast the $RHS$ specifies all the patterns to be present in the graph after the application of a transformation action. Furthermore, we state that $LHS \setminus RHS$ are those patterns which are deleted and $RHS \setminus LHS$ those which are created through a transformation action (c.f. [15]). The operator $\setminus$ is in this case defined as a set operator, which removes

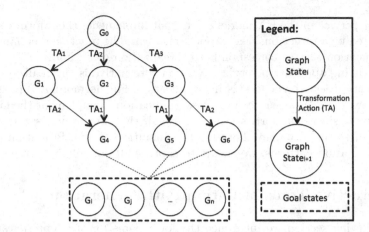

**Fig. 3.** Graph transition system $GTS$ with an initial state $G_0$, applicable transformation actions, and a set of states with goal nodes.

all the patterns present in the second set from the first set. Building the conjunction $LHS \cap RHS$ is the set of patterns that do not change the graph. $NAC$ is used to prohibit the application of a transformation onto any $G_*$ that contains the patterns specified within the negative application condition. The application of a transformation action is a state transition in our $GTS$. Within the $GTS$ the applicability of a transformation action is checked via a graph isomorphism of the specified transformation action to a certain $G_n$ within $GTS$. An applicable transformation action represents an instantiation of a transformation action. We call this applicable action $TA_i$. As a result a transformation action may have several different instantiations in $G_i$. Applying $TA_i$ on $G_i$ results always in the same $G_i + 1$.

## 4.3 Initial and Goal State

The initial state for planning is $G_0$ which is changed through the application of transformation actions. The information necessary for creating $G_0$ is derived automatically from an existing business support map. We define a goal state as a state which allows the execution of a special graph transformation *Planning Finished*, which means that a valid solution has been generated. Even though we use the term state for the termination of the transformation path generation, the state has to satisfy the criteria specified in the *Planning Finished* transformation action instead of being explicitly defined as a state $G_*$ containing specific nodes and edges. Figure 4 shows the nested typed graph pattern for *Planning Finished* that was modeled to provide a stopping rule in transformation path planning. As soon as *Planning Finished* is applicable it is applied automatically and the state is marked as a goal state. The red-dashed rectangles and edges in Fig. 4 represent the $NAC$ of *Planning Finished*. The existential- and all-quantors form a level of nesting for the graph patterns and determine which conditions need to hold for the pattern to match. For details regarding such nesting levels we refer to Habel and Pennemann [11]. Figure 4 was created using the tool GRaphs for Object-Oriented VErification (GROOVE[1]) that we also used to check the soundness of the transformation actions and mappings from existing enterprise architecture models to the graph formalisms. Regarding cyclic and infinite graph transition systems we modeled the transformation actions of $GTS$ in a way that prohibits the recursive application of the same $TA_i$ for every sequence of transformation actions. We realized this by removing and adding information via $LHS$ and $RHS$ of the transformation actions. Furthermore, the upper bound of applicable transformation actions is given by the number of transformation patterns (b), (d) and (g) present in $G_0$.

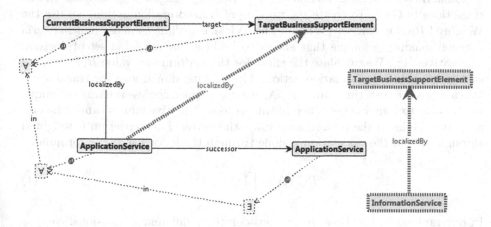

**Fig. 4.** Nested typed graph pattern for *Planning Finished.*

## 4.4 Different Modes of Resource Allocation for Transformation Actions

For the three transformation actions *functional enhancement of an existing application service, develop new application service and new application,* and *develop new application service for existing application* we allow for different modes of resource allocation. We modeled these transformation actions with the same $LHS$ and $RHS$, but with three different execution modes: Normal, double, and quadruple. However, the state resulting from the same transformation in a different mode is the same for all three modes. The transformation actions *reuse existing application service* and *replace an application service with an application service* are not available in different modes, as they consist only of a fixed amount of effort which cannot be varied through raising resource employment. Different resource modes are considered in the ranking of actions (see Table 1) through using different scaling factors. In the double resource mode $s_d$ is used for scaling up the variable costs and $s_t$ for scaling down the variable time. $s_q$ scales up the variable costs in the quadruple resource mode and $s_u$ scales down

---

[1] http://groove.cs.utwente.nl/.

the variable time in the quadruple resource mode. We assume that doubling the resources does not cut the duration time in half and does not result in the same costs as in a lower resource mode. If the scaling factors would be set negative they could be used to scale down the costs or scale up the time. However, this would not reflect reality in projects.

## 4.5    Ranking Applicable Transformation Actions

In order to support the EA architect in selecting transformation actions, we provide a ranking of them. We rank them according to the efforts resulting from a transformation action. Technically the ranking assigns edge weights to the transitions in $GTS$. To create the ranking of transformation actions we use the Weighted Product Model (WPM). The WPM is a dimensionless multi-criteria decision making technique that allows to build a ranking for a set of decision alternatives [18]. We calculate the effort for the performance value $R(P_{PD_{TA}})$ of each applicable transformation action. The ranking dimensions for transformation actions are cost, time, and risk. As we use a dimensionless ranking technique we are able to combine the different dimensions. Negative efforts cannot be created and the lower the performance value the better. Each criterion is weighted through $w_j$ and the calculation is done through the following WPM formula:

$$R(TA) = \prod_{j=1}^{n} (a_{TAj})^{w_j} \qquad (1)$$

In our ranking $n = 3$, because we consider three different dimensions. $a_{TA1}$ is the value for the dimension cost, $a_{TA2}$ as the value for the dimension time, and $a_{TA3}$ as the value for the dimension risk. In order to be able to compute the ranking of the transformation actions it is necessary to acquire the weighting preferences $w_j$ from an enterprise architect for each dimension. Preferences can be derived by either applying ratio comparisons or difference comparisons ([18], Chapters 4 and 5).

For the cost dimension we consider project costs and operation &maintenance costs. These represent the second hierarchical level of the IT cost taxonomy from Närman et al. [14], as estimations on a very detailed level are difficult to make at this point of decision making. Project costs have fixed costs $C_f$ and may have variable costs $C_v$. The operation &maintenance costs are either $C_s$ as expected costs for a new application service and $C_a$ as expected costs for a new application. Those costs may be taken from a service catalogue of the enterprise's IT department. Variable costs depend on factors present in $G_0$. The value for the risk dimension is $Z_P$ and assigns to each transformation action a risk value. The transformation actions *reuse existing application service* and *replace an application service with an application service* have only fixed costs for their application $C_f$. Variable costs $C_v$ are calculated by multiplying the duration time of a transformation action with the costs per time. The complexity of an information object is expressed through the number of schema entries it has. Given these definitions of the variables we are able to create a ranking for

**Table 1.** Ranking efforts of transformation actions in normal, double, and quadruple resource mode.

| Transformation Action | Resource Modes | | |
|---|---|---|---|
| | Normal | Double | Quadruple |
| Replace an application service with an application service | $(C_f \times 2)^{w1} \times$ $(T_f \times 2)^{w2} \times$ $(Z_{P_{ReplaceAS}})^{w3}$ | x | x |
| Reuse existing application service | $(C_f)^{w1} \times (T_f)^{w2} \times$ $(Z_{P_{ReuseAS}})^{w3}$ | x | x |
| Functional enhancement of an existing application service | $(C_v + C_f)^{w1} \times$ $(T_f + T_v)^{w2} \times$ $(Z_{P_{EnhanceAS}})^{w3}$ | $((s_d \times C_v) + C_f)^{w1} \times$ $(T_f + (s_t \times T_v))^{w2} \times$ $(Z_{P_{EnhanceAS}})^{w3}$ | $((s_q \times C_v) + C_f)^{w1} \times$ $(T_f + (s_u \times T_v))^{w2} \times$ $(Z_{P_{EnhanceAS}})^{w3}$ |
| Develop new application service for existing application | $(C_v + C_f + C_s)^{w1} \times$ $(T_f + T_v)^{w2} \times$ $(Z_{P_{NewASOldA}})^{w3}$ | $((s_d \times C_v) + C_f + C_s)^{w1} \times$ $(T_f + (s_t \times T_v))^{w2} \times$ $(Z_{P_{NewASOldA}})^{w3}$ | $((s_q \times C_v) + C_f + C_s)^{w1} \times$ $(T_f + (s_u \times T_v))^{w2} \times$ $(Z_{P_{NewASOldA}})^{w3}$ |
| Develop new application service and new application | $(C_v + C_f + C_a)^{w1} \times$ $(T_f + T_v)^{w2} \times$ $(Z_{P_{NewASNewA}})^{w3}$ | $((s_d \times C_v) + C_f + C_a)^{w1} \times$ $(T_f + (s_t \times T_v))^{w2} \times$ $(Z_{P_{NewASNewA}})^{w3}$ | $((s_q \times C_v) + C_f + C_a)^{w1} \times$ $(T_f + (s_u \times T_v))^{w2} \times$ $(Z_{P_{NewASNewA}})^{w3}$ |

every transformation action using the WPM. Table 1 shows how the ranking is calculated for the different resource modes. Each cell entry allows to calculate the ranking value given the necessary input.

### 4.6   Interactive Selection Process

Given the current and target business support map it is now possible to start the automated part of the transformation path generation by creating the $GTS$. All applicable transformation actions are computed and ranked. A list of them ordered by the ranking, including information necessary to gather the context of the transformation actions, is shown to the enterprise architect. The architect may filter or rearrange the list according certain preferences, for example alternative transformation actions or resource modes. Afterwards, the enterprise architect selects a transformation action manually and the list is updated automatically. To reduce the execution time for computing the resulting $GTS$ we only rank newly applicable transformation actions and automatically remove no longer applicable.

## 5   Use Case

In the following use case the enterprise wants to change the business support for its process *Customer Project Handling*. The drivers for the change are automating the process as far as possible and a demand for replacing old application services. The process *Customer Project Handling* was refined into its process activities (x-axis) starting with the *project planning* activity and ending with the activity for *project closure*. Figure 5 shows the modeled current and target business support map. Application services and one information service, highlighted by a star symbol, were modeled by an enterprise architect in the business support maps. The application that implements the respective application service is depicted in brackets. Figure 5 omits the roles (y-axis) which are responsible for the different activities. Besides the general manager only the role of the project manager is involved in the process. Within the current business support map the process activities *project planning* and *project permission* do not localize an application service via their business support elements. The process activity *project billing* localizes two application services via its business support element. Each process activity in the target business support map localizes at least one application service. For example, the *project tendering* activity in the current business support map is supported by the *tender processing* application service, which is implemented by the application *OFFER*. The application service is to be replaced by the application service *project overview* implemented by the application *TimeTracker*. For the process activity *project billing* an information service was specified. No application realizes this information service via an application service it implements. The information service for *bill completion* uses the information object *Bill* which has five schema entries. Information objects with one to five schema entries result in an effort baseline with one person-month. Six to ten schema entries result in one and a half person-month and information objects with more than eleven entries result in two person-months effort. Therefore, we derive for the *Bill* the effort baseline of one person-month.

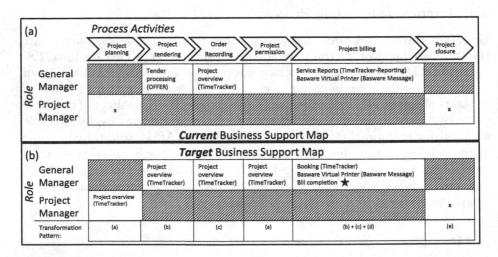

**Fig. 5.** The current and target business support map for the process *Customer Project Handling.*

For the modeled information service *bill completion* four alternative transformation actions are applicable. The first alternative allows to reuse the *booking* application service as it already realizes an information service which uses the information object *Bill*. All the other transformation actions can be executed in the different modes of resource allocation. The second alternative is the

**Table 2.** Value setting in the use case to allow for a ranking of transformation actions.

| Weighting factors | Scaling factors | Fixed values |
|---|---|---|
| $w_1 = 0,5$ | $s_q = 1,2$ | $C_f = 7.500$ |
| $w_2 = 0,35$ | $s_d = 1,1$ | $C_s = 2.500$ |
| $w_3 = 0,15$ | $s_u = 0,3$ | $C_a = 7.500$ |
| | $s_t = 0,55$ | $T_f = 1$ |

functional enhancement of the application service *service reports* implemented from the *TimeTracker-Reporting* application. Thirdly, it is possible to realize the information service via a new application service by an existing application. In the use case the applications *TimeTracker-Reporting*, *TimeTracker*, or *Basware Message* could implement such a new application service. As a fourth alternative it would be possible to create a new application which implements the necessary application service. Table 2 shows the setting of the different values, which allow to calculate the different efforts of each transformation action.

The suggested transformation actions would be to start with (1) replacing the *tender processing* application service, followed by (2) the replacement of *service reports*, and (3) building a new application service for the application *Basware Message*. The first two transformation actions have the same effort. In contrast the third transformation action has the same effort as the transformation actions that would build a new application service for the application *TimeTracker* and *TimeTracker-Reporting*.

# 6   Discussion

We presented a solution for an interactive transformation path generation using the weighted product model and graph based planning approach in the context of enterprise architecture planning based on business support maps. Our contribution allows an automated ranking of transformation actions against each other according to the criteria of cost, time, and risk. The information necessary for a ranking is extracted from enterprise architecture models and the different factors can be weighted to the preferences of an enterprise architect. Furthermore, we allow for the consideration of different modes of resource employment for certain transformation actions, to be able to consider different speeds for changes of different importance and urgency. Our solution is also capable of introducing new elements in the architecture, which is not considered in existing IT consolidation approaches. Additionally, we introduced a less restrictive goal-oriented transformation path planning as in [13]. In this paper we presented a detailed planning which corresponds to bottom-up planning of changes. However, changes are also top-down driven and it should be possible for an enterprise architect to express top-down changes in a similar way. For this we use business support maps on a different level of detail, i.e. on a value chain level of processes and organization units. For further details we refer to [7].

Currently, we do not consider ongoing projects as part of the current and target enterprise architecture. However, a consideration of them is relevant as the current ongoing transformations need to be aligned with future transformations and should even be considered in the effort function. A consolidation with the ongoing and finished projects is desirable. It would also allow to create a feedback loop and an improvement for the precision of future rankings. We would like to extend the mechanism presented in [8] to support this task. Furthermore, we do not provide a mechanism for parallel transformation action execution. The possibility for parallel execution can be extracted from the $GTS$ by checking whether the execution of a transformation action changes $G_n$ in a way that prohibits the execution ($LHS$ or $NAC$) of another transformation action. Additionally, resource constraints are currently not considered. They would prohibit the execution of certain transformation actions. However, these constraints could be included by introducing a resource lock and release mechanism as used in many scheduling approaches.

Future work will address the introduction of value function to allow for a consideration of benefits. This includes the consideration of a more complex decision space, which requires an optimization approach like the binary programming approaches used by Franke et al. [9] and Iacob et al. [12]. Finally, we want to apply the solution in several more use cases at different types of enterprises in order to evaluate its general applicability.

# References

1. Aier, S., Gleichauf, B.: Application of enterprise models for engineering enterprise transformation. Enterp. Model. Inf. Syst. Archit. **5**(1), 56–72 (2010)
2. Aier, S., Winter, R.: Virtual decoupling for it/business alignment - conceptual foundations, architecture design and implementation example. Bus. Inf. Syst. Eng. **1**(2), 150–163 (2009)
3. Bucher, T., Fischer, R., Kurpjuweit, S., Winter, R.: Analysis and application scenarios of enterprise architecture: An exploratory study. In: 10th IEEE International Enterprise Distributed Object Computing Conference Workshops (EDOCW 2006), p. 28. IEEE (2006)
4. Buckl, S., Ernst, A., Matthes, F., Schweda, C.M.: An information model for landscape management – discussing temporality aspects. In: Feuerlicht, G., Lamersdorf, W. (eds.) ICSOC 2008. LNCS, vol. 5472, pp. 363–374. Springer, Heidelberg (2009)
5. Chen, W., Hess, C., Langermeier, M., Stülpnagel, J.V., Diefenthaler, P.: Semantic enterprise architecture management. In: 15th International Conference on Enterprise Information Systems (ICEIS 2013), pp. 318–325 (2013)
6. Dam, H.K., Le, L.S., Ghose, A.: Supporting change propagation in the evolution of enterprise architectures. In: 2010 14th IEEE International Enterprise Distributed Object Computing Conference (EDOC 2010), pp. 24–33 (2010)
7. Diefenthaler, P., Bauer, B.: Gap analysis in enterprise architecture using semantic web technologies. In: 15th International Conference on Enterprise Information Systems (ICEIS 2013), pp. 211–220 (2013)

8. Diefenthaler, P., Bauer, B.: Using gap analysis to support feedback loops for enterprise architecture management. In: Kundisch, D., Suhl, L., Beckmann, L. (eds.) MKWI 2014 - Multikonferenz Wirtschaftsinformatik. University of Paderborn, Paderborn (2014)
9. Franke, U., Holschke, O., Buschle, M., Narman, P., Rake-Revelant, J.: It consolidation: an optimization approach. In: 2010 14th IEEE International Enterprise Distributed Object Computing Conference Workshops (EDOCW), pp. 21–26 (2010)
10. Gringel, P., Postina, M.: I-pattern for gap analysis. In: Engels, G., Luckey, M., Pretschner, A., Reussner, R. (eds.) Software Engineering 2010. LNI, pp. 281–292. Gesellschaft für Informatik, Bonn (2010)
11. Habel, A., Pennemann, K.-H.: Nested constraints and application conditions for high-level structures. In: Kreowski, H.-J., Montanari, U., Orejas, F., Rozenberg, G., Taentzer, G. (eds.) Formal Methods in Software and Systems Modeling. LNCS, vol. 3393, pp. 293–308. Springer, Heidelberg (2005)
12. Iacob, M.E., Quartel, D., Jonkers, H.: Capturing business strategy and value in enterprise architecture to support portfolio valuation. In: 2012 16th IEEE International Enterprise Distributed Object Computing Conference (EDOC 2012), pp. 11–20 (2012)
13. Lautenbacher, F., Diefenthaler, P., Langermeier, M., Mykhashchuk, M., Bauer, B.: Planning support for enterprise changes. In: Grabis, J., Kirikova, M., Zdravkovic, J., Stirna, J. (eds.) PoEM 2013. LNBIP, vol. 165, pp. 54–68. Springer, Heidelberg (2013)
14. Närman, P., Sommestad, T., Sandgren, S., Ekstedt, M.: A framework for assessing the cost of it investments. In: Kocaoglu, D.F., Anderson, T.R., Daim, T.U. (eds.) Portland International Center for Management of Engineering and Technology, pp. 3154–3166 (2009)
15. Rensink, A., Zambon, E.: Pattern-based graph abstraction. In: Ehrig, H., Engels, G., Kreowski, H.-J., Rozenberg, G. (eds.) ICGT 2012. LNCS, vol. 7562, pp. 66–80. Springer, Heidelberg (2012)
16. Simon, D.: Application landscape transformation and the role of enterprise architecture frameworks. In: Steffens, U. (ed.) MDD, SOA and IT-Management. GITO, Berlin (2009)
17. Sousa, S., Marosin, D., Gaaloul, K., Meyer, N.: Assessing risks and opportunities in enterprise architecture using an extended adt approach. In: Proceedings of the 17th IEEE International Enterprise Distributed Object Computing Conference (2013)
18. Triantaphyllou, E.: Multi-Criteria Decision Making Methods: A Comparative Study, Applied Optimization, vol. 44. Kluwer Academic Publishers, Dordrecht and Boston, Mass (2000)
19. van der Torre, L.W.N., Lankhorst, M.M., ter Doest, H., Campschroer, J.T.P., Arbab, F.: Landscape maps for enterprise architectures. In: Martinez, F.H., Pohl, K. (eds.) CAiSE 2006. LNCS, vol. 4001, pp. 351–366. Springer, Heidelberg (2006)
20. Wegmann, A.: On the systemic enterprise architecture methodology (seam). In: Proceedings of the 5th International Conference on Enterprise Information Systems, pp. 483–490 (2003)
21. Winter, R., Fischer, R.: Essential layers, artifacts, and dependencies of enterprise architecture. In: 10th IEEE International Enterprise Distributed Object Computing Conference Workshops (EDOCW 2006), p. 30. IEEE (2006)

# Towards Detecting Misalignment Symptoms: An Alignment Perspective-Driven Architecture-Matching Framework

Dóra Őri[✉]

Department of Information Systems,
Corvinus University of Budapest, Budapest, Hungary
DOri@informatika.uni-corvinus.hu

**Abstract.** When assessing the harmony between business and information systems most of traditional studies deal with the presence and the achievement of strategic alignment. On the contrary, exiguous attention is paid to the phenomenon of strategic misalignment, which means the absence or difficulties of business-IT alignment. This paper deals with strategic misalignment between business and information systems. It proposes an enterprise architecture (EA)-based approach to detect the symptoms of misalignment in enterprise architecture models. The proposed framework aims to perform an EA-based systematic analysis of mismatches between the business dimension and the IT dimension. It collects typical misalignment symptoms along the traditional alignment perspectives and connects them to relevant EA analysis types. The paper discusses the typical signs of strategic misalignment between business and information systems detected in different EA domain matches. Suitable EA analysis types are recommended to the detected signs of misalignment.

**Keywords:** Strategic alignment perspectives · Enterprise architecture alignment · Misalignment symptoms · Enterprise architecture analysis

## 1 Introduction

One of the most important issues on information systems (IS) research is the need to align business with information systems. Since information systems facilitate the success of business strategies, the importance of business-IT (or strategic) alignment is unquestionable.

While organizations are continually trying to achieve alignment, they are suffering from difficulties which encumber the achievement of alignment. This observation points out the phenomenon of misalignment, which is referred to as the "opposite" of strategic alignment, i.e. when strategy, structure, processes and technology are not perfectly harmonized. While most of traditional alignment studies deal with alignment achievement, misalignment issues are scarcely covered in the literature. However, organizations are in the state of misalignment as long as they achieve (or at least approach) the state of alignment. This fact indicates that considerable attention should be paid to the phenomenon of misalignment. Misalignment analysis (detecting, correcting and preventing misalignment) is an important step in achieving alignment, since

© Springer International Publishing Switzerland 2015
J. Barjis et al. (Eds.): EOMAS 2015, LNBIP 231, pp. 214–232, 2015.
DOI: 10.1007/978-3-319-24626-0_16

it helps to understand the nature and the barriers of alignment. In addition, it supports organizations in proposing certain steps to (re)achieve alignment.

Besides the low attention on misalignment issues contrary to alignment issues, existing literature on the topic suffers from two additional shortages. Current misalignment assessment frameworks are mainly concerned with incorporating different concepts that were taken from related research areas. To assess the presence of misalignment in an organization several approaches can be used (such as the approaches of [6, 20]). However, the innate ability of the enterprise architecture (EA) concept to support the detection of misalignment signs is scantily addressed in the literature (for exceptions see e.g. [7, 16, 19]). At the same time, well-established alignment methods are rarely incorporated into misalignment assessment methods. Equal importance should be given to the existing and the innovative ways of approaching misalignment, since traditional alignment methods have been proven to be feasible.

This paper aims to present a framework in order to address the above illustrated concerns. The paper discusses the strategic misalignment between the business dimension and the information systems (IS) dimension. It addresses misalignment symptom analysis by proposing an enterprise architecture (EA)-based framework to detect the typical signs of misalignment in an organization. The proposed approach aims to perform an EA-based, systematic analysis of mismatches between business and information systems. The framework is built on the operation of the traditional SAM model [12], i.e. typical misalignment signs are collected along the four traditional alignment perspectives (Strategy Execution, Technology Transformation, Competitive Potential and Service Level).The specific contribution of the paper lies in connecting typical misalignment symptoms to relevant EA analysis types.

The paper first establishes the theoretical background of architecture-based misalignment symptom analysis by the introduction of building blocks and related work. Based on the theoretical foundation a research model is given which connects enterprise architecture (EA) and misalignment assessment by analyzing misalignment symptoms in different architecture domain matches. The research model consists of 6 constituent parts. The operation of the proposed framework is introduced in detail by presenting the operation of the constituent parts as well as the whole framework. Misalignment symptom detection is performed in an alignment perspective-based manner, i.e. typical misalignment symptoms are collected along the different alignment perspectives. The EA-based framework identifies typical misalignment symptoms in the four traditional alignment perspectives. Finally, appropriate EA analysis types – which are by functionality able to detect the symptoms in question – are recommended to the detected symptoms. The framework operation results are presented in a structured manner. The discussion part proposes the justification for the different choices. Both the arguments for the chosen misalignment symptoms and the arguments for the selected EA analysis types are presented in detail.

The paper is organized as follows. Section 2 deals with theoretical context and related work. Section 3 introduces the research model and presents its constituent parts. In Sect. 4 an analysis is given on the operation of the proposed framework. Section 5 deals with discussing the results of the framework. At the end of the paper conclusions are drawn concerning the proposed framework. Future research directions are determined with special attention to validity issues.

## 2 Related Work

The theoretical foundation of the paper consists of two main parts. While the first subsections deal with theoretical background – works related to the problem statement, at the end of the section more specific works are presented which more closely deal with the proposed solution. The theoretical background part commences with the concept of strategic alignment. Special attention is paid to well-known Strategic Alignment Model (SAM) [12]. Strategic alignment subsection is followed by a concise introduction on misalignment. Subsequently, enterprise architecture frameworks and domains are summarized briefly. The second part of the section deals with specific works. Different enterprise architecture analysis types as well as EA alignment methods are presented which are more closely related to the proposed framework.

### 2.1 Strategic Alignment

Strategic alignment is referred to as an ideal situation in which organizations use appropriate IT instruments which provide congruency with their business strategy. Alignment models are holistic approaches which prescriptively define the method of achieving and sustaining the state of alignment. Contrary to the abundance of possible alignment models, there are some particularly influential and well-recognized models, such as the MIT model [18], the Baets model [2] and Henderson and Venkatraman's Strategic Alignment Model (SAM) [12].

The SAM model is often referred to as the most cited alignment model in the IS literature. The model has four key domains of strategic choice (a.k.a. alignment domains): (1) Business Strategy, (2) Organizational Infrastructure and Processes, (3) IT Strategy and (4) IT Infrastructure and Processes. The external axis of the model consists of the business and IT strategy domains, while the internal axis contains organizational and IT infrastructure and processes. Business axis refers to business strategy and business structure, while IT axis consists of IT strategy and IT structure. The SAM model is based on two primary building blocks: (1) Strategic Fit and (2) Functional Integration. Strategic fit dimension means the need to align the external and internal domains of IT, while functional integration refers to the need to integrate business and IT domains [12].

There are four dominant alignment perspectives, so-called cross-domain relationships in the SAM: (1) Strategy Execution, (2) Technology Transformation, (3) Competitive Potential and (4) Service Level. Alignment perspectives cover 3 out of 4 alignment domains in order to define directions with which alignment domains can be analyzed. Figure 1 shows traditional alignment perspectives. The figure can be interpreted as follows: Anchor means that the perspective is driven by that particular domain. Every perspective affects two additional domains: the intermediate domain is called pivot area, while the ending point is considered as the area of impact.

Strategy Execution perspective deals with the supporting role of IT concerning business strategy-based business structure. Business strategy is translated into business processes and infrastructure to which IT processes and infrastructure provide appropriate support. The perspective is business strategy-driven, which means that if there is

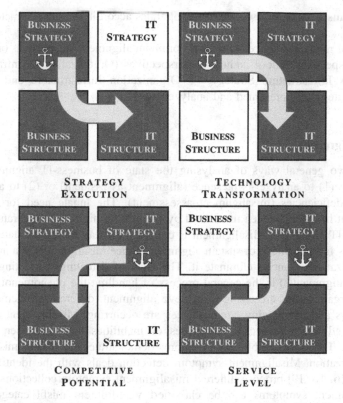

**Fig. 1.** Traditional alignment perspectives (adapted from [10, 12])

a change in business strategy direction, business structure is changed accordingly. In this case IT structure has to be able to adapt to renewed business structure via modified supports.

Technology Transformation perspective is concerned with the business value of IT. In this perspective IT provides innovative solutions in response to the business goals. Innovative possibilities are derived into IT processes and infrastructure which enable the implementation of the innovative solutions. In this perspective business structure does not constrain the implementation of the innovative solution.

Competitive Potential perspective is about emerging information technologies which are able to provide new possibilities to the business. These new concepts affect the business strategy, through which new business structure will be developed. In this perspective IT provides new distinctive competencies to the business. Business strategy is built according to the potentials provided by the IT. The perspective helps to exploit emerging IT capabilities in order to be able to develop new business products and services.

Service Level perspective deals with different ways through which IT can improve business service, or IT can deliver the necessary capabilities to support business products and services. Service Level perspective is intended for implementing an IT service-based organization. Business service levels are defined by collaboration between business and IT. IT service center operates according to the contracted service levels [12].

The SAM model introduced only four dominant alignment perspectives out of the 8 possible perspectives. The 4 additional perspectives (Organization IT Infrastructure, Organization Infrastructure Strategy, IT Organization Infrastructure and IT Infrastructure Strategy) are presented and analyzed by [10].

## 2.2  Misalignment

There are two general ways of analysing the state of business-IT alignment in an organization: (1) to analyze its presence (alignment assessment) or (2) to analyze its absence or deficiencies (misalignment assessment). The innate need for analyzing misalignment has already been mentioned by [8] in their high-profile literature review on business-IT alignment. Misalignment is considered as an undesired state in which organizations fail to achieve or sustain alignment. Since misalignment is a non-desired state, organizations want to eliminate it. The triad of detecting, correcting and preventing misalignment(s) is the general process of handling the phenomenon [6].

While organizations are trying to achieve alignment, different problems, complicating factors and aggravating circumstances are occurring. Misalignment symptoms are considered as inefficiencies, difficulties or inabilities that encumber alignment achievement. The existence of these symptoms demonstrates the state of misalignment in an organization. Misalignment symptom detection deals with the identification of such signs. [6, 16, 19] propose different misalignment symptom collections.

Misalignment symptoms can be classified via different misfit categorizations. Strong and Volkoff [20] give a possible categorization by classifying misalignment symptoms into (1) Functionality, (2) Data, (3) Usability, (4) Role, (5) Control and (6) Organizational Culture misfit types.

## 2.3  Enterprise Architecture

Architecture is regarded as the fundamental structure of a system, including its components and their relationships. Enterprise architecture (EA) is the fundamental construction of an enterprise, described by its components and their relationships [21]. It is an organizing logic of enterprise business processes and IT infrastructure in order to review, maintain and control the whole operation of an enterprise. This organizing logic acts as an integrating force between business planning, business operations and the enabling technological infrastructure. Enterprise architecture integrates information systems and business processes into a coherent map. It also helps to capture a vision of the entire system in all its dimensions and complexity. EA is concerned with coordinating the many facets that make up the fundamental essence of an enterprise [21].

An enterprise architecture framework is a collection of methods to create and manage enterprise architecture. Several enterprise architecture frameworks are available, e.g. the Zachman Framework [25], the TOGAF framework [21] or the DODAF framework [11].

TOGAF (The Open Group Architecture Framework) is a commonly used holistic architecture framework which describes architecture building blocks, their relationships, as well as the method to build and maintain enterprise architectures. The framework has four main components: (1) Architecture Capability Framework, (2) Architecture Development Method (ADM), (3) Architecture Domains and (4) Enterprise Continuum. Different reference models (e.g. Technical Reference Model, Standards Information Base, The Building Blocks Information Base) support the implementation of the framework [21].

Architecture domains are different conceptualizations of an enterprise. The TOGAF approach works with the architecture domains of (1) Business Architecture, (2) Data Architecture, (3) Application Architecture and (4) Technology Architecture [21]. In their approach Business Architecture is served by Data, Application and Technology Architectures. Figure 2 shows the main structure of the architecture domains according to the TOGAF framework.

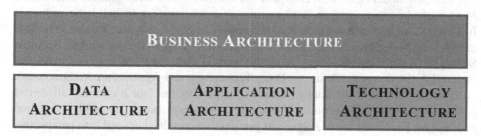

**Fig. 2.** Architecture domain structure according to the TOGAF Framework (based on [21])

### 2.4   Enterprise Architecture Analysis

EA analysis methods provide different ways of assessing EA models. [5, 22] proposes a general process for EA analysis. The process consists of three steps: (1) EA Assessment Scoping, (2) Evidence Collection and (3) EA Analysis. [5, 13, 14] give different EA analysis categorizations according to e.g. (1) quantitative and qualitative, or (2) static and dynamic groupings. [3, 14, 23] propose different EA analysis types. According to the object being investigated (e.g. Dependency, Coverage, Interfaces, Heterogeneity, Complexity and Conformity) different analysis procedures are introduced. Table 3 will show which of the possible EA analysis types will be used in the framework introduced in this paper. Tools for supporting the process of EA analysis are presented by [4, 5].

### 2.5   Enterprise Architecture Alignment

Architecture alignment methods combine different alignment analysis types, misalignment assessment frameworks and EA analysis techniques in order to propose EA-based tools for (mis)alignment assessment. The Kalcas framework [7] deals with semi-automatic data and business process architecture alignment. It is an ontology matching-based model which supports the alignment of business architecture and data architecture via detecting potential alignments and misalignments between the architecture domains. LEAP [9] is an approach which enables architecture alignment. It includes a text-based language and a method to match as-is and to-be architecture stages as well as to simulate logical and physical EA models. SEAM framework [24] proposes a description about an ideal situation in which alignment exists between the business and IT domains. Decoupling mechanisms [1] focus on the integration of business and IT architectures. These instruments collect requirements for architecture alignment and propose artefacts for alignment architecture. In [17] an EA metamodel is introduced for different business-IT alignment situations. The metamodel consists of enterprise entities, entity attributes and entity relationships.

## 3    EA-Based Misalignment Assessment Framework

In this section an introduction is given on the components of the proposed framework. The research model deals with enterprise architecture-based misalignment assessment. Meta-methodology is used as a supporting research concept to build the proposed framework. Architecture domains are interpreted into SAM domains in order to be able to match SAM domains in an architectural style. It means that the domains of Business Strategy, IT Strategy, Business Structure and IT Structure are matched with the underlying EA domains (Business, Data, Technology and Application Architectures). After setting up the SAM domain-matching approach, the four traditional alignment perspectives (Strategy Execution, Technology Transformation, Competitive Potential and Service Level) are used. Alignment perspectives are decomposed into perspective components according to the necessary SAM domain matches. Misalignment assessment is implemented by misalignment symptom detection. Typical misalignment symptoms are collected to every traditional alignment perspective. After collecting

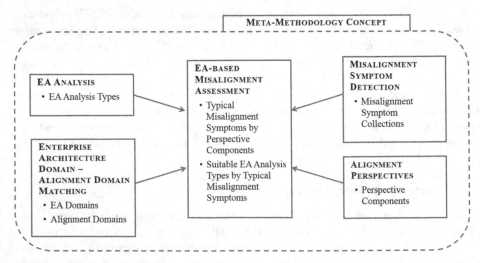

**Fig. 3.** The construction of Enterprise Architecture-Based Misalignment Assessment Framework

typical misalignment symptoms to the perspective components, suitable EA analysis types are recommended to the misalignment symptoms. Figure 3 shows the research model of the proposed framework. The components of the framework will be introduced in this section.

## 3.1 Framework Building with Meta-Methodology Concept

Meta-methodology concept [15] is used to support the preparation of the proposed framework. Meta-methodology is considered as a method to build different research methods. The concept is based on the view that with the input of content knowledge the proposed model produces new knowledge. The model is controlled by best practices, environment factors and project scope, while EA framework elements and tools provide supporting resources.

The methodology is used to combine concepts, related research models and empirical data collections in order to define a proposal for EA-based misalignment assessment.

## 3.2 Matching of Architecture Domains and Alignment Domains

The second step of building the proposed framework deals with the matching of EA domains and alignment domains. In this phase enterprise architecture domains are interpreted into alignment domains in order to be able to match alignment domains in an architectural style. It means that the domains of the SAM model (Business Strategy, IT Strategy, Business Structure and IT Structure) are matched with the underlying EA domains (Business Architecture, Data Architecture, Technology Architecture and Application Architecture). Figure 4 shows the process of matching alignment domains and enterprise architecture domains.

**Fig. 4.** Matching of alignment domains and enterprise architecture domains (based on [12, 21])

## 3.3 Decomposition of Alignment Perspectives

To approach EA-based misalignment assessment in an organized manner, alignment perspectives are used as an organizing logic. Traditional alignment perspectives are decomposed into perspective components, i.e. the correspondent matches of the SAM domains. To ease further reference, perspective components are coded according to the alignment perspectives. Table 1 shows the coding of the perspective components along the four alignment perspectives.

**Table 1.** Coding and decomposition of alignment perspectives (based on [12])

| Code | Alignment Perspective | Perspective Component |
|------|-----------------------|------------------------|
| P.1.1 | Strategy Execution | Matching of Business Strategy and Business Structure domains |
| P.1.2 | Strategy Execution | Matching of Business Structure and IT Structure domains |
| P.2.1 | Technology Transformation | Matching of Business Strategy and IT Strategy domains |
| P.2.2. | Technology Transformation | Matching of IT Strategy and IT Structure domains |
| P.3.1 | Competitive Potential | Matching of IT Strategy and Business Strategy domains |
| P.3.2 | Competitive Potential | Matching of Business Strategy and Business Structure domains |
| P.4.1 | Service Level | Matching of IT Strategy and IT Structure domains |
| P.4.2 | Service Level | Matching of IT Structure and Business Structure domains |

### 3.4 Misalignment Symptom Collection

Matching alignment domains along the alignment perspectives reveals different misalignment symptoms in the underlying EA models. Figure 5 shows general types of misalignment symptoms between the different alignment domains. General

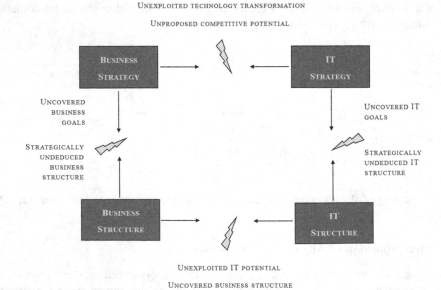

**Fig. 5.** The matching of different alignment domains results in general types of misalignment symptoms (based on [10, 12, 17]).

misalignment symptoms are typical symptom groups that can be identified on the related alignment domain matches.

General symptom types can be deducted into specific misalignment symptoms. In this paper specific misalignment symptoms are used during the EA-based misalignment assessment. Specific misalignment symptoms found in related works are assembled into a symptom catalogue. The symptom catalogue consists of specific misalignment symptoms which were observed in organizations and published in the previous literature on misalignment [6, 16, 19]. To ease further reference, misalignment symptoms are coded. Table 2 shows the misalignment symptom catalogue used in the proposed framework.

**Table 2.** Misalignment symptom catalogue (based on [6, 16, 19])

| CODE | MISALIGNMENT SYMPTOM |
|------|----------------------|
| S.01 | Undefined organizational mission, strategy and goals |
| S.02 | Undefined business process goals, business process owners |
| S.03 | Lack of relation between process goals and organizational goals |
| S.04 | Undefined business roles or responsibilities |
| S.05 | Undefined or multiple hierarchy or lines of reporting |
| S.06 | Application functionality does not support at least one business process activity |
| S.07 | Business process task supported by more than one application |
| S.08 | Critical business process does not depend on scalable and available applications |
| S.09 | Inappropriate application functionality |
| S.10 | Insufficient IT resources |
| S.11 | Lack of IT skills and competencies |
| S.12 | Lack of skills to develop or innovate certain types of products |
| S.13 | Poor IT planning and portfolio management |
| S.14 | Under capacity infrastructure |
| S.15 | Lack or poor systems performance monitoring |
| S.16 | Out of date technological infrastructure |
| S.17 | Insufficient IT resources |
| S.18 | Technological heterogeneity |
| S.19 | Incompatible platforms or technologies |
| S.20 | Frequent periods while applications are unavailable |
| S.21 | Information consistency or integrity problems |
| S.22 | Undefined business service levels |

## 3.5 Enterprise Architecture Analysis Types

The next component of the proposed framework is the collection of relevant EA analysis types. EA analysis types are able to reveal misalignment symptoms in the underlying EA models. In this subsection 8 possible EA analysis types are introduced which mostly deal with the structure of EA models. These analysis types are used in the proposed framework as recommended EA analysis types. The content of the EA analysis catalogue derives from related literature on EA analysis [3, 14, 23]. In order to ease further reference, EA analysis types are coded. Table 3 shows possible EA analysis types with a brief description about the content of the analysis.

**Table 3.** EA analysis types (based on [3, 14, 23])

| CODE | EA ANALYSIS TYPE | BRIEF CONTENT |
|------|------------------|---------------|
| A.01 | Dependency analysis | Analysis of directly or indirectly linked EA entities, relationship analysis and impact analysis. |
| A.02 | Network analysis | Analysis of EA model network elements and EA domain networks. |
| A.03 | Coverage analysis | Analysis of business structure coverage (by supportive application systems). |
| A.04 | Interface analysis | Analysis of interfaces between application systems. |
| A.05 | Complexity analysis | Analysis of architecture complexity by architecture components and relationships. |
| A.06 | Enterprise interoperability assessment | Analysis of interoperability between architecture entities and architecture domains. |
| A.07 | Enterprise coherence assessment | Analysis of coherence between architecture entities. |
| A.08 | Heterogeneity analysis | Analysis of IT assets heterogeneity. |

### 3.6    Enterprise Architecture-Based Misalignment Assessment

The proposed framework for enterprise architecture-based misalignment assessment is built on the operation of the above introduced framework components. EA-based misalignment assessment is performed in an alignment perspective-based manner and is implemented by misalignment symptom detection. Typical misalignment symptoms are collected to every traditional alignment perspective based on the interpretation of the constituent perspective components. Typical misalignment symptoms arise from the above proposed misalignment symptom catalogue (see Table 2). After collecting typical misalignment symptoms to the perspective components, suitable EA analysis types are recommended to the misalignment symptoms. Relevant EA analysis types arise from the above introduced EA analysis catalogue (see Table 3). The relevance of the proposed EA analysis types is based on two aspects: (1) the operation and features of the EA analysis types and (2) the interpretation of the misalignment symptom in question. Figure 6 displays the two main phases of EA-based misalignment assessment.

## 4    Operation of the Framework

This section provides the operation results of the proposed EA-based misalignment assessment framework. A detailed analysis is given on misalignment symptoms and relevant EA analysis types via matching alignment domains along the four traditional

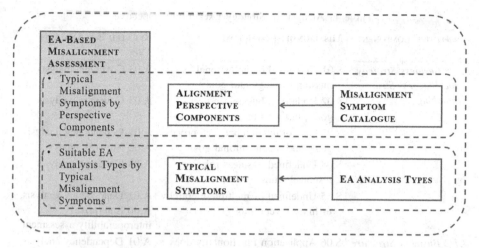

**Fig. 6.** The main phases of EA-Based Misalignment Assessment

alignment perspectives (Strategy Execution, Technology Transformation, Competitive Potential and Service Level). As a first step typical misalignment symptoms are introduced to each alignment perspective according to the results of corresponding alignment domain matches. As a second step suitable EA analysis types are recommended which are – by functionality – able to detect the corresponding misalignment symptom. The results of the proposed framework are introduced in a well-structured manner. The four subsections show the results according to the four traditional alignment perspectives. Within the subsections analysis results are presented according to the related perspective components.

### 4.1 Analysis of Strategy Execution Perspective

Table 4 shows typical misalignment symptoms as well as suitable EA analysis types to the perspective components of Strategy Execution perspective.

### 4.2 Analysis of Technology Transformation Perspective

Table 5 shows typical misalignment symptoms and relevant EA analysis types related to the Technology Transformation perspective.

### 4.3 Analysis of Competitive Potential Perspective

Table 6 shows the analysis results related to the Competitive Potential perspective. After introducing typical misalignment symptoms to the perspective components, suitable EA analysis types are recommended.

**Table 4.** Analysis of Strategy Execution perspective

| PERSPECTIVE COMPONENT | MISALIGNMENT SYMPTOM | RELATED EA ANALYSIS TYPE |
|---|---|---|
| *P.1.1 Business Strategy and Business Structure matching* | S.01 Undefined organizational mission, strategy and goals | A.03 Coverage analysis |
| | S.02 Undefined business process goals, business process owners | A.03 Coverage analysis |
| | S.03 Lack of relation between process goals and organizational goals | A.01 Dependency analysis, A.02 Network analysis |
| | S.04 Undefined business roles or responsibilities | A.03 Coverage analysis |
| | S.05 Undefined or multiple hierarchy or lines of reporting | A.01 Dependency analysis, A.06 Enterprise interoperability assessment |
| *P.1.2 Business Structure and IT Structure matching* | S.06 Application functionality does not support at least one business process activity | A.01 Dependency analysis, A.03 Coverage analysis, A.08 Heterogeneity analysis |
| | S.07 Business process task supported by more than one application | A.01 Dependency analysis, A.03 Coverage analysis, A.08 Heterogeneity analysis |
| | S.08 Critical business process does not depend on scalable and available applications | A.01 Dependency analysis, A.03 Coverage analysis |
| | S.09 Inappropriate application functionality | A.03 Coverage analysis, A.07 Enterprise coherence assessment |

### 4.4 Analysis of Service Level Perspective

Table 7 shows typical misalignment symptoms together with relevant EA analysis types related to the Service Level perspective.

## 5 Discussion

Collecting typical misalignment symptoms and recommending suitable EA analysis types along the four traditional alignment perspectives provided us with several insights regarding the nature of misalignment assessment. In this Sect. 1 out of 4 perspective-based analysis – the Technology Transformation perspective – is evaluated in detail. The justification of the choices is based on the operation of the proposed framework.

Misalignment symptoms collected to Technology Transformation perspective consist of the results of Business Strategy – IT Strategy and IT Strategy – IT Structure matches. While the former mainly dealt with missing resources (e.g. skills and competencies), the latter consisted of the lack or poorness of necessary IT management capabilities, such as IT portfolio management, capacity management and monitoring

**Table 5.** Analysis of Technology Transformation perspective

| Perspective Component | Misalignment Symptom | Related EA Analysis Type |
|---|---|---|
| *P.2.1 Business Strategy and IT Strategy matching* | S.10 Insufficient IT resources | A.05 Complexity analysis, A.08 Heterogeneity analysis |
| | S.11 Lack of IT skills and competencies | A.02 Network analysis, A.03 Coverage analysis, A.05 Complexity analysis |
| | S.12 Lack of skills to develop or innovate certain types of products | A.03 Coverage analysis |
| *P.2.2 IT Strategy and IT Structure matching* | S.13 Poor IT planning and portfolio management | A.03 Coverage analysis, A.05 Complexity analysis, A.08 Heterogeneity analysis |
| | S.14 Under capacity infrastructure | A.02 Network analysis, A.03 Coverage analysis |
| | S.15 Lack or poor systems performance monitoring | A.02 Network analysis, A.05 Complexity analysis, A.07 Enterprise coherence assessment |
| | S.16 Out of date technological infrastructure | A.03 Coverage analysis, A.04 Interface analysis, A.05 Complexity analysis, A.06 Enterprise interoperability assessment, A.08 Heterogeneity analysis |

assets. Considering that Technology Transformation perspective is about the value and transformational proposition of IT to the business, the properness of collected misalignment symptoms can be justified as follows. On strategic level the inappropriate operation of the transformational perspective can be manifested in missing or insufficiently provided IT resources, skills and competences, since this state means that IT is incompletely prepared to provide innovative solutions in response to the business goals. Considering the IT domain matches the lack or poorness of certain IT management capabilities, capacity problems and technological infrastructure obsoleteness indicate problems in preparedness of the IT organization to implement technological transformation. Without e.g. well-managed IT portfolio management IT does not have the necessary knowledge to evaluate possible technology transformation options. Similarly, without appropriately adjusted capacities and up-to-date technological infrastructure IT-driven transformations cannot be implemented.

Suitable EA analysis types related to the strategic matching consist of coverage analysis, complexity analysis, network analysis and heterogeneity analysis. Coverage analysis helps to detect missing IT support, i.e. in certain matches of business elements (e.g. business units, business products, business areas) supportive IT capabilities are missing. In this sense the lack of missing resources, skills and competencies can be

**Table 6.** Analysis of Competitive Potential perspective

| PERSPECTIVE COMPONENT | MISALIGNMENT SYMPTOM | RELATED EA ANALYSIS TYPE |
|---|---|---|
| P.3.1 IT Strategy and Business Strategy matching | S.10 Insufficient IT resources | A.05 Complexity analysis, A.08 Heterogeneity analysis |
| | S.11 Lack of IT skills and competencies | A.02 Network analysis, A.03 Coverage analysis, A.05 Complexity analysis |
| | S.12 Lack of skills to develop or innovate certain types of business and products | A.03 Coverage analysis |
| P.3.2 Business Strategy and Business Structure matching | S.01 Undefined organizational mission, strategy and goals | A.03 Coverage analysis |
| | S.02 Undefined business process goals, business process owners | A.03 Coverage analysis |
| | S.03 Lack of relation between process goals and organizational goals | A.01 Dependency analysis, A.02 Network analysis |
| | S.04 Undefined business roles or responsibilities | A.03 Coverage analysis |
| | S.05 Undefined or multiple hierarchy or lines of reporting | A.01 Dependency analysis, A.06 Enterprise interoperability assessment |

detected as well. Network analysis is able to reveal difficulties in architecture component networks. Missing skills and resources can be also detected via missing relationships in an architecture network model. Complexity analysis deals with assessing the density of architecture models by quantitatively enumerating architecture components and entity relationships. Corresponding misalignment symptoms are able to be detected by complexity analysis since architecture complexity also refers to the sufficient quantity of IT resources. Lastly, heterogeneity analysis is capable of detecting the lack or insufficiency of IT resources since it particularly deals with the heterogeneity of IT assets and resources.

Suitable EA analysis types related to the IT strategy and IT structure matching consist mostly of the same analysis types as of at the strategic matching. Additional analysis types comprise interface analysis, enterprise coherence assessment and enterprise interoperability assessment. Enterprise coherence assessment is suitable to detect performance monitoring issues as it generally assesses the coherence of an EA

**Table 7.** Analysis of Service Level perspective

| PERSPECTIVE COMPONENT | MISALIGNMENT SYMPTOM | RELATED EA ANALYSIS TYPE |
|---|---|---|
| *P.4.1 IT Strategy and IT Structure matching* | S.13 Poor IT planning and portfolio management | A.03 Coverage analysis, A.05 Complexity analysis, A.08 Heterogeneity analysis |
| | S.15 Lack or poor systems performance monitoring | A.02 Network analysis, A.05 Complexity analysis, A.07 Enterprise coherence assessment |
| | S.18 Technological heterogeneity | A.08 Heterogeneity analysis |
| | S.19 Incompatible platforms or technologies | A.04 Interface analysis, A.06 Enterprise interoperability assessment |
| | S.14 Under capacity infrastructure | A.02 Network analysis, A.03 Coverage analysis |
| | S.16 Out of date technological infrastructure | A.03 Coverage analysis, A.04 Interface analysis, A.05 Complexity analysis, A.06 Enterprise interoperability assessment, A.08 Heterogeneity analysis |
| *P.4.2 IT Structure and Business Structure matching* | S.20 Frequent periods while applications are unavailable | A.05 Complexity analysis, A.07 Enterprise coherence assessment |
| | S.21 Information consistency or integrity problems | A.01 Dependency analysis, A.06 Enterprise interoperability assessment, A.07 Enterprise coherence assessment, A.08 Heterogeneity analysis |
| | S.08 Critical business processes are not supported by scalable and highly available applications | A.01 Dependency analysis, A.03 Coverage analysis |
| | S.22 Undefined business service levels | A.03 Coverage analysis, A.07 Enterprise coherence assessment |

model. Poor performance monitoring causes incoherence in an EA model by e.g. the lack of appropriate monitoring assets or KPIs. In this sense enterprise interoperability assessment is able to reveal problems concerning systems performance monitoring. Interface analysis is capable of assessing out of date technological infrastructure, since it can detect missing or unoffered interfaces which, in turn point out the obsoleteness of applied technology. Similarly, enterprise interoperability assessment is able to detect out of date infrastructure elements as it deals with interoperability issues between architecture entities and domains. In case of obsolete technological infrastructure interoperability problems will emerge which reflect the misalignment symptom in question.

# 6  Conclusion and Future Work

This paper dealt with EA-based misalignment assessment. After introducing theoretical context and related work, a framework was proposed on architecture matching-driven misalignment symptom detection. It was followed by an analysis in which the framework was used to connect typical misalignment symptoms to traditional alignment perspectives. After collecting typical misalignment symptoms relevant EA analysis types were recommended which are able to identify the misalignment symptoms in question. The main contribution of the paper was that it connected typical misalignment symptoms to relevant EA analysis types along the perspectives of the SAM model.

As part of future work the approach will be evaluated against some set of testable criteria. In addition, the proposed framework will be tested and validated in real-life situations. Via analyzing real enterprise architecture models examples will be given showing the applicability of the framework. By means of the case study method different cases will be built in order to demonstrate the operation and usage of the proposed framework. Concrete examples of mismatches found in the test EA models will be provided. EA domains will be matched and appropriate EA analysis types will be performed in order to detect misalignment symptoms in test organizations. After collecting misalignment symptoms by matching the EA models of the test organizations, a general assessment will be given on alignment performance. In addition, adequate misalignment correction and re-alignment activities will be offered to the test organizations.

Besides validating the proposed framework, there are additional directions for future work. Firstly, the framework can be extended by analyzing the supplementary alignment perspectives, i.e. the Organization IT Infrastructure, Organization Infrastructure Strategy, IT Organization Infrastructure, IT Infrastructure Strategy perspectives. Secondly, the introduced framework can be refined by expanding misalignment symptom catalogues and recommended EA analysis collections. In addition, the matching of alignment domains and EA domains can be further cultivated. Finally, additional examination methods can be established in order to approach EA-based misalignment assessment from different perspectives.

# References

1. Aier, S., Winter, R.: Virtual decoupling for IT/business alignment – conceptual foundations, architecture design and implementation example. Bus. Inf. Syst. Eng. **2009**(2), 150–163 (2009)
2. Baets, W.: Aligning information systems with business strategy. J. Strateg. Inf. Syst. **1**(4), 205–213 (1992)
3. Buckl, S., Matthes, F., Schweda, C.M.: Classifying enterprise architecture analysis approaches. In: Poler, R., van Sinderen, M., Sanchis, R. (eds.) IWEI 2009. LNBIP, vol. 38, pp. 66–79. Springer, Heidelberg (2009)

4. Buckl, S., Buschle, M., Johnson, P., Matthes, F., Schweda, C.M.: A meta-language for enterprise architecture analysis. In: Halpin, T., Nurcan, S., Krogstie, J., Soffer, P., Proper, E., Schmidt, R., Bider, I. (eds.) BPMDS 2011 and EMMSAD 2011. LNBIP, vol. 81, pp. 511–525. Springer, Heidelberg (2011)

5. Buschle, M., Ullberg, J., Franke, U., Lagerström, R., Sommestad, T.: A tool for enterprise architecture analysis using the PRM formalism. In: Soffer, P., Proper, E. (eds.) CAiSE Forum 2010. LNBIP, vol. 72, pp. 108–121. Springer, Heidelberg (2011)

6. Carvalho, G., Sousa, P.: Business and Information Systems MisAlignment Model (BISMAM): an holistic model leveraged on misalignment and medical sciences approaches. In: Johannesson, P., Gordijn, J. (eds.) Proceedings of the Third International Workshop on Business/IT Alignment and Interoperability (BUSITAL 2008). CEUR, vol. 336, pp. 104–119. CEUR-WS, Aachen (2008)

7. Castellanos, C., Correal, D.: KALCAS: a framework for semi-automatic alignment of data and business processes architectures. In: Morzy, T., Härder, T., Wrembel, R. (eds.) ADBIS 2012. LNCS, vol. 7503, pp. 111–124. Springer, Heidelberg (2012)

8. Chan, Y.E., Reich, B.H.: IT alignment: what have we learned? J. Inf. Technol. 22(2007), 297–315 (2007)

9. Clark, T., Barn, B.S., Oussena, S.: A method for enterprise architecture alignment. In: Proper, E., Gaaloul, K., Harmsen, F., Wrycza, S. (eds.) PRET 2012. LNBIP, vol. 120, pp. 48–76. Springer, Heidelberg (2012)

10. Coleman, P., Papp, R.: Strategic alignment: analysis of perspectives. In: Murray, M., Weistroffer, H.R. (eds.) Proceedings of the 2006 Southern Association for Information Systems Conference, pp. 242–250. MPublishing, Michigan (2006)

11. DoDAF Architecture Framework. http://dodcio.defense.gov/Portals/0/Documents/DODAF/DoDAF_v2-02_web.pdf

12. Henderson, J.C., Venkatraman, N.: Strategic alignment: leveraging information technology for transforming organizations. IBM Syst. J. 32(1), 4–16 (1993)

13. Lankhorst, M.: Enterprise Architecture at Work. Modelling, Communication and Analysis. Springer, Heidelberg (2013)

14. Niemann, K.D.: From Enterprise Architecture to IT Governance. Elements of Effective IT Management. Friedr. Vieweg & Sohn Verlag, Wiesbaden (2006)

15. Noran, O.: A decision support framework for collaborative networks. Int. J. Prod. Res. 47 (17), 4813–4832 (2009)

16. Pereira, C.M., Sousa, P.: Enterprise architecture: business and IT alignment. In: ACM Symposium on Applied Computing, pp. 1344–1345. ACM, New York (2005)

17. Saat, J., Franke, U., Lagerström, R., Ekstedt, M.: Enterprise architecture meta models for it/business alignment situations. In: 14th IEEE International Enterprise Distributed Object Computing Conference, pp. 14–23. IEEE Press, New York (2010)

18. Scott Morton, M.S.: The Corporation of the 1990s: Information technology and organizational transformation. Oxford Press, London (1991)

19. Sousa, P., Pereira, C.M., Marques, J.A.: Enterprise architecture alignment heuristics. Microsoft Architects J. 4, 34–39 (2005)

20. Strong, D.M., Volkoff, O.: Understanding organization-enterprise system fit: a path to theorizing the information technology artifact. MIS Q. 34(4), 731–756 (2010)

21. The Open Group Architecture Framework (TOGAF). http://theopengroup.org/

22. Ullberg, J., Franke, U., Buschle, M., Johnson, P.: A tool for interoperability analysis of enterprise architecture models using Pi-OCL. In: Popplewell, K., Harding, J., Poler, R., Chalmeta, R. (eds.) Enterprise Interoperability IV. Making the Internet of the Future for the Future of Enterprises, pp. 81–90. Springer, London (2010)

23. Wagter, R., Proper, H., Witte, D.: A practice-based framework for enterprise coherence. In: Proper, E., Gaaloul, K., Harmsen, F., Wrycza, S. (eds.) PRET 2012. LNBIP, vol. 120, pp. 77–95. Springer, Heidelberg (2012)
24. Wegmann, A., Regev, G., Rychkova, I., Lam-Son, L., de la Cruz, J.D., Julia, P.: Business and IT alignment with SEAM for enterprise architecture. In: 11th IEEE International Enterprise Distributed Object Computing Conference, pp. 111–121. IEEE Press, New York (2007)
25. Zachman, J.A.: A framework for information systems architecture. IBM Syst. J. **26**(3), 276–292 (1987)

# Author Index

Printed in the United States
by Bookmasters

Printed in the United States
By Bookmasters